Teaching Music: The Urban Experience makes a significant contribution to the existing scholarship focused on teaching music in urban schools. The unique challenges and rewards of *teaching music* in urban schools are shared through the voices of dedicated practicing music teachers, while DeLorenzo critically unpacks the associated pedagogical and philosophical issues. This book belongs in the library of every music teacher who cares about being an effective teacher for all children.

★★

Constance L. McKoy, PhD
Professor and Director of Undergraduate Studies
School of Music, College of Visual and Performing Arts
The University of North Carolina at Greensboro
Co-Author of Culturally Responsive Teaching in Music Education:
From Understanding to Application (2016, Routledge)

TEACHING MUSIC

This timely book explores teaching music in the urban setting along with interviews and journal accounts from urban music teachers in a variety of specializations. Written for pre-service music education students and music teachers new to urban teaching, this is a must-read for those considering teaching in the urban schools. Selected topics include culturally responsive teaching; White teachers working with students of color; nurturing pedagogy for at-risk youths; working with ESL students and immigrant families; creating a democratic and socially just music classroom; and developing habits of teaching that promote resilience and confidence in the emotional, social, and academic well-being of young musicians. A valuable resource for music teaching, this book features an accessible blend of theory and practice with authentic stories from the field.

Lisa C. DeLorenzo is a Professor of Music Education and Graduate Coordinator of Music Education at the John J. Cali School of Music at Montclair State University, NJ. Her first book, *Sketches in Democracy: Notes from an Urban Classroom*, was named a Critics Choice Book Award given by the American Educational Studies Association. She is also the editor of *Giving Voice to Democracy in Music Education: Diversity and Social Justice*, published by Routledge, and has worked with urban youth over the past 25 years. Dr. DeLorenzo received the Mandela Award for Outstanding Leadership in Diversity at Montclair State University for her work with Black and Latino youths. In addition, she is a former fellow of the Institute for Educational Inquiry, founded by John I. Goodlad, where she studied school renewal built on principles of democracy. Her areas of scholarship include urban music teacher education, democracy, and social justice.

> A seminal and important work. Professor DeLorenzo's brilliant insight about, and work with, at-risk youths is revealed in how she uses their natural (and necessary) resilience to the affronts of society and their desire for creative expression in an increasingly complex world, weaves that knowledge with her area of expertise (teaching music in urban settings), and brings out in these young adults an emotional, social, creative, and academic confidence and well-being. Simply amazing. DeLorenzo even takes a dollop of my more gritty, in-your-face street gang research of a quarter century ago, updates it to today and, in her unique way, comes out with a mélange of creative insight that is sheer, radiant genius.
> – Author M. Rutledge McCall (*Slipping Into Darkness*)

TEACHING MUSIC

The Urban Experience

Lisa C. DeLorenzo
With Meredith Foreman, Robbin Gordon-Cartier,
Larisa Skinner, Christine Sweet, and Peter J. Tamburro

LONDON AND NEW YORK

First published 2019
by Routledge
2 Park Square, Milton Park, Abingdon, Oxon OX14 4RN

and by Routledge
52 Vanderbilt Avenue, New York, NY 10017

Routledge is an imprint of the Taylor & Francis Group, an informa business

British Library Cataloguing-in-Publication Data
A catalogue record for this book is available from the British Library

Library of Congress Cataloging-in-Publication Data
A catalog record has been requested for this book

ISBN: 978-0-8153-5476-5 (hbk)
ISBN: 978-0-8153-5477-2 (pbk)
ISBN: 978-0-429-19673-7 (ebk)

Typeset in Bembo
by Apex CoVantage, LLC

To Mom and Dad,
my first and best teachers.

CONTENTS

FIGURE AND TABLE

Figure

Table

ACKNOWLEDGMENTS

I am grateful to you for your help and support in writing this book:

- To the journalists who, despite their hectic schedules, voluntarily shared their experiences so that others could learn: Robbin Gordon-Cartier, Meredith Foreman, Larisa Skinner, Christine Sweet, and Peter J. Tamburro
- To Marissa Silverman and Tina Jacobowitz, for your tireless help in reading and giving feedback on my chapters
- To my other readers, Nick Michelli, Zoë Burkholder, Bryan Powell, Nancy Tumposky, and Lauraine Hollyer, for your generous help
- To M. Rutledge McCall and Constance L. McKoy for having faith in my writing
- To Ms. Pernas, Mr. Mango, Ms. Serpone, Ms. Gopal, and Jessica Finkelstein, for your willingness to interview and provide feedback for this book
- To my editors at Routledge, Heidi Bishop (Commissioning Editor) and Annie Vaughan (Editorial Assistant), for helping with the publication of this book.
- To my daughter, Molly, for always keeping me mindful of what a pre-service teacher needs to know
- To my family, for your constant support of my writing

1

INTRODUCTION

When I graduated from college with my music teachers certificate, there was no question about where to teach. I wanted to be within ten miles from home, preferably in the town where I grew up. Because my home was situated in White, middle class suburbia, my only information about inner cities came from media reports and opinions from other like-minded people. Crime, violence, and racial diversity convinced me that one step into the city was one step closer to my demise. Besides, not one of my education professors or field experiences ever hinted at an alternative to teaching in the suburbs. It simply wasn't an option.

For my first teaching job, I taught in a rural school district forty minutes from my hometown. Traveling among three schools, I also taught kindergarten in a one-room schoolhouse. Driving to school, I often saw deer grazing along the side of the road and farmhouses dotted sporadically across the landscape. Our faculty room even had a quilting rack where we spent time making baby quilts for various friends on the faculty. Needless to say, it was about as far from an urban setting as one can get.

After completing a doctorate, I began teaching music education at a mid-sized university that places great importance on urban teaching and working with diverse student populations. However, my primary experience working with children of color was as a college summer camp counselor with adolescents from low-income urban areas in Philadelphia. Clearly, this was not sufficient preparation for my teacher education students. Consequently, I decided to take a sabbatical year to teach ninth grade general music in a low-income neighborhood within a nearby city. My experiences are chronicled in an earlier book, *Sketches of Democracy: Lessons from an Urban Classroom.*[1] Suffice it to say that the year was a more intensive learning experience than any in my collective forty years of teaching music. Although I loved my first years of teaching in the rural school district, teaching urban students captured my heart and lead to numerous teaching projects in other urban schools.

My past and present experiences with urban youth cover a range of venues. I have taught music in urban schools both professionally and on a voluntary basis, have designed a summer music camp that brings urban youth to the college, and have mentored student teachers in urban schools for over thirty years. Most importantly, I have listened carefully to urban teachers of all races as they talk about their "kids." All of these experiences, in addition to a concentrated study of literature on numerous aspects of urban education, have informed my writing and my teaching of teachers.

In my experience as a university music teacher educator, I find that many students imagine themselves teaching in schools similar to their own schooling experience. New graduates often apply exclusively to suburban or rural schools because, according to some of my music education students, "the students from urban/rural schools are more interested in learning," "there are more resources in the school," "the schools are safer," and "discipline problems are manageable." Whereas the media ignites many of these stereotypical ideas, especially in reporting school violence, it is critical that pre-service teachers become more responsibly informed about the larger picture of urban teaching.[2]

This book is written for music education students and beginning music teachers who believe that all children have a right to powerful music experiences but may not know how to engage with the complexities of an urban setting. Given that most teachers are from White, middle class backgrounds, there are many more hurdles to negotiate than for those who have grown up in an urban environment. It is not unusual for these teachers to experience tremendous culture shock when stepping into an urban school for the first time. There are so many things to learn about students and families who may have a different style of communicating or particular needs unlike any experienced by these new teachers.

All that aside, there is no experience comparable to helping a child or adolescent find his/her/their inner musical self in a world that can be as chaotic as it is confusing. Urban life for those who are poor may be challenging, but it need not keep wonderful teachers from teaching remarkable children. The stakes are high, but the rewards are vast. That is precisely why good urban music teachers prefer urban teaching more than anything else.

What is this book about?

This book explores what it means to teach music in urban schools. In order to enrich the content of this book and provide additional first-hand knowledge, I asked five urban music teachers in New Jersey public schools to keep journals during the 2015–2016 academic year. Of the five, two are African American who grew up in low-income urban areas, and three are White who grew up in primarily White suburban areas. In addition, this cohort of teachers represents a variety of teaching levels and specializations, including middle school general/choral music and middle school to high school instrumental music. At the time of this writing, their teaching experience ranged from four to thirty years in urban schools.

Together as a writing team, we hope that these stories, along with additional chapters on relevant issues in urban education, will speak directly and honestly about what it means to teach music in the urban school. While we hope that this book will encourage a new perspective on urban teaching, we made no effort to "sugar coat" the challenges that music teachers in urban schools face. As Joe Kincheloe remarks in the book *19 Urban Questions: Teaching in The City*: "Teacher educators should be brutally honest with those contemplating going into urban teaching. . . . Urban teaching is hard work."[3]

It would be inaccurate, however, to suggest that all urban schools throughout the country reflect the stories contained in this volume. Our schools, in northern New Jersey, are a small sampling of the nation as a whole, though there is considerable literature that supports our experiences in navigating the urban system. The findings from this literature weave together the stories contained herein. Much of the content, although directed toward urban teaching, is highly relevant to teachers across a variety of contexts and settings. Our purpose, then, is to provide a realistic picture of teaching music in the urban school that highlights both the challenges and the rewards. We do this with the understanding that, although not everyone is suited for urban teaching, good teachers need not always look to the suburbs for a fulfilling career.

As a White university music education professor, I realize the risks in writing a book that attempts to unravel some of the complicated issues of teaching children of color in urban settings. I took this risk because I felt that if I were going to encourage my primarily White, middle class students to teach in underserved urban areas, I had an obligation to write this book from my perspective as a White teacher educator.

Consequently, discussions about such topics as race, sexual orientation, immigration, and classroom management within the context of the urban setting have the potential for creating unintended stereotypes or superficial arguments. For that reason, I have tried to present as much information as possible from scholars in the field, many of whom are non-White, while also honoring the many conversations that I've had with urban music educators.

The book is thematically organized according to issues that arise from the journal entries. These themes and accompanying chapters include the following:

- *Nurturing Pedagogy: Acknowledging the Gifts of Every Child* – What does caring look like, and how do good teachers empower students through culturally responsive teaching?
- *Helping Troubled Students Succeed* – How do teachers work with students whose behavior stems from urban stress and traumatic events?
- *Narrowing the Opportunity Gap for Urban Students* – How can teachers provide equitable music opportunities for students from low-income or impoverished families?
- *Learning to Roll with the Punches* – What role does flexibility play in a teacher's daily routine, and how do teachers maintain a successful music program despite unexpected detours?

- *When White Teachers Teach Students of Color* – How can White teachers develop the skills and sensitivity to teach for the unique needs of students of color?
- *Democracy, Social Justice, and Hip Hop* – What are the commonalities and relationships among democratic practice, teaching for social justice, and hip hop?
- *The Good Teacher* – What can we learn from successful music teachers in the urban schools?

Those who have taught music in the urban schools have much to tell us about what it means to persevere and succeed in a cultural context that is often far removed from their own life experiences. Although the framework of urban schools may initially seem overwhelming and unyielding, creative teachers can make huge differences in the lives of children. It is precisely those rewards and the power of music in the process that illuminate the raw beauty of urban music teaching.

What is it like to teach music in an urban school?

I knew, whether it was Newark or somewhere else, that I was going to be an urban teacher someday. I love the culture, the students, and the challenges that come my way. I feel so fulfilled coming home each day knowing that I have given my 100% to that community and that my knowledge of music brings joy to those that have the opportunity to participate.

– *Mrs. Skinner*

★★★★★★★★★★★★

On the first day, I learned that, in addition to teaching my 170+ band students in 4th to 8th grade, I will now be teaching all 6th to 8th grade general music classes . . . an ADDITIONAL 225 students! I had no warning this would happen, so I didn't order teaching supplies from last year's budget.

– *Ms. Foreman*

★★★★★★★★★★★★

I will never forget the smile on DeShaun's face – a boy who came up to me a couple weeks ago and asked to sing the opening solo in our choir's performance of "Glory" (from the movie Selma), never having sung in front of an audience before and not even been a part of choir. He heard the boisterous applause and hollering of his 400 peers just a few notes into his debut. His peers, up until then, only knew him as a class clown, a fighter, and a hall walker. I don't know if that moment changed his life or not, and I may never know, but it changed mine. DeShaun, and other experiences like that, are the reasons why when I look at other jobs at other "better" places, I have a hard time imagining myself anywhere else.

– *Mr. Tamburro*

Taken from several music teachers' journals, these excerpts offer a small glimpse into the life of urban music teachers. They capture the quixotic nature of teaching in the inner city with its joys, challenges, frustrations, and hope. Urban schools are complex. In terms of teaching, Anna Richert notes:

> Teaching is hard work. So hard, in fact, that it takes a lifetime to learn to do it well. One reason it's so hard is because of the uncertainty of the work. Every-day – all the time – teachers encounter problems that are not easily solvable[4]

We can safely say that good teaching is hard work wherever the setting, but teaching in the urban schools brings a whole different dimension to the concept of schooling. For teachers who did not grow up in an urban environment, walking into an urban school is akin to traversing the rapids in a swiftly moving current. The culture, the kinds of jokes, the style of communication, the differences in expectations, the rules of the school, the rules of the street, the paperwork, the bureaucracy, the sheer number of students . . . even with college preparation, the initial experience becomes a culture shock for many music teachers.

This should not, by any means, turn music teachers away from urban teaching. One needs, however, to reframe his/her/their own experiences in order to see teaching from a new perspective. That is, urban teachers must prepare to be learners as well as teachers. The students, the faculty, and the community have wisdom that should be respected rather than endured. Fortunately, music is a powerful medium for reaching and nurturing students. And, if taught with sensitivity to the cultural context, music can transform students in ways that could have never been imagined.

Profile of an urban school

What does urban mean? Although there is no agreed-upon definition, the consensus seems to indicate that urban settings are unique based on their size and density of residents. H. Richard Milner has suggested that urban settings fall into three categories: (a) those with a significantly large population such as New York or Los Angeles; (b) those that encounter similar issues but are slightly smaller in size; and (c) smaller communities that are beginning to encounter issues present in the larger cities, such as a sizeable number of residents for whom English is a second language or who continue to communicate in their native language.[5] The stories in this book primarily represent the second category – smaller cities designated as urban in terms of low household income; large, complex school districts; and problems consistent with large inner cities.

Kincheloe describes many features that characterize urban schools[6]:

- High population density
- Bigger and serve more students
- Profound economic disparity; high concentrations of poverty existing in close proximity to affluence
- Appalling lack of resources
- Undermined by ineffective business operations

- Poor urban students more likely to experience health problems
- Higher student, teacher, and administrator mobility
- Higher immigrant population
- Linguistic diversity
- Transportation problems
- Teachers less likely to live in the communities surrounding the schools

Urban schools, however, are not all alike. Some public schools actually benefit from their urban status in terms of additional monies allocated by the state. Where the arts are highly valued, especially in schools designated as arts-intensive, arts programs often reflect high-quality human and material resources. For example, one of the teachers featured in this book works in a public high school designated as a School for the Performing and Fine Arts. The music classrooms are spacious and are equipped with the latest technology and Steinway pianos. Students have access to practice rooms; instruments provided by the schools; and opportunities to study piano, music history, and music theory.

Some urban schools, however, are not so fortunate. There is often little money for ensemble music, few or no small group lessons, one or two ensembles (usually band and choir), not enough time in the schedule for select ensembles, musical instruments that are dilapidated or in need of repair, and lack of basic equipment such as a piano or a high-quality sound system. Hardworking, creative teachers can secure resources through grants (e.g. *Mockingbird Foundation* or *Mr. Holland's Opus Foundation*), ask families to donate used instruments they might have tucked away in a closet, approach community organizations such as Rotary to help fund the music program, and so forth. Mrs. Skinner, one of the teachers writing for this book, for example, states:

> *My past two jobs, I've had to find instruments myself. At my first school there was nothing and the principal said, "We don't have money." I had to ask everyone we knew to find instruments – I went to Robbie's Music Store and had to beg for cheap music stands.*

She also contacted the managers of a nearby Home Depot, who donated a whole set of buckets for African drumming lessons. The takeaway here is that teachers with initiative can greatly improve their situation while connecting with community organizations and other funding sources as well.

As Kincheloe describes earlier, there are certain characteristics germane to urban schools. Strong, centralized bureaucracies, for example, put decision-making in the hands of those furthest away from the students. This means that teachers often have less input into rules or policies that govern them. In addition, many teachers leave within their first few years of teaching.[7] Consequently, students not only have different music teachers throughout their program but often novice and inexperienced teachers as well. This makes it difficult to build a cohesive music program within the school and across the district.

Other challenges include a large cadre of learners and their families who are not yet fluent in English (see Chapter 2). There may be a high rate of mobility (families who move out of the district, those who travel to their home country, or new families moving into the district during various points in the school year). Health problems abound – children are often sick because medical services are expensive, especially for families who do not have health care coverage.[8]

Regarding school, the time spent in arts programs is often reduced to support instruction directly related to high-stakes testing. Kate Fitzpatrick-Harnish aptly criticizes this practice, stating: "The idea that some students need more math, reading, and science but less art, music, and beauty in their lives than other students do is condescending and demeaning."[9]

Impact on the music teacher

Adapting to constant change may be the teacher's greatest challenge. For instance, a new teacher hired to teach general music at the middle school may find that his/her/their job has been changed to elementary general music to fill the gap for a music teacher who suddenly left at the end of August. A teacher hired for instrumental music may find that the instruments are not adequate for the number of students who registered for the instrumental program and a rental program is beyond the means of most parents. The general music teacher may find that his/her/their music room has been converted to a kindergarten classroom to accommodate for an influx of children coming into the school.

Although many of these changes are also part of the suburban school landscape, they prevail more often in the urban schools. In addition, these changes often "surprise" the urban teachers on the first day of school leaving them to scramble for supplies and appropriate lesson plans. Mr. Tamburro, whose journal is presented in this book (see Chapter 5), identifies the ability to adapt as one of the urban teacher's strongest skill.

Despite the challenging external issues, good teachers roll with the punches, primarily because of the students. "Star teachers" are urban educators who inspire, challenge, and transform students.[10] The key to quality urban teaching lies in the teacher's ability to help enable students to live independent and productive lives. This means that, in addition to teaching musical content, teachers also help students learn productive coping mechanisms and develop action-oriented skills to facilitate positive change in their community, school, or family.

Any success, no matter how small, is a triumph. For many students, music class is one place where they can imagine, create, and explore. Under the leadership of a good teacher, the music class can become a safe space where students are nurtured for who they are rather than solely on what they achieve. It goes without saying that good teachers know their students well – an advantage for music teachers who work with children/adolescents over the course of several years.

Part of nurturing students has to do with changing one's mindset from a deficit model (the perceived academic/social deficiencies that student have) to one that celebrates students' strengths. That is, instead of seeing the child/adolescent as a troublemaker, or one who can't speak English, or a child in band who can't read music, the teacher must recalibrate his/her/their thinking to recognize the strengths that the student brings to the music room.

The "troublemaker," as initially identified by the teacher, may be highly creative but lacks the emotional stability to productively express his/her/their ideas through music. The student who communicates in a foreign language can often communicate more fully through the musical medium. The student who doesn't read music but wants to play in the band may have an incredible "ear" and can learn to read more quickly than other students. Although these are merely examples, they illustrate the importance of looking at children for what they can do rather than what they cannot.

"Revolutionary love" – that's how Jeffrey Duncan-Andrade and Ernest Morrell describe teachers who inspire change for the student's well-being and empowerment in society.[11] It is a love that energizes teachers to do whatever it takes to help students learn. "When we love children," states bell hooks, "we acknowledge by our every action that they are not property, that they have rights – that we respect and uphold their rights."[12]

Good urban teachers understand that empowerment comes from learning how to negotiate barriers in life. Inner city kids need political and social skills to make substantive changes in their lives and in their communities. If students understand their rights and ability to facilitate societal change, the teacher empowers students to take action rather than fall victims to their circumstances. "Even in the worst situations, brilliant teachers can change students' lives." [13]

Impact on the learner

Kincheloe talks about the challenges that confront city students:

> No one can go into urban schools successfully without understanding and appreciating the everyday challenges many city students endure. . . . Some are overwhelmed by the challenges, swallowed up in the abyss of violence, drugs, and capitulation to short terms needs. Many others persevere, developing amazing coping strategies, construct methods of concentration amidst the chaos and even delay gratification in the pursuit of long terms goals.[14]

Two main assumptions about urban students negatively influence public opinion and those who might initially want to teach in an urban setting. The first assumption involves the culture of urban students and the value they place on education. There is an unfortunate misconception among pre-service teachers and much of the public that students of color in urban areas do not care about learning. However, researchers have shown the opposite – that these students want to learn but the school environment itself is uninspiring both in terms of rigid, formulaic teaching and low expectations for what students can achieve.[15] According to Jeanne

Theoharris, "Part of the appeal of believing that urban students do not care about education is that the responsibility for change lies with them and not the rest of the nation."[16]

The conditions of many urban schools have an impact on any student's motivation to achieve. Classrooms that are freezing in the winter but stifling in the late spring or early September, bathrooms in disrepair, too many students jammed into a too-small classroom or forced to share basic materials – when these all-too-often conditions exist, learning takes a backseat to surviving. When students don't feel safe or come to school hungry, learning takes on a secondary role. Essentially, when students' basic needs are not met – food, safety, and shelter – their learning environment is compromised. Moreover, "The focus on poor values, baggy clothes, broken English, and fears of 'acting white' offers a tremendous amount of psychic comfort to a society that does not want to provide these young people with a quality equal education, but still wants to maintain that all people are treated equal."[17] In other words, judging students for what they wear or how they behave provide an easy excuse for avoiding the issue of inequality in schooling practices.

The second assumption, closely related to the first, involves the value that urban families place on education. "If parents did care," some pre-service teachers say, "they would come to parents' night or other school events. They would monitor their child's homework or music practice and initiate contact with the school when needed." Most urban parents, however, want their children to get ahead in this world. They see education as a way for their children to have a better life. Negative judgments made in terms of parental/guardian absence at school events doesn't account for the fact that many parents are working more than one job, have little ones at home that need supervision, or feel intimidated by the school itself. For those parents who had negative experiences in school as children/adolescents, speak little English, or had children at a very young age, the school can be a frightening place and one associated with personal failure. More than ever, teachers need to forge partnerships with families. Kopetz et al. agree: "Teachers must recognize that the job of educating children is very difficult and cannot be achieved in isolation. Partnership with the home is imperative."[18]

Although there is often a tendency to focus on problems in the family structure, it would be highly misleading to say that urban children come from dysfunctional homes. Like their suburban/rural counterparts, many children come from loving homes – whether single parent or devoted caretakers in the extended families. Despite long working hours and time spent on public transportation, families do their best to guide their children toward an education that they might not have had. Teachers will also encounter, however, students who are homeless, live with alcoholic parent(s), encounter drugs, or are abused. Again, these problems are not endemic to urban students but seem to fuel the stereotypes that pre-service students hold when thinking about teaching in an urban school.

Misconceptions about student and family engagement in the school can result in teachers blaming the student/families for problems at school. Blaming is tantamount to giving up on the student or thinking that nothing can be done. In essence, blaming the students or families for problems at school keeps teachers from taking steps toward positive measures to connect with students and their families. What students need are responsible adults in their corner who believe that all things are possible. While the teacher cannot "fix" problems at home, he/she/they can support students academically and emotionally, even if those students initially reject the help.

What can I expect as a new urban music teacher?

The first years of teaching are rocky for most new teachers but especially challenging in an urban school. Becoming knowledgeable about the lives of students and understanding that urban teaching takes many twists and turns can go a long way in preparing a mindset for the differences between urban and suburban schools. Why a student doesn't practice at home, for example, may have nothing to do with forgetfulness but rather that he/she lives in crowded conditions or has to work after school to contribute to the family income. When parents do not come to concerts, it frequently means that they have unavoidable obligations that prevent them from attending a school event. Clearly, all of this has an impact on the day-to-day course of schooling.

For this reason, flexibility and the ability to adapt to constantly changing conditions are among the most important dispositions that a teacher can have. In addition, approaching urban teaching with the attitude that students and families bring numerous personal assets to the classroom creates a learning environment in which students can embrace what makes them special.

We are fortunate to be teachers of music. Teaching music in the urban setting is a powerful medium for reaching students who might otherwise fall through the cracks. It can offer a safe place for students who experience turbulence and uncertainty in their daily lives. It can also provide an avenue for students to gain confidence through successes that they may not have in other areas of their schooling.

Indeed, teachers of urban students need perseverance to ride the waves and the courage to take risks in the pursuit of both learning music as well as helping students to love themselves.

> *It's the kind of challenge that I love because I'm doing more than teaching music. Music teaches you about life and hard work and it elevates you to be your best self. It teaches about community and working together, thinking, understanding, critical thinking.*
>
> *— Ms. Sweet*

★★★★★★★★★★★★★★

> *The rewards are watching the kids become really decent people. Watching them help each other in class. The beauty of ensemble playing teaches kids how not to leave the least able behind. That builds character. It's rewarding seeing them become people.*
>
> *— Mrs. Gordon-Cartier*

To succeed in reaching those who may feel unreachable is a feeling like no other, for it is the students that make the challenges in urban teaching all the more rewarding.

Discussion questions

1   What are your feelings about teaching music in an urban school? What have you heard, experienced in fieldwork, or read that may influence your thinking?
2   Where did you grow up, and how would you describe your town/diversity of your school?
3   What are the rewards and challenges for urban music teachers? Identify some of the questions you have about urban music teachers at this point.

References

1 DeLorenzo, Lisa C. 2012. *Sketches in Democracy: Lessons from an Urban Classroom.* Lanham, MD: Rowman & Littlefield.
2 Hampton, Bonita, Long Peng, and Jean Ann. 2008. "Pre-Service Teachers' Perceptions of Urban Schools." *Urban Review,* 40: 268–295. doi: 10.1007/s11256-008-0081-2
3 Kincheloe, Joe L. 2007. "Why Teach in Urban Settings?" In *19 Urban Questions: Teaching in the City,* edited by Shirley R. Steinberg and Joe L. Kincheloe, 226–280. New York: Peter Lang: 267.
4 Richert, Anna E. 2012. *What Should I do? Confronting Dilemmas of Teaching in Urban Schools.* New York: Teachers College Press: 4.
5 Milner, H. Richard IV. 2012. "But What Is Urban Education?" *Urban Education,* 47: 556–561. doi: 10.1177/0042085912447516
6 Kincheloe, Joe L. 2007. "Why a Book on Urban Education?" In *19 Urban Questions: Teaching in the City,* edited by Shirley R. Steinberg and Joe L. Kincheloe, 1–27. New York: Peter Lang: 5–8.
7 Sleeter, Christine. 2008. "Preparing White Teachers for Diverse Students." In *Handbook of Research on Teacher Education: Enduring Questions and Changing Contexts* [3rd ed.], edited by Marilyn Cochran-Smith, Sharon Feiman-Nemser, D. John McIntyre, and Kelly E. Demers, 559–582. New York: Routledge; Wilkinson, Gayle A. 2009. "Supportive Induction Slows the Revolving Door." *Research in Comparative and International Education,* 4 (1): 97–110.
8 Kopetz, Patricia B., Anthony J. Lease, and Bonnie Z. Warren-Kring. 2006. *Comprehensive Urban Education.* Boston: Pearson.
9 Fitzpatrick-Harnish, Kate. 2015. *Urban Music Education.* New York: Oxford University Press: 5.
10 Haberman, Martin. 1995. *Star Teachers of Children in Poverty.* West Lafayette: Kappa Delta Pi.
11 Duncan-Andrade, Jeffrey M. R. and Ernest Morrell. 2008. *The Art of Critical Pedagogy: Possibilities for Moving from Theory to Practice in Urban Schools.* New York: Peter Lang.
12 hooks, bell. 2000. *All About Love.* New York: William Morrow and Company: 30.
13 Kincheloe. "Why a Book on Urban Education?" 10.
14 Kincheloe, Joe L. 2007. From Fear to Hope: The Challenges Urban Students Face. In *Teaching City Kids,* edited by Joe L. Kincheloe and kecia hayes, 3–38. New York: Peter Lang: 20.

15 Theoharis, Jeanne. 2009. "I Hate It When People Treat Me Like a Fxxx-Up: Phony Theories, Segregated Schools, and the Culture of Aspiration Among African-American and Latino Teenagers." In *Our Schools Suck: Students Talk Back to a Segregated Nation on the Failures of Urban Education*, edited by Gaston Alonso, Noel S. Anderson, Celina Su, and Jeanne Theoharis, 69–111. New York: New York University Press.
16 Ibid., 110.
17 Ibid., 90.
18 Kopetz, Lease and Warren-Kring. *Comprehensive Urban Education*: 85.

2

NURTURING PEDAGOGY

Acknowledging the gifts of every child

Part 1: From the classroom of Ms. Foreman

Ms. Foreman grew up in the city where she teaches. Speaking candidly, she talks about her earlier experiences: *The city was twenty times worse than it is now. There were a lot of gangs, prostitution, and drugs. A bar on each end of the block. I would see dancers go by and when they fell down, we would laugh. That was until I learned about drugs.*

In terms of Ms. Foreman's current school community, she explains that *students are good with each other because they live together in the neighborhoods. Some get bussed in from other neighborhoods. Many of the neighborhoods are mixed socioeconomically. Wearing uniforms makes a big difference in terms of whether students are from an upper or lower socioeconomic status. The uniforms help offset class distinctions regarding what students wear to school.*

Ms. Foreman teaches in an arts-intensive school. This doesn't mean that her job is easy, but it does mean that she has a very supportive Supervisor of Arts who really stands up for his teachers. At the time of this book, she had a forbidding schedule with fourth through eighth grade band, sixth to eighth grade general music, two special needs classes, and an after-school "killer" jazz band, which is one of the showpieces of the school. Originally hired to build the band program, Ms. Foreman never expected to also teach general music. This was a surprise add-on after several years as a successful band director.

Despite the stress of meeting so many students' needs, she freely admits: *The reward is knowing that I'm touching them in a way beyond music class. All of the students I teach fall in love with band and although they don't always continue, they stay in touch. I get to see a transformation of kids through music because I have them for so many years. I had a boy tell me that I was his greatest female influence. At the end of the year, I get emotional because I had the students for five years. I'm one of the only consistent adults in their lives.*

One disappointment at the school is the lack of support from some of the faculty. *A lot of teachers feel that the arts are a sub-category, and they tell this to the kids. Then the kids feel they don't have to give 100%. In addition, an administrator might pull a student out of band class because of a school-related problem. This can happen even if you have an upcoming concert and the student has a special solo.* She cites another example: *There was a student that was here since kindergarten who was very difficult to manage. However, at the end of eighth grade, she won a special award for art. All the teachers were shocked. I said, "Every student has a gift, and it's our job to foster that."*

She continues: *Some students are introverted when they come to band, but by the end they are more social, have more confidence, and have more friends. If we could figure out what is special about every kid then we could figure out how to teach them. Even if they come with no interest in music class, you can find ways to open them up to music by showing an interest in their interests — by letting them know that what they want to do is important. All kids are teachable, and you just have to get them to buy what you're 'selling.'*

Talking about challenges, she explains: *In general music, the kids come with their own perception of general music. They start with the idea that they don't like it and they were never good at it. I decided I wanted it to be a completely different class for them — something that they had never done before. First, I made a PowerPoint that showed kids playing different instruments. They were all excited. We started with glockenspiels so they could use their note reading skills that they had learned in other general music classes. I gave recorders to sixth graders. After attending a professional development workshop with "Little Kids Rock," I found that the organization's mission and mine were similar: to get all students involved in music through forming a modern band in the class. I got 25 guitars from the organization, and I already had a keyboard lab. Although there are always one or two kids that don't want to try, at the end of the year most of the kids were still asking to play other instruments. It made life so much easier for me. I wanted to give them as much attention as I give the band kids. It was a great solution, and I never got as far as I wanted.*

One day I was teaching piano to a special needs class, and I asked each student to come up to me so I could show them what to do before they sat at their individual keyboards. Katherine, who never says anything, said "Let's get ready to rumble!" It was an aha moment. It helped me know that she liked what she was doing.

In the same class, a new student came in the middle of the year. Coming from a rough neighborhood school, he changed the climate of the whole class. It was difficult, and his classroom assistant wasn't very helpful. Eventually, we got him under control. Then, he stole something from the band room — it was a day when I was ill and out of school. When I got back, another student came to me and said, "My piccolo is gone." The new student had taken the piccolo and discarded it in the boys' bathroom trash can. When we found it, and he confessed, he got suspended. I felt hurt because I was always nice to him. He didn't apologize for a while but did calm down a little after the incident.

As one of two African American teachers who journaled for this book, I asked Ms. Foreman to talk about the advantages or disadvantages that she experiences as a teacher of color. She said, *I'm in a unique position because I grew up in this district and students like that I know where they come from. Teaching the young African American girls and boys — they look up to me and see me as a model of success. It makes me feel empowered.*

I try to give them something that inspires them. Being a Black teacher among students of color makes a difference, but it's not always cut and dry. I had some Black teachers that I didn't like and some White teachers who I loved. But I think it makes a difference in the beginning. If students know you care about them and love them, they can read that.

Ms. Forman's journal, 2015–2016

September

I'm eager to start a new school year. The teachers were required to come back a week before the students for professional development workshops. I must admit these "in-house" workshops are always a disaster, leaving the teachers more confused than when we started. However, all teachers came into the building with smiles, and that was refreshing to see. At the end of the day, we all care deeply for the students, and that is the one commonality amongst everyone in the building.

Let's talk about my new class schedule. . . . I was COMPLETELY BLIND-SIDED!! Apparently, the new guidance counselor was given a copy of the master schedule from last year and told to create a new schedule. She received very little assistance from anyone familiar with how the school runs successfully. On the first day, I learned that in addition to teaching my 170+ band students in 4th to 8th grade, I will now be teaching all 6th to 8th grade general music classes – an additional 225 students! I had no warning this would happen, so I didn't order teaching supplies from last year's budget. I spoke to the new guidance counselor to try and explain how the band program works.

Guess what? She did not care that I wasn't supposed to be teaching general music or that I didn't have supplies to do so effectively. In fact, the guidance counselor told me: "Good luck finding extra money." The principal? She never bothered to answer any of my emails or talk with me about the issue. I feel disrespected and unappreciated for all of the work I've put in building the band program for the last 10 years.

I informed my music supervisor about the changes, and the truth is, in large districts like this, every building administrator (e.g. principal) has the liberty to govern the way he or she chooses. This includes creating the school's schedules, discipline policies, uniform policies, etc. No two buildings are exactly the same. My supervisor told me he will push for another music teacher next year (part-time position). There are currently two of us, but the school houses about 780 students. It was inevitable that I would get one or two non-instrumental classes, but I wasn't mentally prepared for nine.

I've made up my mind, however, to make this a good year, and I know that approaching everything with a positive attitude and positive energy will ultimately be contagious. I've thought of a plan. I called my supervisor back and asked him if I could teach the middle school general music classes as if they were beginner band classes, and he said "ABSOLUTELY!" I can teach them all how to play instruments and "sell" it to them by saying that they will now have the opportunity to apply the skills (note reading and rhythm) they have learned in general music all these years with a real instrument. The problem is . . . I don't have 225 extra band instruments lying around. And I certainly would not trust every kid in the school with a $300 instrument without first volunteering to join the band.

I had no choice but to spend my own money. I'm not conflicted about the purchase because it was for peace of mind. I know that the students will respect me more if I appear to have things under control. I want to be able to have a presentation ready on the first day of school that will make this class legitimate in their eyes. I found a great deal on practice glockenspiels for under $20, so I bought enough for one class. The plan is to store the instruments in the classroom and have each class share them.

My supervisor has agreed to help me purchase 225 recorders with books for the students, and I also plan to take them to the piano lab during the third marking period for beginner piano classes. Hopefully the information they learn on the glockenspiel will carry over to the piano smoothly. I am also going to attend a professional development workshop for "Little Kids Rock" in November. I plan to teach the eighth graders how to play guitar in January to keep them interested throughout the rest of the year. However, we will only switch to guitars if they master the glockenspiel and recorder. My biggest concern is getting them excited about participating in something new and challenging that will take them out of their comfort zone. By now, they already have a perception about music. Either they like it or they don't. We'll see what happens.

October

Just as I expected . . . the schedule has changed four times since the first day of school. Turns out, I wasn't the only one with a messed-up schedule. Things are so disorganized that it's hard to stay positive. I'm starting to see the negative effects this new schedule is having on the band program. I am not able to rehearse with them as a full ensemble regularly. I haven't been able to start the new fourth grade students yet because I'm still adjusting to the 225 non-band students on my schedule. Parents are anxiously calling the school to find out when their child can join the band. It's nice to hear that the parents and students are eager to get started. I am overwhelmed, but I still feel a sense of hope.

My returning band students are so amazing! They know that things are different, but they don't see the overall damaging effects yet. It's a great thing because they are still happy to be involved and in love with playing music. They voluntarily come to the band room during recess to practice their music. Sometimes they come just to eat their lunch, hang out, and talk. They smile every day and are eager to share what they've learned over the weekend. They are supportive of each other and they just want to be good musicians. I feel so blessed to have that love and appreciation flowing in my direction every day. It combats the negative feelings that try to sneak into my mind throughout the week.

The general music classes are interesting. It's like teaching a bunch of fourth grade beginner classes, except they are older. I have to train them to behave accordingly in the band room. In fact, I had a talk with the students the other day about their lack of focus (truthfully, it's only three or four kids that create the distraction). I told them that I feel like they are waiting for me to scream and yell at them. Their immediate reaction was an affirmative head nod.

I knew this was an opportunity for a teachable moment, so I said, "Do you know that we teach people how to treat us by our choices and our actions?" No one said a word as they listened with curiosity. I said, "If the only thing you respond to is screaming and yelling, then that's exactly how people will talk you. Don't you know that it's disrespectful to scream and yell in someone's face? Why would you train someone to disrespect you like that? It's a backward process, and there is something wrong with that kind of thinking." They all silently stared at me while processing what was said. They told me I had a good point. I continued by saying, "I refuse to treat you like that. I'm going to train you to respond to patience and respect. If you make a bad choice there will be consequences, and if you do the right thing there will be rewards. Don't disrespect me, and I won't disrespect you. It will take you some time, but I'm sure you'll get use to my teaching style."

I had this talk with all of my classes that week, and they all reacted the same way. I'm seeing a positive change in them. They are all interested in playing, but we still have to work on the chattiness of some classes. They are not trying to be rude to me. They are just too friendly with each other. I told them they all have to perform in the spring concert at the end of the year for the final exam. Since then, they have been trying very hard to grasp the concepts and focus. I feel like there is a lot of potential, but it is frustrating feeling like I'm starting over again. This is similar to the first year of building the band program 10 years ago. I'm trying to teach a group of non-performing students how to participate in a rehearsal even though they didn't volunteer to be here. Challenging task, I know. I just think it would be amazing if the entire middle school learned how to read music and play an instrument proficiently. That would be really neat. Who knows? There may be some future band members coming out of this group. I guess we'll wait and see.

November

The third month of the school year has been filled with interesting occurrences. It's the month where the bulk of the performance material is learned for the winter concert, and it's also the month where we have many days off due to the annual teacher convention, holidays, and government elections. As a band director, this is the time when I really get to see what kind of year I'll have with my students. I truly get the sense of their level of dedication, musical knowledge, camaraderie toward one another, and emotional stability. All of these aspects set the tone for the rest of the year because I make adjustments to my teaching style and approach based on their behavioral responses thus far.

I feel a little bad for the advanced students because my schedule doesn't allow the time to teach and explore more advanced material. I constantly have to remind myself that high school will teach them more advanced material and that I have done well by providing them with a solid foundation and advanced skills for their age. Luckily, the majority of them are in the after-school jazz band, doubling on another instrument, so they have advanced music and a new instrument to keep them stimulated until the sixth graders catch up.

I must say the sixth grade band students pleasantly surprise me every day! They are SO dedicated and talented. They don't like not being as good as the older students, so they have been practicing endlessly and catching up rather quickly. I think the concert will go well, but it's still a wild card. Only time will tell.

The inconsistency of having multiple days off during the month of November has had a negative effect on the general music classes because I am only scheduled to see them once a week. In some cases, I haven't seen the students in two weeks, so they are two lessons behind everyone else. The "best" part is that the district still expects us to give everyone a grade each week – no excuses. My name has appeared on the missing grades report several times, and I don't feel guilty about it. How am I supposed to give a fair grade to students who I haven't taught in two weeks? I only end up teaching two lessons before I have to administer a benchmark test or quiz. I feel bad for them sometimes – especially the students struggling to connect with the class.

All grades and transcripts are electronic these days, so I can check to see how my band students are doing on a regular basis. When the students are not passing a class, I call them to my classroom and ask them to explain why they are failing the subject. I encourage them by stating, "If something gives you a hard time, then you simply have to work harder. . . . Just like you do in band." I tell them to ask someone for help (the teacher, a friend, or come to me and I'll help). I always say, "You don't have to get straight A's, but you do have to pass. . . . No excuses. Simply doing all of your homework and projects will accomplish that goal. I'm going to be checking every week from now on." This usually helps because the students are shocked that I cared enough to personally check on them. They don't want to disappoint me or be taken out of band for "Intervention" because they feel like it would let me and the other students down.

One day, I decided to check the grades of all the students I have for general music. When I asked how they were doing in school, the majority of them had no idea. Most of the students throw their tests papers away after seeing the grade and never think twice about it. My findings prompted me to talk to each class about the importance of checking their grades on the computer system weekly. I took the last fifteen minutes of all eleven classes to call students one by one to see their grades on my computer. If a student was borderline or failing, then I encouraged them bring up that grade so they won't have to go to summer school. I discussed a plan of action and told them to let me know if they needed help.

I learned that a few of the students who needed help academically were also giving me a hard time in music class by showing up late and not actively participating during the lesson. One boy in particular made an impression on me. On the second day of class, he told me he was late because he "got lost" (he's been in the school for five years. There is no way this seventh grade student was lost!). I told him to get a hall pass, but he was unsuccessful because his previous class was lunch. I lowered his class participation grade and told him not to come to my class late again or he'd have to spend his lunch period with me.

After that uncomfortable encounter, he reluctantly showed up to class on time with a chip on his shoulder. Clearly, he did not want to be in music class. His attitude slowly changed after the day I showed him his grades and gave him an action plan for the subjects he was failing (science, language arts, and social studies). I spoke to him discretely and sincerely, even though deep down I was annoyed that he was giving me a hard time each week. I let him know that he still had time to fix it and that I would help him if he needed it. A week later, he came to my classroom on the way to dismissal to say that he passed his language arts and science tests. He said he pulled his grades up above seventy but still needed to work on social studies. I gave him a high five, celebrated with him, and thanked him for sharing the news with me. He was proud of himself, and I could tell he couldn't wait to tell someone the good news.

I was touched by that interaction; when he left, I smiled and thanked God for that connection. Honestly, I was shocked to see him because I didn't think he cared about one word I was saying. Now, he comes to my classroom at the end of the day with other students just to say hello, and he actively participates in music class. It sounds like a scene out of a movie, but it actually happened. Simple gestures go a long way, especially when they are sincere and one does not expect anything in return. Hopefully he stays on the right path.

December

Though I enjoy teaching general music students how to play the glockenspiel, I feel that I need more in the bag to keep them engaged long term. I sincerely want to keep these classes "instrumental" in nature, so I've also been teaching rhythm (and note reading) with the use of various hand drums and drumstick patterns. Sometimes we form small percussion ensembles with mixed instrumentation, and it takes two lessons to get through the exercise. Sometimes I have to re-evaluate my goals: Should I try to get them to perform the task perfectly, or should I be content knowing that they are trying their best with little-to-no musical training?

I am a perfectionist, so my instinct is to rehearse until it is performance ready. Sometimes when you push them too hard, they give up; however, if your expectations are too low, then you train them to put forth minimal effort and they never reach their potential. Learning the dynamic of each class is an ongoing process because some classes experience more growth than others due to their level of interest and not necessarily their ability. The trick as a teacher is to find a way to get them to buy what you are selling! Sometimes, if the students feel that you care about them on a personal level, they will try simply because they like you as a person.

In an effort to provide more options for my general music students, I attended a workshop hosted by the program "Little Kids Rock." I was initially attracted to the idea of getting a classroom set of free instruments, but after going through the workshop and learning their philosophy and curriculum, I'm intrigued. I think it will be a good bridge between the general music and instrumental music classes. I ordered twenty-five acoustic guitars and guitar racks. The school already has five electric guitars and an electric bass. We also have twenty-four working electric pianos and a drum set. Now I have to practice guitar and figure out a goal for the students. They are very excited to start learning in the new year.

December was a challenging month for the band students, but I was strangely calm this year. Judging from their practice habits, I had a feeling they would be okay for the concert. The district does an annual holiday video to showcase different music programs across the town. This is a great idea, in theory, but as usual things never run organized and smoothly. No one had any idea when the taping would occur until a week before, so the art department had to scramble to decorate the stage while music teachers scrambled to finish teaching students the endings of each piece. We were scrambling to finish teaching the pieces because the videotaping happens weeks before the winter concert!

Days after everyone stressed themselves out for the performance, we received an email saying, "We did not realize the date scheduled for taping is a half day for the students. The new schedule will be announced shortly." Scenarios like this happen all the time, so we just learn to shake it off and adjust. The video performance went pretty well except that my "favorite" new bass clarinet student squealed on the most exposed part of the piece! It was frustrating, but it was a learning experience for him and I'm all about learning from our mistakes. In the end, high school technology students edited the video, so those measures were inaudible due to a variety of other issues.

The band students had three performances for the Winter Concert, and they nailed each one! I am ecstatic with the progress of the sixth graders. I have a really good feeling about this year. They are supportive, funny, friendly, and kind to one another. I know this will go a long way in fostering a healthy learning environment throughout the year. I'm trying to teach them to be self-sufficient, and it's working. They help each other and only come to me with questions when they need guidance on a new concept or to settle a disagreement. I resolved years ago that the students are rarely the issue at this school. It's the administration that stresses everyone out!

Let's talk about the new bass clarinet student I mentioned moments ago. I'll call him CJ. New students come into the building every year either from other districts or from other schools in the town. Oddly enough, I don't usually get new students that join the band. In some cases, the student had a bad experience in their former music program. In other cases, the student chooses to wait until they have been acclimated to the routine of a new school.

In this case, he jumped right in. It was great to see, but I should have been a bit more suspicious after he continuously sang his own praises. He says he was the best player at his other school. As time went on, I watched CJ's behavior and interactions with other students and noticed that he may not fit in so well with the other seventh grade students. He is easily one of the quirkiest kids I've ever had. He doesn't take kindly to anyone trying to help him with the music, his jokes can be borderline offensive, he calls out during rehearsals – usually about something that didn't need to be said. One day he waited for a girl to drop popcorn on the floor so he could eat it.

I went to guidance to see if he has an IEP, and he doesn't. He's just immature and quirky. Oh, did I mention he squeaks on the clarinet ALL THE TIME??!! I find that I'm annoyed with him most of the time, but I see that he's really trying his best so I get over it. Just before winter break, many of the students bought gifts of appreciation. I received handmade cards, artwork, scarves, lotion, music charms, teddy bears, necklaces, etc. Guess what? CJ bought me . . . a bar of SOAP! At first, I was very confused and conflicted. I didn't know if I should be appreciative or offended. He told me, "I hope you like my gift. I paid $25 for it myself and its gourmet." I wanted to say, "Twenty-five dollars? Take it back!"

But I was touched. It was definitely only something he would think to buy as a gift, and honestly it was very thoughtful. He knew I liked nice fragrances, so he invested in something he knew no one else would buy. I saw a different side of him in that moment. He infuriates me, but I see potential in him. I just need to remember that patience, acceptance, guidance, and a little bit of tough love is the way to go.

February

February is shaping up to be another eventful month. At the beginning of the year, I promised myself that I would not agree to extra performances simply because I knew my rehearsal time would be limited. I told myself I would only take on extra responsibilities if my students were ready and I felt they would truly benefit from the experience. In the past, we'd have twelve performances a year for different events including visitors in the building who represent different political affiliations, annual concerts, special schoolwide assemblies, community service trips, competitions, Board of Education meetings, etc.

So far, this year I've turned down five invitations simply because we were not ready. On February third, the principal paid me a visit during class time, not to observe the students, but to say, "Foreman, the band has to perform in two weeks at the Board of Education meeting and we never tell them 'No.' You're going to have to figure something out," I told her, "I don't know if I'll be able to make that work, but I will try and let you know." The truth is I had every intention of saying "No." We just had a winter concert a month ago. Since then, I've only seen the kids four times because of winter break and this ridiculous schedule. Everyone always tells you what they want, but no one ever offers a helping hand around here.

Later, I asked her for permission to pull the students from class for extra rehearsals during the day. She ignored my emails. I asked her if I could stay after school with the students, and she didn't want to stay past 4:30 p.m. Finally, my vice principal chimed in and warmly offered to stay after school with us until 5 p.m. She spoke with teachers to remind them about upcoming rehearsals during the day. I agreed to the performance, but mostly because I knew it would benefit the students to perform in public to a new audience.

The jazz band has the most challenging piece to perform, so I decided to push them to complete their competition piece three months ahead of schedule! The students worked hard and absolutely nailed the performance! They received a standing ovation, and I could not have been prouder. After the performance, we did not receive an email or visit from the principal to congratulate the students. Things just resumed back to normal . . . until the next time they need something above and beyond the call of duty.

In general music land, I'm starting to notice a lack of enthusiasm creeping into some of the classes. I forgot to factor in that the students are learning to play a brand-new instrument with the opportunity to practice only one day a week. The problem with the guitar program is that no one can take an instrument home to practice because there are only enough instruments for one classroom at a time.

Truthfully, I wouldn't trust some of the general music students with acoustic guitars in soft cases. They did not sign up to learn the instrument and their parents did not sign permission slips, so technically they would not be responsible for any damages. However, there comes a time when you have to practice a few things to get to the next level. Let's face it, going from a G chord to a D chord on the guitar is not the easiest thing in the world to do with students who have varying degrees of interest, coordination skills, and background knowledge of the instrument.

It's taking longer than I planned, but they will get it. I need to figure out how to keep them from losing interest. One day a week is pretty tough. I will have to modify my plans and goals for the class. Initially, I wanted all of the students to perform on guitar in the spring concert, but at this rate I don't think it will happen. Some classes are better than others, but the students are not retaining the information from week to week. I think I will switch things up a bit and take the students to the piano lab next marking period. I will give them incentive by saying they have to learn a certain set of chords on guitar first before switching to piano. If I can get the students to perform the same chords on piano, then I'll have more options for the spring concert. Perhaps some can sing while others play. I'll run it by them and see how they react.

March

I witnessed an interaction between two students that made me smile. I watched one of the eighth grade students show patience and kindness to CJ. I've been watching him over the past few months and watching the way he interacts with the other students. All of the interactions usually end with someone saying "CJ, stop!" or "Why did you do that?" Sometimes, the students will simply ignore him or limit their interactions to one or two sentences because he tends to tell jokes that always seem to fall flat. He tries too hard to fit in, and his social awkwardness makes it difficult to connect with him.

We played a music festival this month that featured many artists and performers across the county. The students worked very hard to prepare a high school level piece of music. Rehearsals were productive/progressive, and students were very complimentary and supportive with one another. The piece begins in a very stately way with drums, cymbals, chimes, tuba, and . . . bass clarinet. On the first note, I heard an ambient squeal coming from the back of the ensemble. Two seconds later, the squeal was not so ambient. It was loud and persistent.

Luckily, the baritone saxophone student next to CJ jumped right in and covered the part. CJ realized something was wrong with his instrument and eventually stopped playing altogether. After the performance, while loading the instruments onto the storage truck, a sixth grade student came to me and "Something is wrong with CJ; he's crying." I passively grabbed another instrument and said, "He's probably upset about the performance, he'll be okay. We all have bad shows." The student grabbed my arm to get my undivided attention and said, "No, he keeps cursing at everyone." I was confused as to why he would be cursing at other people so I went to find him.

Low and behold, I hear an eighth grade student say, "Don't worry about it CJ. Calm down, it could have happened to anyone." His response was, "Shut the *uck up! It didn't happen to anyone. It happened to me. Why is my instrument always messed up? I hate this s*it, leave me the *uck alone!" Students were trying to console him while trying to hide their confused laughter at the same time. It was a very strange sight.

After quickly assessing the situation, I called his name and said, "What's wrong with you? What are you doing?" He turned to me and said, "I'm always the one messing everybody up!" My response to that was, "So, now you think it's okay to curse them all out?" He looked at me and said, "No." Then I told him, "Relax – you're more upset than anybody else here. We don't care about it anymore. It happens. We all have bad performances. Get over it!" It sounds a little harsh, but it worked. He immediately stopped crying and came back to his senses. Later, he told me he may have banged his instrument on the side of the truck when we were unloading. I wanted to put him in a headlock on the spot!

During lunch period, some students prefer to eat in the band room and practice their instruments. I watched as the students had group discussions about what they did in science class or who their favorite teachers were. Inevitably, CJ would say something that derails the conversation completely and everyone would try to ignore it and carry on. After the parking lot incident, I noticed one eighth grade girl taking the time to be more attentive with CJ. She would respond to his off-the-cuff comments and engage his thought process. It was interesting to see because, for the first time, he was being validated by a peer. Other students would join their conversation or friendly debate. I didn't say anything to her about it for two weeks, but she treated him that way consistently and I thought it was remarkable.

Eventually, I thanked her for making CJ feel a part of the group. I told her I noticed she's been taking the time to be kind and patient with him. I assured her that it would leave a lasting impression on him because it validates him as a person. She smiled and said, "It's not a big deal!" She doesn't think it's a big deal, but it is bigger than she thinks. She is the most popular eighth grade girl in the school. She is a bright light, sociable, smart, talented, and very pretty. By the end of the month, I noticed other students treating CJ with more respect and patience. Boys and girls alike. She has been in the band program since fourth grade, and she had been mentored by older students before. It makes me very proud to see that.

In general music, all of the students are progressing nicely in the classes. The guitar students are working in groups to perform strumming patterns and chord changes to simple pop tunes. So far, everyone has gotten an A or B on the assignment. It is interesting watching the tough students fear failure in front of their peers. I'm learning that there is a lot of talent in these classes. They just need to be pushed out of their comfort zone. I have been approached by several guitar students who say they would like to join band next year. I predict there will be a few more come September.

The band students are working tirelessly to learn the competition music and additional spring concert charts. The jazz band is working on improvisation and standard blues progressions. The machine is trucking along! PAARC testing is going to begin very shortly. Administration is already training the staff on Proctor and Examiner protocol. The students are getting nervous about the exam, and I'm worried about how much class time I will lose as a result. Moreover, how far will the students regress once the regular schedule kicks back in?

The general music students worry me more than the band students. I will be sure to rehearse with the band students during lunch recess, but general music students are already at a severe disadvantage. I may have to re-evaluate my plans once again before this is all over. The students have learned how to play several instruments throughout the school year. Maybe this will simply be a music appreciation course in the end. Maybe my job is to simply expose the students to a variety of instruments they would not normally have the luxury of trying. I want them to have a greater sense of music appreciation by the end of the year. If they are able to perform in the spring concert, that will be a bonus.

April

It's hard to believe I am in my tenth year of public school teaching! In some way, this is the most challenging year of all because it has been mentally and emotionally draining. I must say, the students are amazing. I've learned to stop stressing about the things that are out of my circle of influence and simply be in the moment. Make the most of what I have in front of me. As I look at the students, I notice they have no idea what's going on behind the scenes. They are just happy to be here with their friends and playing music. If I assess them objectively, I can honestly say they are achieving the same amount of success they have in the past. They are moving at a slower pace, but they are getting there. There are concepts I have not been able to introduce to the band due to lack of ensemble time, but it's all coming together anyway. It's really amazing to watch the older students step up and carry the band on their shoulders. It brings tears to my eyes when I think about it because I was so stressed about the schedule earlier in the year. I didn't want everything that I worked so hard for to crash. I didn't count on the values and hard work that were also instilled in them over the years. This is a treat!

I was recently invited to conduct the 2016 New Jersey Region II Middle School Honors Jazz Ensemble, otherwise known as Region Jazz Band! I also judged my first jazz competition at the middle school level in Pennsylvania. I have always wanted to work with my peers on this level, but I never knew how to get my foot in the door. Both experiences were eye opening for me because it allowed me to see how far my students have come and how far we still have to go.

We are getting closer to the end of the year festivities, and I feel even more stressed because I am unable to complete the important tasks that have absolutely nothing to do with directly teaching the students. I still have to collect fundraising money, collect final payments for a competition, update spreadsheets, give benchmarks, update the gradebook for all 375 students, make sure checks are sent to the bus company for the competition, make sure the check is sent to Festivals of Music, speak to the head of food services to verify a date for the annual Band Awards dinner, verify concert dates, verify paperwork for guest clinicians from Montclair State University, speak to the head custodian about the setup for various events, proctor the PARCC exam, and create permission slips for upcoming rehearsals and performances. I'm sure there is more, but this is everything currently in the front of my thoughts. In short, this is the WORST time to get sick! I was however, comforted by thoughtful emails sent from students saying they "miss me and hope I get well soon."

When I came back to school, it seemed some things have changed. The overall tone amongst the students was laziness and apathy. After PARCC testing, everyone was out to lunch, including some teachers. "It's only April guys, snap out of it!" Students were beginning to behave recklessly in the hallways. Students stopped doing their homework; tardiness and absences increased. This went on for a few weeks. I even noticed a shift in some of my band students who seemed to be going through the motions during rehearsals. It's strange, and I don't like it. I told the students I expect them to at least give me the same energy I give to them during rehearsals. I said, "I don't always feel like standing up in front of you, teaching, and putting up with some of your attitudes, but I do it because I made a commitment and you depend on me to follow through." They got the point once I threatened to pull music from the concert that they loved to perform and worked tirelessly on. After a stretch of non-productive rehearsals, they got it together and came back stronger than ever.

May

I have an eighth grade student that re-joined the band this year after a three-year hiatus. He was removed from the band program by his teachers and the principal because he was failing math and language arts. He clearly loved music as a young boy and still loves music as a teenager. Every year, he would come to my classroom and ask if he could join the band. He would always say "I wish I was still in band." This broke my heart because I knew that my class wasn't the reason he was failing, and it should not have been used as a consequence. In fact, my class never met at the same time as math or language arts, so it should not matter if he was in band or not. That's like telling a kid they can't take gym or art because they are failing math and language arts. It would NEVER happen.

This double standard has always existed for me at this school. Every year I fight for the students even though the benefits of the class are clear and unwavering. Some new staff member comes in (this year it was the guidance counselor), and I have to begin the fight all over again. The one good thing that came out of this horrible schedule is that it allowed him to join again due to a loophole. I am so happy he is here! He is one of the most teachable students I've had in a long time.

I needed a keyboard player for the jazz band, so he learned it. I needed a guitarist for one tune, so he learned it. I needed a suspended cymbal player for one of the competition pieces, so he learned it. He's always there to help set up chairs and equipment, carry bags, organize the fifth grade students, and more. He is so respectful, kind-hearted, and talented. It's the fourth marking period, and he is still failing math and language arts for the year. He is in danger of not graduating. I feel badly for not paying closer attention throughout the year. I've been so overwhelmed with other responsibilities.

A part of me is frustrated with the system. Apparently, he was never good in math and language arts. How does a kid get all the way to eighth grade when he has always struggled academically? I am in one of the good schools in our district! He should have been tutored or offered remediation classes. We have offered free after-school academic programs in the past. Why didn't his parents enroll him? I feel like the ball was dropped on so many levels with this kid. It's sad to me because he has so many great qualities that he should be excelling! He just needs someone to put forth a little extra effort and take him under their wing. I pray he finds that in high school.

For the first time ever, two of my mentors have come to work with my jazz band students. I am both intimidated and eager to share what we have been doing here at my school. The competition is on June 4th, and I recently gave my students a new piece to learn. I performed this piece with the Region Jazz Ensemble last month and fell in love with it. One day, I was listening to the piece in the band room when a student asked if we were going to perform it. I said, "It's a little tricky for us to do in less than a month." She smiled and walked away. As she approached the back of the room, I said, "Wait, do you think we should try it?" She said, "Yes," so I decided to let the band vote on it. I knew it would require a huge commitment from them as the state competition was quickly approaching. The band voted unanimously "YES" as they fell in love with the piece, too!

I may have momentarily lost my mind! I'm usually finishing up performance pieces at this time, not starting fresh with new music less than a month before the big day! The new piece was not completed, and I contemplated pulling it from the program several times, but there comes a point when you just have to go for it. The students have been working so hard on their parts that it would be a crime not to let them do it. One Friday, I received an email from a student with a video attached. It was the entire saxophone section practicing the new piece in someone's back-yard! The message read, "We've been at it for four hours already and we're not done yet!" I was blown away! I shared the video with my supervisor and closest friends. Did I mention, they sounded AMAZING!?

I love them dearly, and they never hesitate to show me the same kind of love every day. A few eighth grade students came into my room the other day crying. I thought they failed a test or got bad news about graduation. When I asked what was wrong, they stated, "It's almost over and we don't want to leave you." I encouraged them to make the most of each day and to continue making new memories to hold onto forever. Deep inside, I was sad as well. I've known them for almost five years, and I've seen them grow into remarkable young people. For the first time, the valedictorian and salutatorian are both band students! We hugged, and I told them how proud they make me. They told me they would not have achieved it if I weren't in their lives. One more month to go, and I'm already fighting back tears

My response

From September to May, Ms. Foreman's journal entries illustrate an ethic of care that undergirds all her decisions and interactions with students. Care, in this journal, is demonstrated in several ways. The most common idea about care is showing love and understanding for the student: "I love them dearly, and they never hesitate to show me the same kind of love every day." Pre-service teachers often equate this form of care in student-teacher interactions.

However, there are other forms of caring that carry the same importance in creating a nurturing environment. Holding students to high standards – reassuring them that they are capable of challenging work – is particularly necessary in the urban school where students are stereotyped as less intelligent or lazy. According to Ms. Foreman, "They just need to be pushed out of their comfort zone."

John Goodlad, a nationally recognized author for education reform, introduces pedagogical nurturing as one of the four dimensions of teaching. He, like other well-known writers Nel Noddings and Gloria Ladson-Billings, recognized that caring is not only essential to child development but learning as well. Students learn when they sense that teachers believe in them and take time to know them beyond a score on a test. Students learn when they are challenged because someone believes they are capable of rigor and hard work.

Ms. Foreman had a challenging set of circumstances in that she found out the first day of school that her schedule, along with her instrumental responsibilities, included a substantial number of general music classes. She knew what it took to build a band program based on care and trust, yet the addition of general music classes threatened to undermine the level of care she was able to give to her instrumental students. At the same time, she sought ways to care for her general music students through a new curriculum, purchasing instruments and seeking out professional development for enhancing her classroom teaching skills. The conflict that she, and many other music teachers face, has to do with time – time to give the most to every child under her care.

Ms. Foreman is a master teacher who built a thriving program in an urban middle school. Hopefully, her tenacity in working through the frustrations and challenges while keeping a positive mindset becomes obvious as one reads through her journal. Her love for her students, whether in checking individual grades or challenging students to play daunting repertoire or even telling CJ to "get over it," exemplify nurturing pedagogy at its best. Most importantly, the students know that she cares about each one of them. "Simple gestures go a long way, especially when they are sincere and one does not expect anything in return." This is perhaps the most essential piece in authentic teaching.

Part 2: Nurturing pedagogy: Acknowledging the gifts of every child

Liking children is not hard. Love for children is more complex. It is an act of compassion that recognizes each child's potential for success and supports each child during periods of frustration, joy, and vulnerability. According to bell hooks, "When we love children we acknowledge by our every action that they are not property, that they have rights – that we respect and uphold their rights."[1] The dimensions of love include care, kindness, recognition, respect, commitment, and trust[2] – all of which are intrinsic to the educator who sees students beyond a simple academic measure. Through care and affirmation, we communicate love to students for who they are and who they aspire to be.

There are times when children seem to push you away, ignoring your invitation to learn or rejecting your advances to help. More often than not, this rejection has nothing to do with you, the teacher, but is, rather, an outward signal that something else is not right. It could be lack of proper nutrition, an overwhelming feeling of failure, a need to look tough in front of others, or inexperience with a caring adult. Caring, in this case, requires inner tenacity and patience to parse through the layers of resistance that many children have developed to survive. Understanding the purpose of these layers is essential for establishing yourself as the adult in the room and the person children can begin to trust. This is the hard work of love.

Caring and receiving care are essential human needs that music teachers can model not only through everyday interactions but also through music itself. We work in a medium that is both expressive and community building. When children experience a sense of belonging, they begin to see themselves as a part of a larger whole. Making music is our greatest tool for tapping into these needs and nurturing the inner child in each student. Music can soothe, music can ignite passion, music can give courage. In short, music can be a conduit for reaching even the most troubled child.

Children cannot engage in meaningful music making when they show disregard for others or lack of empathy. Nel Noddings, a foremost authority on care in schooling, writes, "What children need to learn is how to sympathize and empathize with other people and to understand their own inclinations toward cruelty and violence."[3] How do children learn to care? They learn by modeling significant adults in their lives. Teachers, among others, are significant adults in children's lives.

Whether it involves music, math, social studies, or language arts, children cannot learn if they lack the most foundational element of getting along in a social environment.[4] For that reason, it is not unrealistic to gear some music lessons toward the collaborative and cooperative nature of making music. Talking honestly, without judgment, about dispositions of care such as listening to others without interrupting, acknowledging different points of view, and demonstrating respectful behavior toward the teacher may need to preempt a more musical goal in the teaching process.

In my teaching, for example, safe handling of electronic keyboards became a mechanism for teaching about care for each other.[5] Additionally, actively listening to each student play helped develop respectful attentiveness and support among students in the class. The excitement of finding new timbral possibilities or familiar tunes on the keyboards encouraged students to share with others. As such, they became partners and tutors at the same time. Although I set out to teach some basic keyboard skills, the goal of demonstrating human kindness was just as important.

Culturally responsive teaching

Caring evolves from a keen desire to know and understand the lives of your students. It is not enough to know a child's name and his/her/their in-school behavior. Informed teaching requires that music teachers also learn about the cultural context of the community and the students they teach. This is grounded in the belief that culturally responsive teaching and educational equity are inextricably linked. To foster this connection, teachers must develop a deep understanding of their own beliefs about, for example, race/ethnicity, sexual orientation, ableism, or religious affiliation, with the intention of developing behaviors and curriculum that respond to the cultural needs of their students.[6]

Although some teachers associate the term "culture" primarily with geographic location (i.e. China), the essence of cultural responsiveness is to not only know students' heritage but to also recognize the oppressive forces that work against marginalized groups. A culturally responsive teacher acknowledges that there is a power component whenever groups are marginalized. Sensitivity to the biases, discrimination, and other barriers that students face is part of cultural responsiveness on the part of the teacher. In a larger sense, culture represents "the ways that groups of people identify themselves based on commonalities."[7] These groups are porous so that any one person may be a part of more than one. For instance, Black females may confront challenges with regard to race and gender but could also encounter bias if they identify as LGBTQ. For more of this discussion, see Chapters 5 and 6.

When teachers hold conscious or unconscious stereotypes about students who have different backgrounds or value systems, they may act on a different set of expectations from others in the class. Gloria Ladson-Billings,[8] one of the most oft-quoted educational researchers on culturally responsive teaching, identifies three central tenets of cultural responsiveness in the classroom: First, teachers must never waver from holding high standards for the students; second, teachers must demonstrate that they have developed cultural competence regarding students' lives beyond a simple academic measure; and third, teachers must have a sense of socio-political consciousness, the recognition that learning takes place in a context that is community driven and politically charged. These dispositions provide a comprehensive view of culturally responsive teaching.

Every person has a story or lens through which they see the world. For the music teacher, it is tempting to teach exclusively from his/her/their own experiences rather than learning about how students' experiences and lifestyles influence their learning process. Here is a brief example: As a young teacher, I took a short trip to Arizona where I had the opportunity to teach on a Hopi reservation. Using best teaching practice (as I knew it at the time), I taught a fifth grade general music class starting with some exploratory experiences with sound production that led to an improvisation with atypical instruments. Although highly successful in my previous teaching with White students, it fell flat with the Hopi children. What I didn't know was that in Hopi culture, the children are taught to support the group rather than express their own individuality. Thus, asking the children to explore and create sound episodes was completely out of their comfort zone and counter to their cultural context. Not only was I inexperienced in terms of the Native American culture and ways of learning but also with the power differential of a White teacher teaching Hopi children.

Bobby Starnes, who spent years on the Chippewa-Cree reservation, states two important ideas that I have taken to heart:

> The first is how very little we know about the ways Native American chil-
> dren learn. We don't recognize the chasm that exists between their needs and
> our traditionally accepted curricula and methods. The second is how difficult
> it is for even the most skilled and dedicated white teachers to teach well
> when we know so little about the history, culture, and communities in which
> we teach – and when what we do know has been derived from a white
> education. In such cases, solid teaching skills, good intentions, hard work, and
> loving the kids just aren't enough.[9]

Although there are many types of culture represented in the classroom, this chapter focuses particularly on cultural responsiveness as related to race and ethnicity.
Teachers across the nation have different experiences with students depending on
the location of the school and the number of students of color in the classroom. In
terms of race and ethnicity, some teachers may teach classes where students represent many races/ethnicities. Others have classes populated primarily by students of
one or two different races/ethnicities (with the understanding that White is also a
race).

A colleague of mine who taught fifty-five high school students of color in her
music class put time aside each week for students to share some music from their
cultures.[10] The students listened to many different styles of music and learned why
the music was significant to the contributing student. Importantly, the students
became teachers in those moments and taught the class how to dance to salsa and
Bollywood music; how to freestyle rap; how to create reggaetón beats and lyrics;
and how to create and engage with EDM (electronic dance music). It is important
to note that such student-led teaching flips "power roles" and places authentic
importance on who the students are and where they are coming from. The students
celebrated their own identities and cultural backgrounds and helped others understand – through active music making and reflecting – why such musical means were
so important.

What are some other ways that music teachers can learn about their students?
Here are a few suggestions, some more relevant than others depending on how
many racial/ethnic cultures are represented in the music class. Reading related
books on the particular culture can be very informative, especially when the read-
ings give clues to the value systems and how children learn. A music teacher's open
curiosity about students' culture gives students reassurance that their lives matter.
On the other hand, there is no substitute for first-hand knowledge. Whether it is a
highly diverse classroom or one with a concentration of one or two races/ethnici-
ties, the school-community connection and what children do out of the classroom
is a vital resource.[11] Adults from the community, for instance, can provide historical context that greatly enhance the music teacher's understanding of the context

in which their students are raised. Many members of the community are already engaged in music native to their heritage through lullabies, work songs, family music making, or professional performing. They can enrich a choral curriculum, for instance, by teaching the language and meaning of the text. They can demonstrate instrumental prowess on native instruments, they can provide a source of support for helping music teachers understand the values and learning style of the children under their care, and they can tell stories and folktales that often have underlying moral messages that illuminate the beliefs of the culture.

Some music teachers feel confident that teaching a few non-Western music making activities during the year demonstrates their connectedness to multicultural education. Too often, music teacher-development workshops and teacher preparation classes approach diversity through games, songs, and music listening that are, in many instances, "sanitized" (e.g. translated to English or simplified rhythms/ melodic patterns such as adjusting an odd-meter song to traditional duple or triple time). Stephen Benham writes:

> In *music* education, this narrow focus has resulted in the perception that addressing cultural diversity in the classroom is more of a materials (curricular) issue than it is of developing teaching methods and styles that are culturally diverse. And arming teachers with a set of multicultural songs, dances, or other cultural icons, is certainly easier than helping teachers to develop an understanding of, and the ability to work within, culturally diverse settings.[12]

As Benham acknowledges, teaching for cultural responsiveness goes beyond a single multicultural activity. For teachers who are uncomfortable teaching multicultural music, though, this may be the first step. Cultural responsiveness, however, is far more complex.[13] Vicki R. Lind and Constance McKoy explain, "It's not simply adding on a few new 'pop' songs or incorporating 'world music.' Rather, it involves infusing the ideals of culturally responsive teaching into every aspect of the classroom."[14]

Geneva Gay and Kipehoge Kirkland[15] have identified three components when integrating cultural knowledge in a pedagogical setting. First, cultural responsiveness assumes that in order to engage students in deep learning, teachers must understand the integral connection between multicultural education and equal access to learning opportunities. This means that teaching from a multicultural perspective is part of insuring that all students are equitably served. Second, teachers must become highly conscious and reflective of their own teaching and the ways in which they interact with students. And third, teachers need to continually question what is to be taught, how it is to be taught, and who their teaching primarily addresses. In order to engage in culturally responsive teaching, music teachers must not only acknowledge its import in teaching the whole child but also develop heightened awareness to the needs of all children, how students' identity influences learning, the social-political context in which students live, and the kind of nurturing that engenders self-confidence and a sense of belonging.

The importance of belonging

Culturally responsive teaching is one dimension of nurturing pedagogy. Caring for students also involves making sure that each student has an important place in the school community. Students with a strong sense of self have confidence and a feeling of efficacy – "I can do it" – generally have a positive attitude toward school. These are the dispositions that lend themselves to success both in and out of school. Another critical factor related to school-student self-confidence is the relationships students form from belonging to clubs, extracurricular activities, and school events. For instance, one of the reasons why Ms. Foreman has such a strong relationship with her students is not just because she cares deeply for each student (and they recognize that) but she also understands the value of belonging to something. She actively works at making sure that the jazz band is a second home for her students.

Belonging to a group and feeling that one's membership counts, whether through music, sports, or service activities, has tremendous power in helping students become more connected to the school. Making friends and being part of something helps students develop a positive identity. It is also a telling indicator for active participation in civic or other groups in adulthood.[16] Nilda Flores-Gonzalez notes, "Finding a niche in school is important because the factors needed to develop a school-kid identity are found in these niches: they provide students with socially appropriate roles (e.g. athlete) . . . increase prestige and popularity . . . and provide students with avenues to succeed outside of academics."[17]

Recognizing the interrelationship between belonging and learning enhances the entire teaching process.[18] It is key to retention, feeling good about learning, developing self-confidence, and considering what's good for the group rather than primarily focusing on the self. When students feel good in school, they enjoy learning. According to James P. Comer, "Development and learning are inextricably linked, and takes place best through interactions between a child and meaningful people in warm, supportive environments."[19] This suggests that, while academic content and related processes are generally the first things equated with schooling, a supportive school society for students can be just as important. Cooperative learning and building communities of trust, for example, are not just vehicles for learning content; they appeal to the students' need for belonging to a greater whole.

Here's where music teachers have a powerful tool in their hands. The ensemble, for instance, can become the mechanism not just for learning repertoire but through which students learn that their musicianship is vital to the success of the group. Simply putting a group of musicians together and rehearsing for a performance, though, does not guarantee that students feel part of the group. In other words, to create a community where students support each other as a means to the greater good, the music teacher must consciously teach students to "stick together," help each other, and create a learning space where everyone counts. These qualities are a large part of why Ms. Foreman has such success as a teacher: *[My students] are supportive, funny, friendly, and kind to one another. I know this will go a long way in fostering a healthy learning environment throughout the year. I'm trying to teach them to be self-sufficient and it's working. They help each other and only come to me with questions when they need guidance on a new concept or to settle a disagreement.*

In general music, whether at the elementary or secondary level, creating music in small groups or composing a song with the entire class has the potential for bringing students together and filling their need to belong. As mentioned earlier, a group structure is not enough to create a community of trust. Teachers need to make one thing clear: Making music depends not only on each student's musical contribution but also on the humanity with which students support each other in the process.

Building communities where students feel a sense of belonging is not straightforward or easy. There will be times when students argue, disagree, feel hurt, and are resistant to working together. Linda Christenson reminds us that "Real community is forged out of struggle. Students won't always agree on issues, and the fights, arguments, tears, and anger are the crucible from which a real community grows."[20] And further:

> Students must learn to live in someone else's skin, understand the parallels of hurt, struggle, and joy across class and culture lines, and work for change. For that to happen, students need more than an upbeat, supportive teacher, they need a curriculum that teaches them how to empathize with each other.[21]

The point here is for music teachers to understand that building supportive learning communities take time. Music teachers who begin this process in September may not see the fruits of their labor for several months. There are, however, small steps along the way that let you know you're on the right track, such as a student who speaks in class for the first time or a normally antagonistic student who shares his/her/their music with a classmate without your prompting. "Each experience of support," states Comer, "helps students acquire a sense of being valued and belonging . . . that builds to an increased capacity to learn."[22]

Developing positive connections with students of color

The premise of this chapter is that good teachers take time to learn about their students' culture and community values. This kind of culturally responsive pedagogy stems from an ethos of care and is paramount in understanding what and how to teach. For students of color, cultural responsiveness means understanding the challenges that are unique to the students' racial/ethnic context. This section will address the role of identity in Latino and Black students and its impact on the learning process (for a more in-depth discussion, see Chapter 6).

Latinos currently represent the largest minority group in the United States. In fact, one in every four students is Latino/a.[23] Unfortunately, Latino students also have the highest high school dropout rate.[24] Part of this has to do with poverty, language barriers, and experiencing more failure than success in school. Regarding the language barrier, many Latino students face the double challenge of learning to speak English while also mediating a multicultural environment. Yet, common misperceptions about Latino students abound, including lack of motivation, initiative, and academic ability.[25]

Given these misperceptions, teachers may not only expect less from Latino students but also show a lack of concern for their academic welfare. According to Stephen Benham,

> Negative teacher views of *others* influence every aspect of the teacher-student interaction, including expectations regarding the achievement of *others*, pedagogical approaches to teaching *others*, and willingness to live in or be part of the community where *others* also live.[26]

Benham places special emphasis on the word "others" to amplify the distinction between the culture of the teacher and the culture(s) of others in the classroom.

One aspect that non-Latino teachers often overlook is the sheer diversity within the Hispanic community. Latino families, for instance, come from many different countries, including Mexico, Columbia, Puerto Rico, Guatemala, Dominican Republic, Cuba, Peru, etc., and rarely appreciate being categorized as a single group. According to Mireya Nevarro, "Latinos, as a group in this country, tend to identify themselves more by their ethnicity, meaning a shared set of cultural traits, like language or customs."[27] The cultural differences, while not always apparent to the teacher, may have great importance to the Latino student. A teacher who mistakenly identifies a Columbian child as Puerto Rican or Cuban, for example, may be forcefully corrected. Latino families take great pride in their heritage – who they are and where they've come from. In order to connect with one's Latino students, music teachers will not only need to understand these general aspects of identity but also include repertoire and learning opportunities specific to the students' country of origin.

In order to develop a positive connection with Latino students, one must start with respect for the family culture. In most Latino families, the parents, grandparents, aunts, and uncles have a particularly strong role in raising the child and enculturating the child into the family structure.[28] The familial emphasis on cooperation and getting along is something that music teachers can build upon through cooperative learning and group projects. In addition, a sense of belonging, which has its roots in the strong family structure, is particularly vital in helping Latino students develop positive connections to the school. Music ensembles, clubs, and other organizations facilitate friendships and acknowledge that Latino students have something important to contribute.

Ruben Garza acknowledges, "Building community with Latino students continues to be a key element to their success in the school setting."[29] Building community in the classroom has been discussed earlier, but in the case of Latino (and African American) students, *culturally specific* communities are also valuable.[30] This does not suggest that music teachers group students by race/ethnicity, but it speaks, rather, to the importance of extracurricular groups or organizations that can provide culturally specific support through the school, school district, or community.

Although music ensembles can foster a feeling of community among its members, this alone does not always ensure that students of color will feel welcome. Kenneth Elpus and Carlos Abril, for example, found that fewer Latino students played in a traditional school band setting than White and African American students. Speculating on these findings, the researchers, among other things, suggest that perhaps Western music does not appeal to Latino students.[31]

The rise in popularity of Mariachi bands and Latin percussion ensembles may be one viable response to this information While there are no pat solutions, the larger purpose of providing alternative ensembles is to provide *all* students with experiences that honor Latino composers/musicians. A conscientious effort, then, to develop an understanding of the heritage and musical language of the culture comes from a deep sense of caring about multiples contexts in which students live.

As with Latino students, African American students face many barriers in their schooling. Systemic racism (see Chapter 6) infects not only American society but schools as well. Christopher Emdin notes, "How successful the teacher is in the classroom is directly related to how successful the teacher thinks the students can be."[32] When teachers believe that Black students will not succeed to the same degree as White students, they may accommodate for this by simplifying their teaching and assignments. This is both insulting and damaging to the students' self-perception of their ability to succeed.

Teachers who consciously or unconsciously teach down to African American students demand less effort from them in the classroom and on assignments.[33] Yet, it is rising to a challenge and successfully completing an assignment or problem-solving task that develops students' sense of accomplishment and capability. Students who feel capable engage more tenaciously in problem solving than those who believe they cannot succeed. For African American students, a sense of accomplishment is essential. Lisa Delpit asserts, "See their brilliance: Do not teach less content to poor, urban children but instead, teach more!"[34] As mentioned earlier, holding all students to high standards is crucial in raising students' self-esteem.[35]

In terms of teaching, Delpit (2006) believes that the Black community looks for teachers who they perceive as "strong." She explains further:

> In many African-American communities, teachers are expected to show that they care about their students by controlling the class; exhibiting personal power; establishing meaningful interpersonal relationships; displaying emotion to garner student respect; demonstrating the belief that all students can learn; establishing a standard of achievement and "pushing" students to achieve the standard; and holding the attention of the students by incorporating African-American interactional styles in their teaching. Teachers who do not exhibit these behaviors may be viewed by the community members as ineffectual, boring, or uncaring.[36]

In a student-centered teaching approach, it questionable about what this means in terms of discipline or academic tasks. Delpit, however, explains that she is not advocating for "mean" or "unkind" teachers. Rather, she suggests that some Black students may initially respond more easily to teachers who are direct and concrete about their expectations.

Essentially, music teachers can do a great deal in helping both Latino and Black students acclimate to the music class. There are several basic ideas to keep in mind: First, positive adult relationships contribute to a sense of belonging and a feeling of family. Taking the time to find out about students' goals, their perception of school, etc. demonstrates care for the student as well as validates their identity.[37] Second, learning about the students' culture sends the message, "I care about who you are." Third, expect nothing less than the best from students of color.

One might argue that the aforementioned ideas pertain to all students, and, in a sense, they do. However, students of color have particular racial barriers that their White counterparts do not. It bears repeating that to think of all students as the same without recognizing the special gifts that they bring to the classroom is a way of devaluing the person. Families with children of color, especially those with financial hardships, look to the school as a way of advancement in this society.[38] Cultural advancement through the arts is an important piece of this mission and offers students of color unique avenues for developing resilience and self-fulfillment.

Working with immigrant/refugee students and English language learners

Urban areas often have large pockets of families who have immigrated to the United States. Although many areas in the United States have little diversity, the rising rate of immigrant/refugee students indicate an increase of diversity within most classrooms in the nation, particularly in urban areas. Given this, the urban music teacher will likely encounter a classroom with many immigrant or refugee students.

The terms "immigrant" and "refugee," however, do not mean the same thing. Immigrant students are born into a family that has emigrated from a foreign country to the United States. Refugee children come from families that have fled persecution in their home country. Nevertheless, "All children in the USA are entitled to equal access to a public elementary and secondary education without regard to their or their parents' actual or perceived national origin, citizenship, or immigration status."[39]

One of the more challenging aspects of teaching music is the influx of immigrant/refugee children in the schools who speak little or no English. According to Steven Camerota, Bryan Griffith, and Karen Zeigler:

> The number of children from immigrant households in schools is now so high in some areas that it raises profound questions about assimilation. What's more, immigration has added enormously to the number of public school students who are in poverty and the number who speak a foreign language. This cannot help but to create significant challenges for schools, often in areas already struggling to educate students who come from disadvantaged backgrounds.[40]

For English Language Learners (ELL), teachers must be knowledgeable about the psychological and sociological context of what it means to step from one culture into another. Facility with the English language, however, can influence how one is perceived in terms of social class, intelligence, and level of education.[41] Unfortunately, these students sometimes face a biased opinion, such as English Language Learners who are less able than those who speak English fluently.[42] Because ELL students may not have the verbal skills to participate fully in discussions or follow directives or even ask simple questions, they may also encounter lower expectations or lack of attention on the part of the teacher. When music teachers (or any teachers for that matter) equate "proper English" with intelligence, they do a grave disservice to students who do not meet that standard. At the very least, students lose an opportunity to be heard, which is often central to self-esteem and feelings of self-worth.[43]

Lisa Delpit, co-author of *The Skin That We Speak*, addresses this issue throughout her book. She states,

> Ironically, the more determined we are to rid the school of children's home language, the more determined they must become to preserve it. Since language is one of the most intimate expressions of identity, indeed, 'the skin that we speak,' then to reject a person's language can only feel as if we are rejecting him.[44]

With the rising numbers of ELL students in the schools, music teachers need to think about inclusive music instruction. One great benefit of having immigrant/refugee students in school lies in the rich culture of the arts and multi-perspectives they bring to the classroom. Because they live through at least two cultures, that of American and of their native heritage, immigrant/refugee students develop multiple ways of solving problems and seeing solutions from more than one angle. "This," states Gándara, "is an invaluable skill" and can enhance creative thinking in the classroom.[45]

Learning English, however, is compounded by the psychological toll of attending a school that may have no likeness to the school left behind. For the immigrant/refugee student, the feeling of being uprooted from all that is familiar, including the inability to express one's basic needs, can create a profound sense of isolation from peers and teachers. In fact, some immigrant/refugee students even report a lack of caring or initiative to reach out on the part of teachers.[46] Although many immigrant/refugee children have much success learning English, others are mired in frustration, which contributes to the high level of ELL students who drop out before finishing high school.

Sadly, Chavez writes:

> For children of undocumented immigrants, their subjective understanding of their place in society is that of being "unwanted" and "discardable." . . . These are not unwanted beliefs, but rather the result of experiencing life in

the United States, a life in which their future goals are often placed on hold. Their lives are sidetracked and derailed seemingly without concern by the larger society.[47]

Consequently, teachers must make an extra effort to acknowledge the value of ELL students. One way to help ELL students is to nudge them into joining school-related clubs and extracurricular activities. This is important in helping immigrant/ refugee students acclimate themselves to a school environment that feels so foreign. The lack of English proficiency, for many, can be a large obstacle in joining organizations. According to Gándara, Latino students have a particularly difficult time joining and participating in extracurricular activities.[48] These, however, are the very activities that encourage students to develop friendships and become more integrated into the life of the school. For that reason, music teachers may need to take the lead in helping immigrant/refugee students find an activity that they enjoy. Music activities and ensembles can often create the kind of belongingness that children crave.

Working with ELL students, especially for American-born White teachers, requires the teacher to be "effective operating and teaching within another culture, the *teacher* must be the one who adapts and changes."[49] It is often said that music builds bridges across cultures, and there are many instances where music teachers can connect with ELL through modeling and hands-on instruction. This is not enough, however, for functioning fully in a music learning setting. Music teachers deal with verbal content all the time, such as classroom discussion, musical text in singing, and leading an ensemble rehearsal. For that reason, the challenge lies in how to accommodate ELL students so that they have access to the same experiences as their English-speaking peers. In essence, preserving the dignity of children for whom English is limited supports the humanness of each child and remains central to nurturing, caring behavior.

Music teachers tell their own stories

To explore the challenges and opportunities of teaching ELL students in music class, I invited three urban music teachers to talk about their experience. Ms. Pernas, an urban high school vocal/choral teacher, teaches in a school where 85% to 90% of her classes consist of immigrant and refugee students. She talks about the opportunities of having such a diverse student body: *You get to learn about cultures that you wouldn't anywhere else. You get to hear stories of their lives. By the end of the year, there's always growth for them and for me.*

As a choral teacher, both English texts and a Western tonal framework create unique issues in teaching vocal music. Ms. Pernas explains: *Latin texts seem to work best, but English is the hardest because of the vowel sounds and diphthongs. It is so hard to match a vowel sound with so many languages. I have three students who speak English well, but they sing with a thick accent. Sometimes they stop and laugh, which is good because it means they are self-correcting. Arabic boys sing very high (in a falsetto). They also have*

Eastern music in their ear that involves fluctuating pitch, which makes it difficult for them to sing Western harmony.

Ms. Pernas relies on demonstration and help from bilingual students who can translate for those with limited English proficiency. Although she clearly cares deeply for her students, she knows that sometimes the going is tough: *It's going to be hard, but you have to stick with it. If you let fear run you and kids see that, they are never going to trust you. You have to keep moving forward.*

Another teacher, Mr. Mango, has been teaching music in an urban school for only one year. Speaking with him provided some special insight into the challenges and opportunities of working with immigrant/refugee students as a new teacher. As an elementary general music specialist, Mr. Mango's classes include mostly immigrant students, among whom approximately 10% are refugees. The school is primarily Hispanic with a small number of African American students. Mr. Mango is the only White teacher on the faculty.

You have to know some Spanish, he explains. *I am not fluent, but I know enough to give general commands and I try to learn new words every day. We sing half of our songs in Spanish and the other half in English.* He comments further: *I grew up in a White privileged area. It's nice to see another side of life. You need to have a connection with the kids. If I had taken a job in my hometown, I might not have had the opportunity to really know these students and what they need.*

Mr. Mango tells a story about a first grader who came into school at the end of December: *She had a hard time getting to know other people. For two months, she was worried about where her dad was. She cried constantly and couldn't read or write in English. It turns out her dad was detained then deported. The family left less than a week later. She didn't officially withdraw from school – the family just left because they were scared. A similar thing happened to another student. It is heartbreaking. A lot of kids get sad very quickly because of home life and many of the kids live in motels.*

In terms of advising new teachers who will or are already teaching in urban schools with a large immigrant/refugee population, Mr. Mango is particularly adamant about showing kindness: *They're just kids. Love them as much as any other kid because they just need that.* Here again, the word "love" becomes a compelling connector for nurturing students who especially need to feel love in what can be a very alienating environment.

Finally, Ms. Serpone teaches general music and choral music in a middle school. She admits that teaching students with limited English proficiency is most difficult in the general music setting. Because her teaching style is student-centered with a lot of discussion, her immigrant/refugee students often have trouble participating. In her school, however, English-speaking buddies are placed with those who are just learning to speak the language. In addition, students are urged to use Google Translate for writing assignments: *Sometimes I will translate the prompt in their native language. They will write the assignment in their native language and then translate it back to me in English. The nice thing about the computer is that it helps enormously with the translation process.*

Despite the communication challenges, Ms. Serpone recognizes the rich benefits that foreign students bring to her classroom. She explains: *Working with ELL students is rewarding and an experience that everyone should have. As someone who grew up in a fairly privileged environment, it took me until this year to appreciate this. It's really awesome to see how these students change throughout the year. You are like a parent to them, and they're so grateful for what you've done for them. It brings a different element into what it means to teach because you're really teaching them to be a whole person.*

It is heartening to find that, despite the communication difficulties, these music teachers welcome the stories and cultures of their immigrant/refugee students. They've found numerous ways to assist ELL students through pairing with an English-speaking student, integrating cultural activities into their teaching, learning basic sentences in the students' languages, and relying on Google Translate for tasks that involve writing.

Carlos R. Abril, in his article "No Hablos Inglés: Breaking the Language Barrier in Music Instruction," acknowledges that many undergraduate music education majors do not have the training for working with ELL students.[50] Not surprisingly, showing respect is first and foremost.[51] One can initiate a positive connection by warmly welcoming the new student and immediately including him/her in classroom activities. He states, "A child's first experience in school – positive or negative – can have a profound and lasting effect."

Music teachers should understand that when learning a new language and acclimating to an unfamiliar setting, many students may refuse to speak.[52] This stage is normal because students are observing and absorbing the language, school routines, and ways of behaving in a new situation. Refusal to speak or verbally participate, in these first few months, is not a sign of belligerence or lack of social skills but, rather, an understandable part of learning a new language. Once students begin to participate, music teachers can gently offer many opportunities for ELL students to practice speaking.[53] Choosing songs with a lot of repetition or activities that involve poetry and chants as well as projects that involve cooperative learning is a move in the right direction.

Connecting with immigrant/refugee families

Communication between the teacher and student is as essential as communication with families who may not understand permission slips, announcements, phone calls, or other important information from the school. It is exceedingly difficult for parents or guardians to negotiate the school system when they have been schooled in a different country. They come to America having experienced different roles of the teacher-student relationship and educational values that may be out of sync with their child's new school. This contributes to feeling as an "outsider" when it comes to school-family connections.[54]

"Relatedly," Adelman and Taylor explain,

> immigrant parents and other family members bring varying understanding and attitudes about schooling and about how to interact with school staff. Some of this reflects their own experiences with schools, cultural and religious values, and the reasons they left their country of origin.[55]

For this reason, it is important that music teachers understand how difficult it is for parents to participate in the school, especially when they have limited or no English language proficiency.[56] They, too, are often scared and uncomfortable about how to manage their role in the American educational process. When sensitive to the complex lives of both immigrant/refugee children and their parents, music teachers can find positive ways to integrate them into their program.

Language and knowledge of how American schools work represent two barriers to parent participation and lower-class immigrant parents. Other barriers include differences in social status, race, religion, and ethnicity. According to Comer:

> Although they would like to see their children have a better experience, they don't expect this to happen. Often the education and social status of people who work in the schools intimidate undereducated and poor parents. Differences in race, religion, income, and ethnicity might cause tension. Some parents are under economic stress and have little time or energy.[58]

Because of a language barrier, music teachers may be tempted to avoid phone calls home or speaking with families after a concert. [Some] teachers fear adversarial relationships, or "someone looking over my shoulder."[59] The family, however, is a critical piece to the child's image and attitude toward school.[60] Latino families, for instance, generally hold teachers and education in high regard.[61] Therefore, outreach to families solidifies the belief that teachers have their child's best interest at heart.

It is helpful to translate permission slips and music bulletins into the child's native language. This may be possible through Google Translate. In terms of phone calls or face-to-face interaction, the music teacher may need to ask for help from a colleague who speaks the language. Learning key phrases in the native language helps with the initial greeting, but for important conversations, a translator from the faculty may be necessary. In any case, just greeting the parent with a smile and a handshake goes a long way toward developing a positive connection with the music program.

The consideration in all of this is to acknowledge the importance that immigrant/refugee families have in their child's education and to make every effort to communicate often. Music teachers need the family to support the music program, transport students to rehearsals, come into class to teach a music-related culture lesson, or give permission for a field trip. Just as music teachers make a special effort to communicate with ELL students, the same holds true for communicating with their parents/guardians. Speaking English can be a terrifying experience for those not familiar with the language. Helping families feel a sense of belonging to the school, despite these challenges, can only enhance the students' feeling of belonging and safety in the school setting.

Conclusion

Cultural responsiveness takes many forms: helping students find a comfortable niche in the classroom/school; respecting the home and values that surround them every day; designing curriculum to meet their special needs; and insisting on high standards for all students despite their race, ethnicity, or facility with the English language. The simple act of greeting children warmly and embracing the fact that all children have rights to an excellent education can have a significant effect on how students feel coming to school.

In much of this chapter, I have focused on the need for students to feel a sense of belonging in school. Related to belonging is the need to be understood – that the teacher hears the students' intended message. In a verbal context, understanding comes from actively listening when students speak while also hearing the subtext in their stories. Listening attentively to what children are saying and shaping curriculum to meet their unique needs sends the message that "You matter."

Implicit in nurturing pedagogy is the presence of caring, knowledgeable teaching, and cultural responsiveness. Whether music teachers have 15 students or 115 students, knowing about the cultures represented in the student body forges a bond between teachers and students that contributes to the feeling that music class is a safe place. The bottom line: A student who feels capable and understood is more likely than not to engage in deep music learning.[62] "It is automatic that students must feel a sense of belonging in the school if they are to be truly engaged and motivated to excel. Relationships are crucial."[63]

One of the lessons we learned from Ms. Foreman is that caring is a part of love for the student. It could mean assuring students that they are smart and capable. It could mean holding students to high standards of learning and behavior. And it could mean celebrating the cultural gifts that each child brings to the classroom. In short, teachers who care demand the best from their students and give plenty of encouragement along the way.

When music teachers begin their journey as professionals in the field, they often feel overwhelmed by the school procedures, determining what/how to teach, and even getting to know the names of the many students that they teach. For new teachers, especially those in the urban schools, learning to teach is like having an ocean wave wash over you where you misjudge the height and force of the water. Little by little, you learn to jump before the wave crests, negotiate the undertow, and enjoy the power and magnificence of the sea. As with ocean swimming, getting to know the students, their culture, and their community does not happen all at once. More important is the acceptance that culturally responsive teaching enhances learning and promotes love for the children that you teach.

Discussion questions

1   Nurturing pedagogy is a complex dimension of teaching that goes beyond "being nice to children." What are some actions that music teachers can take to demonstrate care for their students?

2   Why is a sense of "belonging" so critical in the school, and how can music teachers facilitate this in or beyond music class?

3   How would you run a rehearsal if a majority of your students do not speak English? Likewise, how would you give English Language Learners an equitable experience in general music?

References

1   hooks, bell. 2000. *All About Love*. New York: William Morrow and Company: 30.

2   Ibid.

3   Noddings, Nel. 2005. *The Challenge to Care in Schools* [2nd ed.]. New York: Teachers College Press: 55.

4   Carter, Bruce. 2011. "A Safe Education for All: Recognizing and Stemming Harassment in Music Classes and Ensembles." *Music Educators Journal*, *97* (4): 29–32. doi: 10:1177/0027432111405342

5   DeLorenzo, Lisa. 2012. *Sketches in Democracy: Notes from an Urban Classroom*. Lanham, MD: Rowman & Littlefield.

6   Gay, Geneva and Kipehoge Kirkland. 2003. "Developing Cultural Critical Consciousness and Self-Reflection in Preservice Teacher Education." *Theory into Practice*, *42* (3): 181–187.

7   Kelly-McHale, Jacqueline. 2016. "Democracy, Canon, and Culturally Responsive Teaching: Blurring the Edges in the Music Classroom." In *Giving Voice to Democracy in Music Education: Diversity and Social Justice*, edited by Lisa C. DeLorenzo, 216–234. New York: Routledge: 218.

8   Ladson-Billings, Gloria. 2001. *Crossing Over to Canaan: The Journey of New Teachers in Diverse Classrooms*. San Francisco: Josey-Bass.

9   Starnes, Bobby Ann. 2006. "What We Don't Know Can Hurt Them: White Teachers, Indian Children." *Phi Delta Kappan*, *87* (5): 385.

10   Silverman, Marissa. 2013. "A Critical Ethnography of Democratic Music Listening." *British Journal of Music Education*, *30* (1): 7–25.

11   Emdin, Christopher. 2016. *For White Folks Who Teach in the Hood . . . and the Rest of Y'all Too: Reality Pedagogy and Urban Education*. Boston: Beacon Press.

12   Benham, Stephen. 2003. "Being the Other: Adapting to Life in a Culturally Diverse Classroom." *Journal of Teacher Education*, *13* (1): 25.

13   Sato, Mistlina and Timothy L. Lensmire. 2009. "Poverty and Payne: Supporting Teachers to Work with Children of Poverty." *Phi Delta Kappan*, *90* (5): 365–370; Roberts, J. Christopher and Patricia Sheehan Campbell. 2015. "Multiculturalism and Social Justice: Complementary Movements for Education In and Through Music." In *The Oxford Handbook of Social Justice in Music Education*, edited by Cathy Benedict, Patrick Schmidt, Gary Spruce, and Paul Woodford, 272–286. New York: Oxford University Press.

14   Lind, Vicki R. and Constance McKoy. 2016. *Culturally Responsive Teaching in Music Education*. New York: Routledge: 133.

15   Geneva Gay and Kipehoge Kirkland. "Developing Cultural Critical Consciousness." *Practice*.

16   Putnam, Robert D. 2000. *Bowling Alone: The Collapse and Revival of American Community*. New York: Simon & Schuster.

17   Flores-González, Nilda. 2002. *School Kids/Street Kids: Identity Development in Latino Students*. New York: Teachers College Press: 75.

18 Comer, James P. 2015. "Developing Social Capital in Schools." *Society, 52* (3): 225–231. doi: 10.1007/s1211501-015-9891-5; Garza, Ruben. 2009. "Latino and White High School Students' Perceptions of Caring Behaviors: Are We Culturally Responsive to Our Students?" *Urban Education, 44*: 297–321.

19 Comer. "Developing Social Capital." 227.

20 Christensen, Linda. 2008. "Building Community from Chaos." In *City Kids, City Schools: More Reports from the Front Row*, edited by William Ayers, Gloria Ladson-Billings, Gregory Michie, and Pedro A. Noguera, 60–73. New York: The New Press: 61.

21 Ibid., 61–62.

22 Comer. "Developing Social Capital." 227.

23 Gándara, Patricia. 2017. "The Potential and Promise of Latino Students." *American Educator, 41* (1): 4–11.

24 Mosquedo, Eduardo and Kip Téllez. 2016. "Contesting Racism, Marginalization, and Mexican Immigrant Youth Failure: Examining the Elusive Path Toward Earning a Diploma from a Nontraditional High School." In *Cracks in The Schoolyard: Confronting Latino Educational Inequality*, edited by Gilberto Q. Conchas, 96–111. New York: Teachers College Press.

25 Garza. "Latino and White High School Students' Perceptions." 297–321.

26 Benham. "Being the Other." 29.

27 Nevarro, Mireya. 2012. "For Many Latinos, Racial Identity Is More Culture Than Color." *New York Times*, January 14: 11. www.lexisnexis.com.ezproxy.montclair.edu:2048/hottopics/lnacademic/?verb=sr&csi=6742

28 Gándara. "The Potential and Promise."; Tatum, Beverly D. 1997. *Why Are All the Black Kids Sitting Together in The Cafeteria?* New York: Basic Books.

29 Garza. "Latino and White High School Students' Perceptions." 317.

30 Vega, Irene I., Leticia Oseguera, and Gilberto Q. Conchas. 2016. "Race, Brotherhood, and Educational Engagement in the Urban Context: A Case Study of Structured Peer Bonding Among Boys of Color." In *Cracks in The Schoolyard: Confronting Latino Educational Inequality*, edited by Gilberto Q. Conchas, 54–75. New York: Teachers College Press.

31 Elpus, Kenneth and Carlos R. Abril. 2011. "High School Music Ensemble Students in the United States: A Demographic Profile." *Journal of Research in Music Education, 59* (2): 128–145. doi: 10.1177/002242941145207.

32 Emdin. *For White Folks*: 207.

33 Delpit, Lisa. 2006. *Other People's Children*. New York: The New Press.

34 Delpit, Lisa. 2008. "Lessons from Teachers." In *City Kids, City Schools: More Reports from the Front Row*, edited by William Ayers, Gloria Ladson-Billings, Gregory Michie, and Pedro A. Noguera, 113–135. New York: The New Press: 115.

35 Delpit, Lisa. 2012. *Multiplication Is for White People: Raising Expectations for Other People's Children*. New York: The New Press; Ladson-Billings. *Crossing Over to Canaan*. 2001.

36 Delpit. *Other People's Children*: 142.

37 Gushue, George V., Christine P. Clark, Karen M Pantzer, and Kolone R. L. Scanlan. 2006. "Self-Efficacy, Perceptions of Barriers, Vocational Identity, and The Career Exploration Behavior of Latino/a High School Students." *The Career Quarterly, 54*: 307–317.

38 Ladson-Billings, Gloria. 2008. "Yes, But How Do We Do It? Practicing Culturally Relevant Pedagogy." In *City Kids, City Schools: More Reports from The Front Row*, edited by William Ayers, Gloria Ladson-Billings, Gregory Michie, and Pedro A. Noguera, 162–177. New York: The New Press.

39 U.S. Department of Education, *Educational Services for Immigrant Children and Those Recently Arrived to the United States.* 2015. http://www2.ed.gov/policy/rights/guid/unaccompanied-children.pdf

40 Camarota, Steven A., Bryan Griffith, and Karen Zeigler. 2017, January 9. *Mapping the Impact of Immigration on Public Schools.* Report from the Center for Immigration Studies:1. http://cis.org/map-students-immigrant-households

41 Stubbs, Michael. 2008. "Some Basic Sociolinguistic Concepts." In *The Skin That We Speak: Thoughts on Language and Culture in the Classroom* edited by Lisa Delpit and J. K. Dowdy, 63–85. New York: The New Press.

42 Adelman, Howard S. and Linda Taylor. 2015. "Immigrant Children and Youth in the USA: Facilitating Equity of Opportunity at School." *Education Sciences*, (5): 323–344. doi: 10.3390/educsci5040323

43 Hoffman, Adria R. 2011. "Do You Hear What I'm Sayin? Overcoming Miscommunications Between Music Teachers and Students." *Music Educators Journal*, *97* (4): 33–36. doi: 10.1177/0027432111405341.

44 Delpit, Lisa. 2008. "No Kinda Sense." In *The Skin That We Speak: Thoughts on Language and Culture in the Classroom*, edited by Lisa Delpit and Joanne Kilgour Dowdy, 31–48. New York: The New Press: 47.

45 Gándara. "The Potential and Promise." 9.

46 Adelman. "Immigrant Children and Youth."

47 Chavez, Leo O. 2016. "Uncertain Futures: Educational Attainment and the Children of Undocumented Mexican Immigrants in the Greater Los Angeles Area." In *Cracks in the Schoolyard: Confronting Latino Educational Inequality*, edited by Gilberto Q. Conchas, 144–160. New York: Teachers College Press: 157.

48 Gándara. "The Potential and Promise."

49 Benham. "Being the Other." 27.

50 Abril, Carlos R. 2003. "No Hablos Inglés: Breaking the Language Barrier in Music Instruction." *Music Educators Journal*, *89* (5): 38–43.

51 Ibid., 40.

52 Ibid., 38–43.

53 Ibid.

54 Lind and McKoy. *Culturally Responsive Teaching.*

55 Adelman. "Immigrant Children and Youth." 328.

56 Lind and McKoy. *Culturally Responsive Teaching.*

57 Villegas, Ana Maria and Tamara Lucas. 2002. *Educating Culturally Responsive Teachers: A Coherent Approach.* Albany and New York: State University of New York.

58 Comer, James P. 2005. "The Rewards of Parent Participation." *Educational Leadership, 62* (6): 39.

59 Ibid.

60 Quiñones, Sandra. 2015. "Garnering Resilience: Latina/o Education as a Family, School, and Community Affair." In *The Plight of Invisibility: A Community-Based Approach to Understanding the Educational Experiences of Urban Latina/os*, edited by Donna Maris Harris and Judy Marquez Kiyama, 50–77. New York: Peter Lang.

61 Albarran, Alejandra S. and Gilberto Q. Conchas. 2016. "Yes, We Care! Understanding the Role of Community-Based Organizations and Latina/o Parent Cultural Wealth in a Large Urban City." In *Cracks in the Schoolyard: Confronting Latino Educational Inequality*, edited by Gilberto Q. Conchas, 112–127. New York: Teachers College Press.

62 Lind and McKoy. *Culturally Responsive Teaching.*

63 Gándara. "The Potential and Promise." 10.

3

HELPING TROUBLED STUDENTS SUCCEED

Part 1: From the classroom of Mrs. Sweet

Mrs. Sweet has taught for ten years, with eight years of experience in the urban setting. Presently, she teaches high school strings and orchestra in an arts-intensive public high school located in a large urban city. Although students must audition for acceptance into the school, Mrs. Sweet acknowledges that their skills are often at a novice level: *Most of the students who audition have only played for a year and that experience is usually ensemble-based. We have to see if they're raw beginners or they have potential. For instance, some of them don't read music. When they come to the audition, this is what we look for: Do they have a good ear? What are their grades? What kinds of books do they read? In other words, do they initiate reading on their own? If I can tell they are interested in learning and have a good ear, then I will accept them.*

The level of students' technical skill on their instrument is one of Mrs. Sweet's biggest challenges. Because there are only a few middle school string programs in her district, the feeder system is limited and none of the students are able to afford private lessons. *When they come to high school, we're supposed to get them college ready, but it's often not possible. That's a major challenge for me.* A lack of resources adds to the difficulty of her job. Although she received many resources during the first two years of teaching, she now has no budget for supplies. Mrs. Sweet says, *I'm worried that my supplies (rosin, strings, bows) will run out.*

The students come from all over the city. Some live in houses, and others live in apartments. Many students live with relatives other than their parents. Unfortunately, in some of the neighborhoods, there is a shooting every week. For that reason, they aren't allowed to go outside after dark or without a friend. After high school, most students go on to college. A few of them get jobs, and some go to community colleges.

Mrs. Sweet grew up in a racially homogenous neighborhood. Regarding her background, she said: *It was middle class, pretty much all White (I knew of only one African American family). Most of the families were Jewish, Italian, or Irish Catholic. Half the women were stay at home moms, and the neighborhood was small enough so that I knew all of the kids.* Consequently, she came from a background that was completely different from her students.

There is no question about Mrs. Sweet's dedication to her students. She loves her job and speaks enthusiastically about the love and appreciation that students show her. In her words, *It's the kind of challenge that I love because I'm doing more than teaching music. Music teaches you about life and hard work. It elevates you to be your best self.* Despite the challenges of teaching in an urban school, Mrs. Sweet is the kind of caring and nurturing person who has built indelible, lifelong connections with her students. They continue to visit her classroom long after they graduate.

Mrs. Sweet's journal, 2015–2016

October

DATA – the new paradigm for public music education. We must collect data on student growth. The whole evaluation system and our personal development plan are based on scores that our students get on assignments and assessments. How we collect that data is divided into very specific goals, much like that of businesses. I find myself caught up in torrent of thoughts on how I am going to make all of this meaningful and have it make sense to me. I know I am an effective teacher by the concerts, by the applause, the alumni visits, the hugs from parents and students, the community, and a sense of musical excellence that I have instilled in many. But I must prove it on paper. Show how I do it. Be able to document and show a level of growth that reflects all of that.

When common planning with my colleagues, we all discuss the idea of using music theory as a marker for documenting growth, but the argument stands that we have to prepare for concerts and rehearsals. We have to be great under many difficult circumstances. So the question is: How do we prepare our students for a concert, mark their growth at every turn, come up with meaningful SGOs (Student Growth Objectives), and collect data for our artifact folder that now must align with about ten different effective teaching tools – whatever that means.

And then the report comes to mind: *The National Core Standards*. In my professional development plan. I have to include those that align with how my students will grow as well as align the standards with every single lesson plan that I write. My heart starts to race. But I still have more repertoire to choose. And I have to get that student to take her bass home; and another student is not practicing because he had brain surgery, and I am not sure if he is having health problems – I must call the mom tomorrow. The list drags on. Wait, there is more. My service – yes, we have service this year.

Make a document of all the National Core Standards, all six strands, in a week and a half. Cut and paste, cut and paste, so we can see all novice students in a row, all the intermediate students, etc. Color-code the lesson schedule. Not sure what will be next. Wow! My head is spinning. The funny thing is that my students are doing great! Most are practicing a lot. Progress is being made, and a community is growing within the classroom environment. Students are getting the note reading and rhythm down. Things are really cooking. But I am feeling like I am burning out already, and it is only October. And to that I say, "I absolutely love my students, and it is the joy of my day to work with them as well as to receive their hugs."

November

In November, my junior and senior students performed at the New Jersey Performing Arts Center with the New Jersey Symphony. Two weeks before the concert, one of my students had brain surgery to see if the mass in his head was cancerous. He was back to school after a few days. He was a bit disoriented and could only fake his music. I decided to write to members of the symphony about this situation. He really wanted to perform. It was such a magnanimous gesture to me that all the people I contacted got back to me right away and said he should indeed perform! It was amazing. He had a great time, and they taught him the art of "faking" the music. After the concert, I saw one of the mothers of my viola students who is a junior. She was carrying a baby about six weeks old. She said it was my student's baby (my student is a young man). He never told me, and I would have never known by the way he shows up to class and works. Afterwards when I saw him, he gave me a very big hug and his mom said I was his favorite teacher. And that made me cry. I said, "I guess this kind of makes me a grandma since I'm his string teacher mama."

December

Yesterday we had a guest from the New Jersey Symphony Orchestra work with the violins in a masterclass. But at the end of class, when we were all talking festively, shouting erupted from two girls – two of my best junior students. I knew there was some tension between the two girls. Fear gripped me as I thought they might get physical because it's happened in the past with other girls. Punching and scratching began. I called security. It took forever for someone to pick up the phone in the main office.

By then, one girl left, then the other. I planned to tell security that they should stay in my hall in case the girls broke out in a fist fight. It really shook me up. There is no training for this. I went to music school. How does one deal with this and the emotions of fear and disgust that well up? I did what I could do. Contacted the principal, my supervisor, and the mothers of the kids. The only problem was the telephone numbers did not work. Fortunately, when I got to work this morning, the principal came in to hear my side of the story. Both of the girls' mothers had been contacted last night, and all were meeting during my first class this morning. I gave the girls detention – something I thought I would never have to do.

Teaching is being a disciplinarian, a counselor, but also an inspirer. An education is more than just reading the music. It includes how to behave as a professional, how to organize yourself, and much more. I was afraid I could not sleep that night, but I remembered this has happened before. It all worked out.

Recently, a student who had given me so much drama her whole career in high school came back from college to do a documentary on my class. She had become the woman I knew she would be and encouraged her to be. I knew it would all be ok. I slept soundly. I did all I could do. I don't think security ever showed up, though. Sometimes that worries me.

January

My concert was one and a half weeks after Christmas break. What a nightmare that is every year. No one wants to practice over the holidays. Even the really good students don't practice. The first rehearsal I felt my hair turning gray strand by strand. Every note out of tune – every note we fine-tuned meticulously before the break was a squeaky mess. The ensemble was a train wreck. After the first rehearsal, I went to my colleague, almost in tears, wanting to quit my job. I was really worried because I invited the superintendent to the concert.

I think to myself about all the cuts in the middle school string programs. We have auditions in February because this is an Arts High School, and I don't know if anyone will show up. As my old colleague used to say, if they have a pulse we will take them. I thought that very crude at the time, but I really understand now. I feel my heart racing. Presently, my colleagues pulls me out of my reverie and said, " Just make them play scales for a whole class." I look at him like he lost his mind. That is your answer? I don't say it out loud; I just meekly smile and say," Sure,' and leave the room feeling crestfallen. I stare at the wall for a while in despair. How will I get these kids up to speed?

As I calm down, I realize I have been here before. And I realize my colleague is right, but I have to do it my way. The kids need to get back in shape and really fast. What do I do every time I need to get myself ready for a concert? Long slow bows and lots of scales until my fingers are working again. So the next day, calmly I go through all of the scales, then we do the scales in rounds so they can hear the intonation; then we play them in rhythms so they can practice their ensemble. After a few days, things fall into place. Students come during lunch and my preps as well as before school for extra help. I work constantly getting them up to speed. It all works out, the concert is a success, and, low and behold, the superintendent is at my concert. He gives me a giant hug at the end of it and tells me what a wonderful job we did.

The key to all of this is that I had to problem solve and figure out how to keep these kids focused, inspire them, encourage them, keep myself from getting more gray hair, and pull off a successful concert. It's incredibly important to stay focused on remaining calm and being flexible. You must be resilient to constant change because it is a very important skill for teachers.

February

A few weeks ago, a student of mine passed away from brain cancer. After school, I had gone with the school nurse to see him in the hospital, but we were too late. He had already passed. We waited for the mother to come, then we all went up together. It was all so surreal. The hospital was a dismal place to begin with. There he was, lying so peacefully, as his mother wailed from grief. Tears flowed down my cheeks.

It was heart wrenching to come to work the next day. They had grief counselors come in and work with the students to make cards for the family. It seemed so ridiculous to me, but I was mourning, too, and not thinking straight. Students were crying; some were angry; some didn't want to be there. That was one of my worst days of teaching. I felt like I had to take away all their pain. Hold it for them. Protect them from it. But I felt like I was exploding myself.

We had a four-day weekend after that. The next week, school went on as usual. Picking up the pieces, I had to keep going, show up to work. Stay strong. On Sunday, we performed at his memorial service. Seven of my students showed up to play. I made an arrangement of "Don't Worry, Be Happy." It sounded great. We all clung together with the notes as tears threatened to tear all of us apart.

March/April

Every day is an adventure, and if it's not it's a lesson in patience and perseverance. There are moments when I want to walk away and do something else with my life because teenagers can be so difficult and challenging – yet also inquisitive and inspiring. I have finally gotten more comfortable with my own approach to discipline. This was something I struggled with and was the very thing that made me not want to be a classroom teacher. It is a real art.

I remember my first year, eighteen years ago in another school, a teacher told me, "It's a con game." You have to make them believe you are in charge. My mom gave me advice to be an actor: "If I didn't believe I was good at discipline, act like it." "Don't smile on the first day or month or until Christmas" was other advice I had gotten. It really was a series of trials and errors.

Now in my eighth year at this school, I feel confident that I have something that works for me. The very fact that I still question what I do makes me a better teacher because I am constantly reflecting and adjusting how I approach things. Every year students change. You have new students; you have difficult students. You also have students that become difficult. What I have found at the core is that it is very important to be balanced myself. To plan ahead but be ready for anything. At any given of moment, my students can decide to challenge me or gang up on a request that I make.

A few weeks ago, we were creating planning groups. The students were in charge of their groups. One student got very angry because he wanted to be with other boys and threw a fit cursing and raging. The other students were affected, and it was starting to spiral. I immediately sent him to the vice principal's office and called the main office to let them know. Even though my heart was racing, I did not let the students see me sweat. I had been through worse: fights in my class and destructive behavior. Over time I learned what worked: Remove the upset child.

In the past, I would have been upset, too. But I just said, "OK let's move forward" and didn't give the students a chance to speak about the situation. But the next day, when everyone was calm, we talked. The boy was sent to guidance, and a lot of issues came out about why he was so upset. My class was just his tip of the iceberg.

My students have been through a loss, and there is still pain underneath it all on top of all their other personal problems. It's important to be aware, but it's also important for self-preservation to know you can't do everything. Being a good teacher or even a great teacher means that you have to show that we work as a team of teachers. We are a community – we are all here to help in any way that we can together. The students need to see that we look after them. That gives them the space, a safe place to let their mind be creative and to learn. Otherwise they close up and get angry because, instinctively, they want to learn. We are inquisitive beings; at their young age, they are hungry for knowledge.

But they have been distracted by media/technology, maybe because they were left alone as a mother worked two jobs when they were little. Many had to raise themselves. They don't get enough sleep from fear of danger or excess noise – so many factors that distract them from learning. The most important thing I have found in my classroom is to create a home away from home: a warm and welcoming place; a place with rules and expectations of community and helping, good manners, and an open and comfortable place to let the creative mind learn.

May

I threw myself into preparing the students for our concert. One day, the upper classmen were particularly difficult. I couldn't hold it in anymore. I started to cry and said, "You guys have to cut me a break. I lost my friend (a colleague) across the hall. We all feel betrayed and it is difficult for us." There are a few moments you question yourself as an educator. In the public school, we are becoming more and more impersonal, yet we can't help being human. My students all crowded around me; some cried with me because they felt sad or angry, too. We had a big group hug. I felt bad for breaking down, but I also felt stronger to continue on. I showed my vulnerability, and they showed compassion. I really did build a small community in my room.

My response

As with all of the journals, Mrs. Sweet touches on a variety of themes. She talks about the complexity of teaching in an era of accountability. Her concerns about having enough time to prepare her students for a concert while also responding to state assessment mandates is not uncommon for music teachers in the United States. Music teachers, like other teachers, have to multi-task not only in terms of responsibilities set by the state and the school district but also in the many personal interactions with students on a daily basis. *How do we prepare our students for a concert, mark their growth at every turn, come up with meaningful SGOs (Student Growth Objectives), and collect data for our artifact folder that now must align with about ten different effective teaching tools?* Mrs. Sweet's journal begs the question asked by many music teachers: "Why can't I just teach music to my students?"

Another theme has to do with loss – the death of a student. Tragically, most teachers will experience this loss at some time(s) in their teaching career. Nothing is more painful than teaching students when one among them is no longer there. When teachers build a community, as Mrs. Sweet has, the loss is profoundly felt by everyone. Yet teachers have the responsibility for moving forward, while at the same time honoring the student who has died. How does a teacher talk with her grieving students? How does a teacher acknowledge that grief while still maintaining stability in the class?

At times when our very humanity is shaken, there are no easy answers nor prescriptive methods for knowing what to do as a teacher. Every incidence occurs under different circumstances, and student response can range from extreme sadness to anger to withdrawal. Although schools will bring in professional counselors from the community, the teacher remains in the front lines with his/her/their class. Caring for students may mean playing a special piece at a memorial concert, singing a well-liked song in remembrance, or just empathetic listening.

The final theme is also highlighted in the following chapter, "Helping Students in Troubled Times." Mrs. Sweet wrote about two incidences that involved students acting out: fighting in the hallway and an explosive episode in the classroom. Although such incidences can happen at any school, pre-service teachers tend to unfairly link urban schools with unmanageable behavior issues. In fact, classroom management is such an overriding fear among teachers in training that many reject the idea of teaching in an urban school altogether. In an effort to help beginning teachers shift their mindset from a panicked reaction to that of a helping agent, the following chapter addresses the unique needs of urban students and provides suggestions for teaching with confidence and compassion. Mrs. Sweet says it best: *The most important thing I have found in my classroom is to create a home away from home: a warm and welcoming place; a place with rules and expectations of community and helping, good manners, and an open and comfortable place to let the creative mind learn.*

Part 2: Helping troubled students succeed

The classroom management techniques that one learns in college usually focus on student or group off-task behavior within the context of a typically well-behaved class. These techniques are based on the assumption that children will have a bad day here or there but, with positive intervention, can move on and respect the rules of the classroom. Yet, often children/adolescents display aggression, defiance, or opposition in school. Although such children may respond to some of the techniques typically taught in higher education, most do not, creating a frustrating mismatch of students' needs and teacher's learned strategies for coping. Christopher Emdin states, "Teaching in the hood requires a very different skill set that those coming into the hood must first recognize they lack, and then train to develop."[1]

This chapter speaks to the kinds of challenges that both distract students from positive learning as well as disrupt a peaceful environment for the entire class. For the pre-service teacher, management issues constitute one of their strongest concerns. Yet, the intent of this chapter is not to confirm misguided opinions about teaching in the urban school, but rather, to honestly address the types of behavior that pre-service teachers may encounter. Understanding the roots of challenging behavior, then, leads to positive strategies for helping troubled students succeed.

Students with challenging behavior are not exclusive to the urban schools. However, many teacher education students associate student aggression with urban schools because they have been inundated with stories, both published and hearsay, about crime and violence in the city. The misperception that urban students lack control undergirds what pre-service students often say: that urban students do not want to learn and create unmanageable disruptions. Although crime and violence in certain urban areas are real and have a decided impact on children, it is important to *not* associate "bad" behavior with geographic location, socio-economic status, or race/ethnicity. L. Janelle Dance is a researcher who spent a year in the inner city observing and interviewing adolescents about their experiences in the school and community. When speaking with new teachers, she states:

> If teachers are scared, it is probably because they focus on the few students who are violent. A few urban students may be dangerous, but the popular view that the vast majority of urban students are gangsters is based more upon fiction than fact. If teachers became better acquainted with more inner-city students, they would not project the violent actions of the few onto the nonviolent many.[2]

In a multicultural classroom, students from different cultures have ways of communicating with each other that may not reflect the kind of classroom demeanor many would define as a positive learning environment. Loud talking, getting overly excited, or yelling across the room are behaviors that, to some, suggest a classroom out of control. At the same time, when excited about some issue related to music, some of these students may simply be communicating in a style consistent with their culture.

How do beginning music teachers know when to intervene and when to acknowledge that students are responding with passion through their identified cultural forms of communication? There are certain mannerisms that lend themselves to a positive (and possibly boisterous) classroom. These include the ability to hear another person's point of view (whether in agreement or disagreement), treating peers and teachers with respect for who they are, and staying focused on the issue. Likewise, no matter what the culture, the following are not acceptable in building a learning community: Physical or verbal actions that hurt, humiliate, or distract the group from the main discussion/activity at hand, destroying property, and threatening another student or teacher. Loud talking, moderate interruption, or passionate persuasion could actually reflect an exciting, on-task class. Such behavior does not require standard modes of classroom control that represent the kind of environment espoused in many teacher education programs. If we value the child's cultural background, then valuing the communication modes of that culture are equally important when heightening the engagement of the students.

Actions that disrupt the learning of others, however, are problematic. The literature in psychology and education uses several different terms for frequent disruptive behavior, such as aggressive, defiance, and coercion, that may be helpful for teachers in communicating with other school professionals. Specifically, these include verbal or physical assault, overt refusal to comply with a teacher's request/command, or tactics that involve forced compliance and humiliation of another student.[3] In a music class, this might include rude remarks about a student's performance; continual refusal to do what the teacher asks, such as working in a small composition group; or leaving the room rather than sing with the group. Coercive tactics involve the use of negative persuasion to get something, such as band members intimidating a new student in the marching band to hand over supplies (e.g. music, parts of a uniform) that they forgot.

Children/adolescents from high-poverty areas are especially vulnerable to frustration and anxiety that may lead to aggressive behavior.[4] As Christopher Edmin acknowledges in the opening quote, teachers need to approach urban teaching with the understanding that children in urban schools have significantly different needs from those in other school contexts.[5] For that reason, this chapter will address social and psychological issues that affect learning and the different ways that students cope with stress. In addition, this chapter will suggest strategies for helping students gain social skills and how music teachers can teach resilience and self-control.

Wanting to learn

Children do want to learn and to make their parents proud. Education is perceived as a lifeline for overcoming urban poverty, and this fact is not lost on the children or their families. Why, then, do some children or adolescents exhibit problems that get in the way of their learning and achieving? One explanation has to do with what children/adolescents experience outside of the school. According to Hill R. Walker et al., "More and more children from troubled, chaotic homes are bringing well-developed patterns of antisocial behavior to school."[6] When children have not experienced productive ways of negotiating conflict, they often lack the social skills needed to get along with others in the classroom. Ironically, peer attention may not only reinforce aggressive behavior but sometimes contribute to a personal gain in popularity.[7] Consequently, students cope with stress in many different ways.

Signs of urban stress

Children in many areas of the urban community suffer from the risks of violence and poverty. Some come to school without having had breakfast or dinner the night before. Some live in homes that are overcrowded and pose health hazards. Medical care is a luxury so that even a mild illness, such as earaches or respiratory infections, may escalate into more serious illnesses. Asthma and lead poisoning, for instance, are more common among children from poverty-stricken families.[8]

Living with violence, in the home or on the street, also creates considerable stress. The shooting death of a relative or friend is not unusual.[9] Children/adolescents who experience or even witness this event suffer unimaginable trauma. Not surprisingly, such trauma may lead to acting out, withdrawing, or depression.[10]

Accordingly, music teachers need to recognize the stressors that can contribute to challenging behavior. Some of these are listed below:[11]

- Antagonism toward school, rebelliousness
- Resistance or demonstrated hostility to adult influences
- Lack of respect for themselves and educators
- High rates of absenteeism
- Academic skill deficits
- Lack of motivation and/or withdrawal from classroom challenges
- Feelings of inferiority and failure
- Immature behaviors and poor adjustment actions
- Lack of academic or vocational goal
- Little or no interest in outside hobbies, sports, and other activities

Patricia B. Kopetz et al. observe that children who live with chronic violence have trouble concentrating from lack of sleep or engage in aggressive play that imitates what they have seen.[12] They may overcompensate by acting tough or showing a lack of care toward others in the classroom. Some become clinically depressed with symptoms that mirror those listed above. In elementary school, the homeroom teacher may have a greater opportunity to observe these behaviors simply because he/she/they spends more concentrated time with the student. Given this, it is important for elementary music teachers to confer with homeroom teachers when they see a pattern of problematic behavior. In the middle and high school, however, music teachers often see students more than once a week and have a better opportunity for identifying students who are truly troubled as compared to those having a bad day.

Martin Haberman, a well-known teacher educator for urban schools, remarks that, "Feelings of deep frustration are a major characteristic of both adults and children who grow up and live the experience of urban poverty."[13] He explains that constant stress from living in an area where violence is the norm can lead to aggression or withdrawal. Both types of behavior signal a warning that the student needs intervention. If a music teacher notices a cluster of the above behaviors over time, he/she should follow the school's protocol for helping troubled students. This often involves consulting with the homeroom teacher and alerting the school counselor or principal so that he/she can take appropriate action. Similarly, signs of abuse (e.g. bruises on the skin, wearing long sleeves in warm weather) must be reported as well.

Sometimes a student will come to talk about personal issues and begin by saying, "I want to tell you something but you have to promise not to tell anyone." You *cannot* make this promise, but you can listen briefly and encourage the student to talk to the guidance counselor, letting the student know that you will support them, even to the point of walking with the student to the counselor's office. Mrs. Cartier, one of the collaborators for this book, remarks: *A kid comes to class and tells you that her dad tried to choke her. When kids seem that they're about to tell you something, you try to get them to the guidance counselor as fast as possible.*

What about calling the parents? Again, this is only something that a school authority should address. You have no idea how parents or caretakers may be involved nor should you put yourself in a position of speaking for the school. While you do have an ethical and moral responsibility for making sure that the student is in the care of a professional, whether a school counselor or administrator, you need to recognize the limitations of your responsibility so that the care of the student remains a top priority. Teachers are not trained therapists and should never take on that role.

Street-savvy kids

Some areas in the city are more tumultuous than others. For those children/adolescents living in a violent neighborhood, survival depends on learning to read signs of potential danger on the street. Their knowledge of the streets is often far beyond that of the teacher's and can lead to friction or conflict when the teacher misunderstands the codes or language of the students. Dance states, "Students complain that most teachers have no clue that so-called 'disruptive behavior' is sometimes a necessary front for surviving the streets."[14]

Most pre-service teachers, coming from middle class backgrounds, have little or no street experience comparable to that of their urban students. Dance explains,

> Regardless of how well a teacher knows his or her subject matter, unless she (or he) can relate, or cares to relate, to the demands of urban street culture, she may not be able to acquire and maintain the interest of the students who must navigate the streets on a daily basis.[15]

Urban students are looking for the "down" teacher – someone that understands the code of the streets or at least *makes an effort* to learn about the street culture of his/her/their students. In the urban school, this involves not only knowing the student but also the context in which the student lives.

As a White teacher with a suburban middle class background, I had a lot to learn in order to build trust among my urban students. In the next few sections, I share those insights from both my teaching and the writings of other teachers/authors who taught in the urban setting. Although music teachers may not have students who are involved in the activities described below, knowing what students confront and the context of their communities provides valuable insight for understanding the needs of urban children/adolescents.

Gangs

Most schools, whether urban, suburban, or rural, have gang activity in the area. Although music teachers rarely encounter gang-related problems in the classroom, most will come in contact with students who know/join gangs or may be harassed by gang members. Pre-service teachers will probably not discuss gangs in any depth in their programs. I believe, however, that this information is better addressed in the education of teachers than avoiding the subject entirely. In addition, pre-service teachers can find a number of up-to-date resources online that describe the general governance of gangs and the steps that gang members take to identify themselves in the area.

Regarding the school population, Nilda Flores–González discusses two different peer cultures:[16] those that are school oriented and those that are street oriented. The groups are distinguished from one another according to the behaviors they display and the kinds of peer approval or prestige that they gain from these behaviors. For example, school-oriented students have strong records of achievement and partici-pation in school activities. They derive pleasure from academic excellence and/or involvement in clubs and organizations. Street-oriented students are motivated by activities or behavior not sanctioned by the school, that will earn them power and status on the streets.

A street orientation can indicate the presence of gang activity. According to Florez–González,

> In addition to peer influence, the leavers [those that drop out of school] say that joining a gang is inevitable. They see gangs as an inextricable part of growing up in their neighborhood, an inner-city rite of passage into adulthood.[17]

In his gripping book, *Slipping Into Darkness: A True Story from the American Ghetto*, M. Rutledge McCall went undercover in the inner city where he lived among members of the Blood Stone Pirus, a gang on the east side of South Central Los Angeles.[18] His story is brutal, vivid, and compelling as he chronicles the lives and activities of several gang members. Although one must read the book to fully appreciate life in the underworld, McCall does address information from which teachers can benefit. For instance, he states,

> It's easy to say to a gang member, 'Get out, just quit gangbanging and get educated and do right for yourself.' But making the ten blocks to school each morning is a bigger worry than doing well in class. Staying alive is more important home-work than algebra or science. Or a high school diploma for that matter.[19]

The pressure to join a gang is not always a choice in the face of daily violence, neglect, and poverty. Gang life offers the care and protection that neglected children/adolescents crave, especially when siblings are part of that group. When females and males feel powerless and a lack of respect from others, the pull toward joining a gang is even stronger.[20] In an interview with McCall, a gang member confides:

> It was more like a . . . not a forced situation, it was more like a role model thing, because all my role models were gangsters, such as my brothers and my sisters from the 'hood, you know . . . all my friends was banging. And I fell into the click when I was real young, you know. I fell into it when I was about ten . . . [21]

★★★★★★★★★★★★

> And far as I can remember, far as my homeboys you know, they gave me more love than anybody. You know, when I didn't have nothing to eat, my homeboys fed me. When I didn't have nowhere to go, my homeboys gave me somewhere to live. . . . They was my mother and father. You know what I'm saying? My friends, my best friends, my brothers, all that.[22]

Online resources such as *A Parent's Guide to Gangs*, published through the Office of Justice Programs, can be helpful in providing current, succinct information about gang activity.[23] For example, it is no secret that gang members subscribe to rigid rules and may wear clothing or sport tattoos that mark their affiliation. The most important posture for members of a gang community involves constant demon-stration of loyalty to the group. Those who break that covenant may suffer severe backlash from other gang members.[24] Although many schools forbid overt signs of gang affiliation, most students are aware of the gang members among them. For teachers, it may be of some comfort to know that gang members usually contain their activity outside of the school as they try not to bring attention to their loyal-ties inside the school setting.

When asked about gang activity at school, some of the contributing teacher writers experienced little or no presence of gangs in the school: "There isn't a lot of gang activity among students that we know of. A lot of kids have parents that are protective" (Ms. Foreman). Mr. Tamburro, however, responded:

> There are kids in gangs or trying to get into gangs. I don't deal with it directly but the principal or other authorities deal with it. One time, something was going on — one of the kids had said something offensive about another student to his friends. At the end

of school there was a group of 23-yr old men and teenage boys getting ready to rough up the student that he had a problem with.

Also, there's a police officer in front of school every morning and a police officer around at end of school. We have a detective who is around all the time. He was a gang detective with the PD (police department). You see these detectives all the time. They are just checking in. It's when the kids get older (middle school) they are most vulnerable to the gangs and these vultures swoop down and grab them. We have gangs like the Bloods, Crips, and MS 13. All the big ones in New York and LA are here in our town. I know who the kids are but they don't have problems with me in class.

Dance describes three types of street-savvy adolescents that she identifies as "Three Variations of a Gangsta Theme." The descriptions below are useful in identifying where some students stand in terms of gang activity. These categories come from the students that she studied in her research:[25]

1   "Hard" (or "hardcore") refers to the state of being a street-savvy and tough gangster who has actually committed criminal, violent, and ruthless acts. A so-called hard student is typically involved in the illicit aspects of street culture.
2   "Hardcore wannabe" students act hard because it is fashionable or prestigious – that is to say, a superficial means of gaining social esteem in urban youth culture. A student labeled as a "hardcore wannabe" has either no involvement or sporadic, peer-pressured involvement in the negative aspects of street culture.
3   "Hardcore enough" (or "hard enough") denotes the state of being street-savvy and tough enough to convince one's peers that you could be ruthless if you had to but that you choose not to be.

So, what does the music teacher do with this information? First, it is important to know that these divisions exist and that some students may be in the untenable position of having to join a gang or adopt gang-like postures. Secondly, the more street language teachers know, the more convincing they are in learning the culture of their students. "Down" teachers, those who students respect, have high expectations and are able to shepherd students in distress by suggesting viable, realistic alternatives for navigating their difficult lives. The one characteristic that all favorite teachers have in common is the ability to convince students that they genuinely care.[26]

As indicated earlier, gangs and drugs are not endemic to urban schools. Their reach also extends well into the suburban and rural schools. The presence of gang activity, however, may be more intense in areas with high crime and poverty. Music teachers, particularly in urban middle schools and high schools, are likely to interact with some students who fit the scenario of "Hard," "Hardcore Wannabe," and "Hardcore Enough." Given this, music may be especially powerful in reaching troubled students – if only to provide respite from the stress of daily life.

Bullying

"Whereas school violence comes in different forms (e.g. fighting and weapon use), it is daily instances of bullying that students are most likely to encounter."[27] Bullying is nothing new in schools; however, in the past decade, bullying has come to the forefront of the media and policy-making institutions. Bullying is defined as "unwanted, aggressive behavior among school aged children that involves a real or perceived power imbalance. The behavior is repeated, or has the potential to be repeated, over time" (see Appendix A). Bullying can involve any of the following behaviors: making threats, spreading rumors, attacking someone physically or verbally, and purposefully excluding someone from a group. Targets of bullying may include those who are overweight, those with high achievement in school, LGBTQ students, religious affiliations, racial/ethnic conflict, etc.

Although there is no federal law on bullying, each state has adopted legislation and/or policies to protect students from bullying behavior. Some teacher education institutions have also instituted a bullying course to familiarize pre-service teachers with bullying behavior and victimology. Because every state has its own legislation, new music teachers must become familiar with the policies of their school. An online resource, see Appendix A, provides additional information on all aspects of bullying.

Cyberbullying brings a new dimension of bullying to the school and can have severe or deadly consequences. For that reason, many states have included cyberbullying in their anti-bullying policies. There are several reasons why cyberbullying is so heinous. First, it flies under the radar. Unless someone reports cyberbullying to the teacher or the teacher overhears a student conversation, cyberbullying can go unnoticed. Second, cyberbullies that post hurtful or false information about the targeted person reach others who often add their own insults to the fray. Third, in this technologically proficient generation, social media is part and parcel of every student's daily life. There are few students who do not have easy access to the internet via a smart phone or other technological devices. Anything can be posted over the internet, channeling to hundreds of other students in a matter of seconds.

Mrs. Cartier explains:

> One thing that we see is the cyberbullying. For instance, one day some 6th grade girls made a plan to fight in the gym. One of the girls recorded the fight on her telephone – Kids will do things and put it on line. The phones, Instagram, snapchat – these are the things that kids mess with. The biggest thing is doing bad stuff and recording it. If you go online and google "girl fights," all this stuff will come up. This is a big craze everywhere. The digital media shows women fighting like cats and dogs and students see this horrific behavior. Given these images, when our girls fight they fight hard.

For victims of bullying, school is not a safe place. In response, schools across the nation have instituted bullying prevention programs. Music teachers, as with all teachers, should know the signs of bullying and report any type of bullying behavior to the school administrator. Taking responsible action within the school guidelines is critical in protecting all students.

Transition to middle school

The transition to middle school is a particularly vulnerable period for young adolescents. Along with the physical changes in their body as well as a reframing of how their brain processes information, students encounter significant changes in the school climate.[28] Switching to a new, and often bigger, building; having individual schedules; experiencing different discipline codes and expectations in each class; and having fewer opportunities to build relationships with teachers – these are some of the challenges that students face.

Students also begin to socialize along racial lines. While this is a time when most students search for their identity in the world, students of color also struggle to construct their identity as a person of color living in a White dominated society. Beverly Tatum wrote about this phenomenon in her book, *Why Are All the Black Kids Sitting Together in the Cafeteria?*[29] She explains that when students get older, they tend to "hang" with people of similar background and culture. Unfortunately, some teachers misunderstand this stage of development, particularly with Black students, as students who "just don't want to get along." Although close friendships exist among students of all colors, it is important to realize that racial/ethnic groupings are not an indication of impending discipline problems.

As noted above, friendships and peer approval become increasingly powerful for shaping behavior and building confidants. Middle school students, in trying to establish themselves within a changing peer culture, can lapse into "aggression, bullying, and deviant behaviors in order to become more accepted."[30] In a study on the transition from elementary to middle school, many participants indicated that middle school was the point at which they began to get into serious trouble.[31]

Ms. Foreman tells a story from the middle school where she teaches:

> *One kid came in the middle of the year. He came from a neighborhood school that was rough. He changed the climate of the whole class. It was difficult. The classroom assistant wasn't very helpful. Eventually we got him under control. Then, he stole something from the band room – it was a day when I was ill and out of school. When I got back a different student came to me and said "My piccolo is gone." The boy had discarded the piccolo in the boy's bathroom trashcan. When we found it, he confessed and got suspended. I felt hurt because I was always nice to him. He didn't apologize for a while but did calm down a little after the incidence.*

In essence, the stories of the teachers featured in this book and information from writers in psychology and education have similar themes. First, children from low-income families grow up in an environment that is considerably different from the backgrounds of most teachers. Second, an environment that is characterized by violence creates numerous stressors in children and adolescents. Third, when adolescents have no adult role models who respond to conflicts in a reasonable, peaceful manner, the students may come to school with deficits in social behavior (described later in the chapter). Fourth, although gang behavior is generally isolated to the streets, bullying is a preeminent concern for students and teachers. Fifth, the middle school transition can escalate problem behavior among students who are shifting among peer cultures and looking for peer approval in the process.

I want to be a music teacher, not a police officer

If you are ready to give up on urban music teaching at this point in the book, I want to remind you of two things. One, aggression or defiance are typically symptoms of something larger going on in a young person's life and are present in suburban and rural school settings as well. Two, the aim of this book is to prepare you for the nuances of urban teaching, which can involve some challenging teacher–student interactions. Joe Kincheloe states, "No one can go into urban schools to teach successfully without understanding and appreciating the everyday challenges many city students endure and the creative responses they construct."[32]

Policing behavior, effective only under extreme circumstances, is the antithesis of why you wanted to teach music in the first place. Likewise, if you are drawn to urban teaching because you want the "save those poor kids," you may be shocked to find that urban children/adolescents do not want to be saved; they want mature adults who understand the challenges they face yet maintain high standards for behavior and musicianship. They want an adult who maintains a safe and equitable place for them to learn.

What difficult behavior might a music teacher encounter? At an early age, students may use whining and unwillingness to participate in order to get what they want. As students get older, this behavior can progress to bullying, fighting, deception, stealing, or destruction of property. "The longer students are allowed to be aggressive, defiant, and destructive, the more difficult it is to turn them around."[33] How, then, do teachers work with students when they push the boundaries of acceptable behavior? More to the point, how do teachers work with particularly difficult students who show little regard for the teacher or the well-being of the classroom community?

What doesn't work

In general, students who are consistently disruptive either want to *get* something such as peer approval or *avoid* something that the student does not want to do.[34] Unfortunately, the kinds of strategies that work with typical behaviors do not work with serious behavior problems.[35] The first tactic that teachers usually try is to exert power and control over the student(s). For instance, if a student constantly calls out for the purpose of disrupting the class, the teacher might scold the student in front of others, give the student an extra assignment, or send him/her out of the class. "Too often," Rutherford and Nelson write, "the only interventions used with aggressive behavior involve punishment tactics, which do not address the function the behavior may serve the student."[36] Yelling, punishing, or suspending a student may seem to work at the moment but actually provides the kindling for a bigger fire later on. In other words, yelling and punishing quickly lose their power, even to the point where students may laugh at the teacher.

Research shows that suspensions are more harmful than helpful as they only serve to remove students from the situation where they most need to be: *in school*.[37] Suspended students miss valuable instruction, tests, and assignments that only push the student further behind. Moreover, additional studies show that a student who has been suspended "is more likely to eventually drop out of school or end up in the criminal justice system."[38] In short, exerting control and power do little to fix the root of the behavior and often intensify rather than diffuse the situation.

Sometimes the student's anger escalates into a full-blown confrontation with the teacher. Power struggles can take place in front of other students who often perceive that the student, not the teacher, has control. When this happens, the teacher can either challenge the student or disengage with him/her/them. The latter, of course, is preferable.

For instance, one day while I was teaching, Travon got up in the middle of the class and starting yelling to friends outside the window. I told him to sit down and he turned to me, his eyes blazing, and said, "Fxxx You." I wasn't going to challenge him. Travon was not only bigger than me but clearly out of control. I needed to let him cool down before talking with him later. It wasn't a frightening situation in the least but could have been if I had tried to argue or reprimand him.

Here's what I didn't know: Troubled students often perceive a teacher giving directions as a direct provocation rather than a request.[39] This, in fact, is very much what happened with Travon. I asked him to sit down, which was a direct command. There are two types of directions that teachers typically give. The first is an alpha command that is a clear and specific directive. The second is a beta command that is somewhat vague, e.g. "Sometime this afternoon we will rehearse *Siyahamba*, so please be ready." Both types of commands, while often necessary in the classroom, can lead to aggressive behavior simply because the student perceives one command as confrontational or the other as confusing. There is no reason, however, to conclude that teachers should abandon giving alpha or beta commands. More to the point, music teachers can use this information to analyze their style of teacher talk when problems occur.

Other examples of teacher talk that can escalate a situation include reprimanding, arguing, engaging in hostile interactions, or forcing compliance. These approaches are fruitless in dealing with aggressive or defiant students who come to school well versed in the "science" of coercion, often having had extensive practice at home. Sometimes, teachers give instructions or tasks that generate so much non-compliance among a student that the request is withdrawn. This is called the "behavior escalation game and it is a game teachers cannot win and should not play."[40]

What works better

There are many techniques for classroom management that work well with most students. This section, however, discusses ideas for working with troubled children/ adolescents who show aggression, hostility, or defiance. Regrettably, urban schools have been unfairly positioned as places of mayhem and disrespect. Beginning teachers who hold this assumption will probably approach problems as inevitable occurrences rather than behaviors that they can shape along more constructive lines. Good teachers recognize that different students need different approaches. Without question, each child should have a place in an inclusive, respectful learning community.

Learning cannot take place, however, in an environment that is chaotic and unsafe either emotionally or physically. To think about the range of behavior you might encounter, picture a continuum – at one end, students may cry, sulk, pout, whine, or withdraw. Further down the continuum, behavior may include screaming, swearing, spitting, kicking, destroying property, lying, and truancy.[41]

Ross W. Greene, in his best-selling book *Lost at School*, proposes that teachers change their mindset.[42] Instead of viewing the student as uncooperative in following class rules or attending to his/her/their work, Greene suggests that teachers see defiance or aggression as a kind of learning disability. These students lack the kinds of thinking skills that help them mediate their behavior and problem solve social situations that other students have learned. There is, in fact, a developmental lag in areas of emotional responsiveness and reflection. Such behaviors are typified by difficulty in handling change, thinking through one's actions (impulsivity), persisting in challenging tasks, and inaccurately perceiving social cues from others. Whereas the more centered child can adapt to changes in routine or recognize that throwing a chair has consequences, another student may not have those thinking skills in place.

Seeing the troubled child as someone who needs help with social/emotional thinking skills demands a major shift in perspective. It takes away the temptation to blame the child for lack of control and, instead, asks the teacher to help students develop coping mechanisms for dealing with everyday issues in the classroom. Does this mean that the teacher becomes a therapist? Absolutely not. Part of teaching the whole child is helping that child develop confidence in learning. When social/ emotional skills are lagging, however, the student hurts his/her/their own learning or that of other students in the long run.

In the music classroom, we are constantly dealing with content that is expressive and emotional in nature. For that reason, our connection to the affective side of learning is a big part of involving students in authentic musical experiences. Sometimes this is exactly what the troubled child responds to. On the other hand, there are children/adolescents who bring a multitude of problems into the music classroom that detract from the lesson. Although frustrating for any teacher, it is particularly difficult for an arts teacher who needs a high level of trust in order to engage students aesthetically. To look at this from a different angle, helping students adapt emotionally and socially is actually critical to what we do as musicians. We deal with artistic material, which means that we work not just with the cognitive aspect of music learning but the emotional side as well. Perhaps we have a greater obligation to the wellness of our students than previously thought. According to Greene, "Helping kids with behavioral challenges is never easy and is always time consuming. But intervening in ways that aren't working is always harder and more time consuming."[43]

Marvin Marshall's writing echoes many of the underlying ideas in Greene's work.[44] Both view discipline as an opportunity to teach children how to self-monitor their behavior. The emphasis is on teaching skills that students need to acclimate themselves into society – whether that social unit is the classroom or society at large. Marshall sees discipline as tantamount to developing a thoughtful engaged citizenry; preparing students to contribute productively and work collaboratively with others is a hallmark of democracy. Regarding music teaching, then, teachers have a responsibility to children that extends beyond musicianship. Preparing musicians also involves the social/emotional skills to participate fully in a socially just society.

Punishment, coercion, and manipulation have no place in teaching discipline. Notice the importance of the phrase "teaching discipline" rather than "imposing discipline." As with Greene's approach, Marshall believes that children must take ownership of their behavior, not through contracts signed "under duress" but through the development of skills to self-monitor behavior. Although external demands ("If you don't learn the music, you may not go on the field trip") may seem to get results in the short term, they don't teach students to develop internal controls that lead to persistence, thinking before acting, and understanding that respect is earned through the way one treats others. Simply put, "People do better when they feel good, than when they feel bad."[45]

In his own urban teaching, Marshall was continually frustrated with student behavior that not only disrupted the classroom but was also hurtful to other students. He designed a hierarchy of behavior that helped him identify those areas in which students needed help learning to self-regulate their behavior. The model has four levels that progress from the least ability to self-regulate to the highest level of self-regulation. It is important, though, to understand that the names of the levels are meant for teachers only and should not be used with the students. The following excerpts come from Marshall's book, *Discipline Without Stress, Punishments, or Rewards: How Teachers and Parents Promote Responsibility & Learning.*[46]

Level A – Anarchy

Anarchy is the lowest level of behavior. The word comes from Greek and literally means "without rule." This level refers to absence of constructive purpose, aimlessness, and chaos.

Level B – Bossing/Bullying

Bullying is the level above anarchy. A student behaving at this level violates the courtesies of class operations and accepted standards. The bully attempts to boss others by violating others' rights. The sooner a person/teacher stands up to bullying, the easier it will be to handle and the sooner bullying will stop.

Level C – Cooperation/Conformity

Conformity is as essential for classroom decorum as it is for a civil society. No society can exist without some measure of conformity. The term means compliance and cooperation with expected standards. *The term does not mean or connote regimentation.* Rather, it means to be connected and involved with others. It refers to the accommodations people make when they are naturally inclined to accept the values and mores of their immediate group and society. The key concept of level C is that *motivation is external.* Teachers who understand the power of peer pressure can help young people to become more autonomous and to decide against engaging in socially irresponsible acts, both inside and outside of school.

Level D – Democracy

Level D is the highest level. At this level, the motivation to be responsible is *internal.* The person has been integrated to regulation of important actions. Behavior at this level is manifested by qualities of character that individuals habitually recognize as the right thing.

Both Greene and Marshall offer information that positions discipline as a teaching tool rather than a punishment/reward system. The objective here is to help students develop the thinking skills needed to participate fully in a community of learners. For music teachers, these ideas are particularly resonant. Group composing, performance, singing, and ensemble work involve students who trust and support each other. Building a community in music means "We're all in this together." In this light, teaching students to develop self-discipline, whether the ability to practice on their own or listen reflectively to peer contributions, is integral to what musicians do.

The aforementioned approaches are focused on student learners with challenging behavior in the classroom. These approaches are grounded in consistency and building an ongoing relationship with the student. In some of the journals for this book, the teacher writers mention relying on the help of a security guard or administrator. This is for the safety and well-being of all involved. Skirmishes in the hall do not necessarily involve students you know nor should you put yourself at risk with a student who can potentially harm you. In these cases, you will probably need additional support for managing the situation. In addition, when students are cened state of emotional upset, sometimes the best course of action may ιove them from the group or get help from outside the classroom. The key this is to not make things worse.

Conclusion

Children and adolescents who live in areas of crime and violence deal with untold stress beyond the school walls. Because many are victims or witnesses to violence, music teachers can expect some students who may have difficulty getting along with others or participating with full engagement in music activities. Although it is easy for the teacher to take aggression or defiance personally, what troubled students need most is a mature adult who provides firm but caring support in the students' weakest moments.

Discipline through an ethos of care always moves toward resilience rather than victimization. Helping students feel confident in their ability to weather the storm builds resilience. Simply finding a way to momentarily stop the action does little to help students learn the thinking skills that lead beyond a victim mentality. This means that, at times, the music teacher may have to step back from his/her/their lesson plan in order to teach care and empathy (see Chapter 2). Nel Noddings reminds us that "Unless they can respond to caring attempts they will not grow, and they will certainly not learn to care for other."[47]

In democratic practice, there is always tension between the individual's needs and those of the group. When do you put the individual first and when do you put the group first? This delicate balance takes experience – knowing when to push and when to pull back. Rather than just reacting to problems, teaching students how to constructively work through their problems activates thinking processes that lead to self-regulation.

The goal, in essence, is to build a community where students trust and support each other. Community is the cornerstone of music. Our work is inclusive and depends on everyone pulling his/her/their own weight. The most obvious examples are large or small group music activities and ensemble participation. Yet, even individual music making, composing, or solo performance requires a willing and supportive audience. When student behavior disrupts the group process, both the individual and the group are hurt. For that reason alone, music teachers need skills in helping students develop internal mechanisms for making better choices.

All the contributing teacher writers have had good days and bad days. But in light of the passion and love they exude when writing about their students, there are many more good days. They know that teachers can make all the difference in the world. They recognize that no one strategy works for every student and that there is no prescriptive solution for the multitude of interactions that music teachers experience on a daily level. They also understand that caring adults can make connections through music that break through some of the barriers that students have. As Mrs. Sweet writes, *the students need to see that we look after them.*

Discussion questions

1   Have you ever experienced a time when you were so frustrated or upset that you couldn't concentrate on your schoolwork? What kind of support did you need from your teacher(s)?
2   If a student uses street language as his/her/their communication style in the classroom, how would you respond?
3   What are some important things to keep in mind when helping a troubled student to succeed?

References

1   Emdin, Christopher. 2016. *For White Folks Who Teach in the Hood . . . and the Rest of Y'all Too: Reality Pedagogy and Urban Education*. Boston: Beacon Press: 58.
2   Dance, L. Janelle. 2002. *Tough Fronts: The Impact of Street Culture on Schooling*. New York: Routledge: 55.
3   Rutherford, Robert B. and C. Michael Nelson. "Management of Aggressive and Violent Behavior in the Schools." *Focus on Exceptional Children, 27* (6): 1–27.
4   Kopetz, Patricia B., Anthony J. Lease, and Bonnie Z. Warren-Kring. 2006. *Comprehensive Urban Education*. Boston: Pearson.
5   Emdin. *For White Folks*.
6   Walker, Hill M., Elizabeth Ramsey, and Frank M. Gresham. 2003–2004. "Heading Off Disruptive Behavior: How Early Intervention Can Reduce Defiant Behavior – And Win Back Teaching Time." Winter. *American Educator*. Washington, DC: American Federation of Teachers: 1.
7   Rutherford and Nelson. "Management of Aggressive and Violent Behavior."
8   *Child Trends*: Data Bank. 2016, November. "Indicators on Children and Youth." www.childtrends.org; Meliker, J. (Ed.). (2017). "High Prevalence of Elevated Blood Lead Levels in Both Rural and Urban Iowa Newborns: Spatial Patterns and Area-Level Covariates." PLoS One online journal. https://www.ncbi.nlm.nih.gov/pmc/articles/PMC5433780/
9   Benhorin, Shira and Susan D. McMahon. 2008. "Exposure to Violence and Aggression: Protective Roles of Social Support Among Urban African American Youth." *Journal of Community Psychology, 36* (6): 723–743.
10 Eisman, Andria B., Sarah A. Stoddard, Justin Heinze, Cleopatra H. Caldwell, and Marc A. Zimmerman. 2015. "Depressive symptoms, Social Support, and Violence Exposure Among Urban Youth: A Longitudinal Study of Resilience." *Developmental Psychology, 51* (9): 1307–1316. doi: 10.1037/a0039501
11 Kopetz, Lease and Warren-Kring. *Comprehensive Urban Education*: 109.
12 Ibid.
13 Haberman, Martin. 1995. *Star Teachers of Children in Poverty*. West Lafayette, IN: Kappa Delta Pi: 88.
14 Dance. *Tough Fronts*: 70.
15 Ibid., 76–77.
16 Flores-González, Nilda. 2002. *School Kids/Street Kids: Identity Development in Latino Students*. New York: Teachers College.
17 Ibid., 128.
18 McCall, M. Rutledge. 2000. *Slipping into Darkness: A True Story from the American Ghetto* [Kindle Edition]. Edinburgh: Archangel House.

19 Ibid., 6034.

20 Kharem, Haroon. 2007. "What Does It Mean to Be in a Gang?" In *19 Urban Questions: Teaching in The City*, edited by Shirley R. Steinberg and Joe L. Kincheloe, 99–108. New York: Peter Lang.

21 McCall. 2000. *Slipping into Darkness*: 6404. (This selection was rewritten in standard English by the author).

22 Ibid., 6410. (This selection was rewritten in standard English by the author).

23 *A Parent's Guide to Gangs*. (retrieved 2017, January 10). Office of Juvenile Justice and Delinquency Prevention, Office of Justice Programs, US Department of Justice. www.k12.wa.us/safetycenter/Gangs/pubdocs/Parents-Guide-to-GangsOJJDP.pdf

24 Kharem, Haroon. 2007. "What Does It Mean to Be in a Gang?" In *19 Urban Questions: Teaching in The City*, edited by Shirley R. Steinberg and Joe L. Kincheloe, 99–108. New York: Peter Lang.

25 Dance. *Tough Fronts*: 52.

26 Ibid., 75.

27 Duggins, Shaun D., Gabriel P. Kuperminc, Christopher C. Henrich, Ciara Smalls-Glover, and Julia L. Perilla. 2016. "Aggression Among Adolescent Victims of School Bullying: Protective Roles of Family and School Connectedness." *Psychology of Violence, 6* (2): 205. http://dx.doi.org/10.1037/a0039439

28 Blakemore, Sarah-Jayne and Suparna Choudhury. 2006. "Development of The Adolescent Brain: Implications for Executive Function and Social Cognition." *Journal of Child Psychology and Psychiatry, 47* (3/4): 296–312. doi: 10.1111/j.1469-7610.2006.01611

29 Tatum, Beverly. 1997. *Why Are All the Black Kids Sitting Together in The Cafeteria?* New York: Basic Books.

30 Hongling, Xie, Molly Dawes, Tabitha J. Wurster, and Bing Shi. 2013. "Aggression, Academic Behaviors, and Popularity Perceptions Among Boys of Color During the Transition to Middle School." *American Journal of Orthopsychiatry, 83* (2–3): 265–277. doi: 10.1111/ajop.12039

31 Kennedy-Lewis, Brianna L. 2013. "Persistently Disciplined Urban Students' Experience of The Middle School Transition and 'Getting in Trouble'." *Middle Grades Research Journal, 8* (3): 99–116.

32 Kincheloe, Joe L. 2007. "City Kids – Not the Kind of Students You'd Want to Teach." In *Teaching City Kids*, edited by Joe L. Kincheloe and kecia hayes, 3–38. New York: Peter Lang: 20.

33 Walker, Ramsey, and Gresham. "Heading Off Disruptive Behavior." 9.

34 Rutherford and Nelson. "Management of Aggressive and Violent Behavior in the Schools."

35 Walker, Ramsey, and Gresham. "Heading Off Disruptive Behavior."; Greene, Ross W. 2014. *Lost at School: Why Our Kids with Behavioral Challenges Are Falling Through the Cracks and How We Can Help Them*. New York: Scribner.

36 Rutherford and Nelson. "Management of Aggressive and Violent Behavior in the Schools." 6.

37 Duggins. "Aggression Among Adolescent Victims."; Kenney-Lewis, "Persistently Disciplined."

38 Dominus, Susan. 2016. "Halls of Justice." *The New York Times Magazine [Education Issue]*, September 11.

39 Walker, Hill M., Elizabeth Ramsy, and Frank M. Gresham. 2003–2004. "How Disruptive Students Escalate Hostility and Disorder – And How Teachers Can Avoid It." Winter. *American Educator*. Washington, DC: American Federation of Teachers: 2. www.aft.org/periodical/american-educator/winter-2003-2004/how-disruptive-students-escalate-hostility

40 Ibid., 2.

41 Greene. *Lost at School*: 12.

42 Ibid.

43 Ibid., 9.

44 Marshall, Marvin. 2007. *Discipline Without Stress, Punishments, or Rewards: How Teachers and Parents Promote Responsibility and Learning* [2nd ed.]. Los Alamitos, CA: Piper Press.

45 Ibid., 9.

46 Ibid., 73–77.

47 Noddings, Nel. 2005. *The Challenge to Care in Schools* [2nd ed.]. New York: Teachers College Press: 108.

4

NARROWING THE OPPORTUNITY GAP FOR URBAN STUDENTS

Part 1: From the classroom of Mrs. Skinner

Mrs. Skinner has an interesting teaching history. After a year of teaching in an affluent suburban school, she had an opportunity to take a string and chorus position at the International Community School in Bangkok, Thailand. Three years later, she returned to the United States and accepted a position in a mid-sized urban community teaching instrumental and general music. In the following year, her school district opened a new school for gifted and talented students excelling in academics, performing arts, visual arts, and athletics. Mrs. Skinner transferred to this school as the string teacher for grades two through eight. She was just beginning her seventh year of teaching.

Her school is located in the downtown area where there are many small family-owned Latino restaurants, laundromats, bodegas, and apartments. *The neighborhood,* Mrs. Skinner remarks, *includes many apartment buildings, run-down homes, and tightly packed multi-family houses. Most houses are not kept up and have very little yard space for kids to play.* She notes that her own background in a small, primarily White, Midwestern city was very different from that of her students in the school where she currently teaches.

Her "brand new" school is a U-shaped building with three floors. The two art rooms, band room, and stage are located in close proximity on the first floor. Right above, on the second floor, are a chorus/general music room and drama room. The school houses 800 students from all over the city, which includes grades 2 through 8. A majority of the students are of Latino descent, and the teachers represent various ethnicities and races, including many Latino teachers. As a White teacher, Mrs. Skinner is in the minority.

Despite the shiny new rooms and generous space devoted to the arts, the school did not have any instruments until the fourth month of the school year. Mrs.

Skinner comments on the irony of building a string program without instruments: *I wanted the kids to do a winter concert, so I went and found instruments. I had good colleagues outside the district who said, "Yeah, you can use this until you get your instruments." I ended up with about twenty string instruments including violins, cellos, and a bass. I had four small violins for twenty-five kids in the second grade. I split up the class into four teams, and they had to share the instrument.*

In her journal, Mrs. Skinner writes about the rewards and challenges of teaching in a new urban school. Her journal entries also reflect her frustrations in coping with lack of resources. This is not an unfamiliar story, as many urban music programs do not have the basic supplies needed to give students an educational experience in line with their more affluent neighboring communities. While it's clear that an opportunity gap exists, breaking down the barriers so that urban districts have the same opportunities as more affluent ones is something that Mrs. Skinner has been exploring during her time in this position.

Mrs. Skinner's journal, 2015–2016

September 9th

I've always loved the first day of school because everything is new: the kids, the air, the school supplies! As a seventh-year teacher, I can say that this year has been by far the most interesting. Earlier in my career, my first day of school, as a first teacher, was in a suburban, pretty well-off district. The "poorest" students boasted North Face fleeces and instruments of their own. Activities and procedures were well organized, parents were ready and armed with questions, and things were very predictable. During my second and third years, I taught at an American international school in Thailand and, like my very first year, things went as expected. I then came back to the states to finally fulfill my dream of being an urban teacher.

I can honestly say that the seventh year of teaching was one of the biggest challenges I had faced thus far. I came to my new school very excited because I had been chosen to start an instrumental string program from scratch. What a fun challenge! The problem was, I didn't expect a very empty office (not even a phone!) and an even emptier ensemble room. I went to the principal and asked where everything was. She told me that there wasn't anything as of yet and no money to purchase what I needed. I began my journey begging and pleading with other teachers to spare me some instruments. I also called friends to dig up their old college instruments from fifteen years ago that were hidden away in their attics. But as you can imagine, my first day I sat at my desk, stumped – no schedule, no students, and no instruments at my disposal.

It was, however, so exciting to be part of a program at a brand-new school. This school is a gifted and talented school, with students specializing in four main subject areas: performing arts (instrumental music, vocal music, and theater), visual arts (including photography), physical education, and academics. Yet, on that first day, there was a lot of confusion. The schedule was nuts; the students and faculty were all lost in the large, new building; students' schedules did not match with their teachers' schedule; and, of course, there were no instruments (due to cheap contracting during the construction phase of the new building). Oh, and did I mention that we had a flood of sewage spewing out into the main lobby? Amidst the chaos, my performing arts team met together to try and decipher everything, only to get more confused about the way this school was supposed to be run. At least we had music stands!

September 30th

Ever since I can remember, I've always wanted to be a teacher. As a child, I used to set up a classroom in my basement and teach "students" (neighborhood friends) from my mom's old ESL workbooks. I knew I wanted to be a music teacher when I was in middle school. I had an amazing band teacher who I hoped to emulate. I loved playing my violin because it was so much fun! It wasn't until college, though, that I began to consider *where* I would want to teach.

I belonged to a Christian organization during college that gave me many opportunities and experiences in urban environments. I believe that "the moment" I knew it was my dream to teach in an urban district started when I participated in a week-long experience called the New York City Urban Project (NYCUP). For an entire week, my team served in an after-school day care center, tutoring and playing with children from Harlem. We walked through the neighborhoods and interacted with the people living there. We stayed overnight at a homeless shelter, serving them dinner and breakfast the next morning. I was really moved by the whole experience because I had really only seen the bright lights and Broadway shows of Manhattan.

In reflection, I was awakened to the great need for quality teachers to serve children in urban areas. I chose to do my student teaching in Newark with one of the most talented teachers I've ever met. I learned so much from her and the students at that school. I knew, whether it was Newark or somewhere else, that I was going to be an urban music teacher one day. In my fourth year of teaching (after my experience in Thailand), my dream came true. I loved the culture, the students, and the challenges that came my way. I felt, and still feel, so fulfilled coming home each day knowing that I have given my 100% to that community and that my knowledge of music brings joy to those that have the opportunity to participate.

October 16th

I underestimate how much my students love music. It is easy to take for granted things like having a plentiful number of instruments (or not even having to worry at all about inventory if your district rents). It's very easy to become complacent about the ordinary things like practicing, note reading, and morning rehearsals when you don't have to face certain challenges every day. But when you have a huge lack of resources, your perspective changes dramatically. Despite having very few instruments, my students had a good attitude and shared what little we had with each other. Just this week, I was able to borrow some string instruments from three of the other schools until we get our own. Because I now had some instruments (about fifteen violins, six violas, three cellos, and two basses), I could start putting together a lesson schedule. It isn't enough to meet as an entire orchestra, but small-group lessons could at least get off the ground.

I went to the different lunch periods and asked who was interested in joining the orchestra. They had to fill out a form with their daily schedule so I could know when to pull them out of class. I was given strict instructions that I wasn't allowed to pull out of math and elective courses. Over eighty kids from grades five through eight wanted to join! What an awesome problem! I say "problem" only because I don't have nearly enough instruments and it would cause a scheduling nightmare. I accepted everyone who expressed interest. Because it was our first year, I wanted to include as many students as possible in order to establish a musical culture at the school. The kids all received permission slips that their teachers had to sign. The teacher also needed to select an "accountability partner" in the class who would take notes and collect any worksheets the teacher passed out while the string students were with me. So far, the lessons have gone well.

I went to the office one day to check my mailbox, and the principal came up to me. He told me that Devin, one of my violin students, couldn't stop talking about how excited he was to start learning how to play – fast forward to the future three years later, and Devin still plays. Even though he causes trouble throughout the rest of the day, he is completely focused and doing well in my strings elective class! My principal said his aunt came in, gushing with happiness. She is so thankful that Devin gets this opportunity to play. Other students have come to me, enthusiastically expressing how excited they are. I can't wait for our instruments to come in so that we can meet as a full group! If the instruments come soon enough, we may be able to pull together something for the winter concert; however, I'm thinking that we may have to perform as small-lesson groups due to lack of preparation time.

October 27th

I also teach a class piano course. One of my class piano students of two years, Jennifer, came to my room to talk with me about private lessons. She said her mom wanted me to give her lessons after school and asked how much I charge. I told her what I normally charge for private students and told her to ask her mom if that was something they could afford. She came back and told me that her mom had been doing research and was really surprised at how expensive music lessons are. I told her that I don't even charge nearly as much as other people would. However, the fact that this mother is taking her daughter's love for piano seriously moves me.

It just illustrates how students from underprivileged areas don't or can't get ordinary experiences that other children might. I think back to my own musical upbringing and how fortunate I was to take piano, violin, and flute lessons. To become an accomplished musician takes a serious monetary commitment. How can we help to provide these experiences for students who can't afford it? Should I as a professional teacher offer free or reduced lessons? It's a difficult decision for me, not only because I love my students but also because I'm a busy person and need the extra income wherever I can get it. I also don't want to overcommit and spread myself too thin. It's very easy to give and give and give to these kids, But there also should be a limit for your own sanity. If I say yes to one, am I obligated (in my heart I feel that way anyway) to say yes to whomever else may ask?

November 17th

Our instrument order has not come in yet – can you believe that? We wrote a proposal in May of the previous school year, and we are still undergoing problems with ordering. At first, we were given the instructions to write down everything we needed for our program with an extremely generous budget (since it is a new school, we needed *everything*). I got to determine my dream program with every instructional material I could think of.

However, as the months went on, the proposal needed constant revision, whether in a different format or with a different company and their prices. It was a mess. We were promised the instruments before the school year started, and it is now November. I had to beg other string teachers in the district for any extra instruments. We received enough for small-group lessons but still not enough to accommodate the number of students who were participating in the program. At this point, it doesn't look like the instruments or supplies are coming any time soon. Our winter concert is scheduled for December 10th, and the borrowed violins are beginning to show the strain. The strings on the instruments, that probably haven't been changed in 30 years, are starting to break. Thankfully, my students are appreciative of what we have and are displaying patience. We expectantly wait for the mail to arrive every day, hoping there are some boxes filled with instruments.

December 1st: Concert preparations

Our first concert is coming up, and the Performing Arts team is very excited. Posters were hung, announcements sent home, and snowflake decorations adorned the cafetorium (cafeteria + auditorium). Some supplies have arrived: shoulder rests for violins and violas, extra strings, and lots of rosin. Still no string instruments, but at least I can replace a few strings! The band has received some of their clarinets, saxophones, and French horns. The Visual Arts team will have a PowerPoint before and after the concert displaying various projects. My string students, small but mighty, are ready to show the world what they've been working on. Because it is the first concert in the short history of this school, expectations are high!

December 20th

Guess what? Twelve violas and seventy violins just arrived – of course two weeks after the winter concert! Despite the lack of instruments, my fourth grade quartet and advanced orchestra put on a wonderful concert. Everyone felt proud of what they had accomplished in such a short time with few supplies. We even had the opportunity one week later to perform at City Hall for a holiday program! Now armed with the supplies I needed (minus cellos and basses), I was ready to take on beginner orchestra. More than fifty students have been taking lessons with me on the borrowed violins, and now we could finally meet all at the same time.

January 30th

I received a flyer for Montclair State University's Chamber Ensemble Day hosted by NAfME's collegiate chapter. Chamber Ensemble Day is a gathering of middle school instrumental students from schools in the surrounding area. In preparation for Chamber Ensemble Day, students of NAfME create chamber ensembles based on instrument and years played. Although the students don't meet in chamber groups until the day of the event, they do receive the music to prepare.

I handed out the information to my eighth grade string students, and Carolyn, a cellist, signed up. Carolyn is a wonderful student who is hardworking, musically talented, and extremely responsible. I was proud that she took the initiative in giving herself this opportunity; in the end, I think she was glad she did. Many factors can inhibit a student from participating in outside events such as Chamber Day. If bussing is not provided and participation fees paid, it can sometimes be difficult to recruit students. Barriers such as language, financial issues, no means of transportation, and level of playing proficiency can stop students from participating. Students in other districts don't have to worry about the same things that our city kids do. These are obvious disadvantages for performing arts students who come from low-income immigrant families. I see it as my job to knock down as many barriers as I can so that students have these kinds of opportunities.

Despite these disadvantages, Carolyn performed in a string quartet in the recital hall at the John J. Cali School of Music. To my knowledge, no middle school student from our district had accomplished that before. I went to the recital and got an opportunity to meet her father and stepmom for the first time. Her older brother and baby sister were also there.

I think this was the first time her family had ever been to a recital like this because there was an obvious lack of knowledge about concert etiquette. This hasn't been the only time where I've noticed this from parents in our school concerts or in outside performances. The next day, I spoke to the parent liaison about possibly doing a workshop for parents about appropriate concert behavior in English and Spanish. She wholeheartedly agreed that this was absolutely necessary for our parents.

February 20th: The ones who scare you

This is the first time I've encountered a student who makes me nervous. At my previous school, we only had up to sixth grade, and all the students were fairly manageable. Even the ones who had behavioral and emotional disorders did not make me uncomfortable. I was always able to connect in some way to them and develop a relationship of trust and respect. However, at my current school, we have up to eighth grade.

I'm fairly small. Giving a strong command, for me, can be hilariously easy to disobey if you're a defiant student. There aren't many discipline problems at my school since it is a gifted and talented academy where students are accepted based on an audition and test scores. However, there is one student who refuses to follow directions, is disengaged, is a distraction, picks fights, and is inappropriate with other students. Special accommodations with the school behaviorist have been put into place to help him learn how to behave in educational and social settings. Nothing seems to be working yet.

All is not lost, though. I had to substitute for the band teacher, and this student was present in the class. The student had not paid much attention to me and did what he wanted when I asked him to follow directions. However, today I asked him if he could help me move boxes since he seemed to be pretty strong. Not only did he willingly help me, he seemed completely engaged in receiving positive attention. I hope we can have more victories like this in the near future. It is the small steps forward that count. Unfortunately, this student was transferred to another school at the end of the year because of his behavior and actions toward the students and teachers.

March 5th: Higher expectations

I just read an article this morning about the successes of another school in New Jersey. The article focused on the success of the students graduating from that school, many of whom have become successful entrepreneurs and leaders of world relief organizations. The school has received acclamations for its high-quality education – and not just for the core subjects. The arts receive just as much attention and share in the school's claim to fame. Many students come from immigrant families with parents hoping for a better life for their children.

Articles like this make me wonder what it would take for my school, or any other urban school for that matter, to achieve such high levels of successful students who are empowered to change society and be innovators in their particular fields. I believe that most administrators desire their school to be such an establishment; however, our particular situations (in the urban schools) stop us from achieving such goals. Although the median income of the families at my school is much lower than that of the other school in the article, is it possible for us?

Our school is touted as "state of the art" because it is new and has one-to-one laptops, a 3D printing lab, new instruments (finally), lots of resources, etc. Many parents are involved, partly thanks to our wonderful and extremely active parent liaison and our principal's support. Does student success start with the teachers and how we approach our teaching? Maybe it's the opportunities we provide our students such as field trips to enlighten and expose our students to new ideas, social activism, real-life experience outside the walls of the classroom, and opportunities to perform, etc.? Why aren't any of my students in Jr. Region Orchestra or receiving private lessons outside of school? Despite lack of money and possibly transportation, can we provide these experiences and pay the cost for them? Would that make the difference?

June 2nd

Today we just had our district-wide band and string festival at the high school. This has been a tradition among the music department for years. It is a really great opportunity for my students to hear all of the other performing groups from the different schools, especially the high school band. In my second year in this district, we got a new supervisor and plans fell apart. For whatever reason, we weren't allowed to do a district-wide band day. Everyone was extremely disappointed – teachers and students alike. In my third year, I inquired about the possibility of bringing Band Day back, and my supervisor agreed, as long as I organized it. So, working alongside the high school band director, we brought band day back but this time adding a new element – All City Band and Strings. Music teachers recommended a certain number of students and had two evening rehearsals with a guest conductor before performing at Band and Strings Day for their peers and music teachers.

Because of last year's success, we wanted to do All City again. Unfortunately, across the city, instrumental music has been suffering more and more, which greatly affected participation. Instrumental teachers have been scheduled for more general music classes. Some have become so frustrated by the cut in their programs that it seems like they have almost given up. For All City, this means that fewer students are recommended and fewer schools are able to perform at Band Day. Out of the nine schools that offer band, only four schools participated. All City Band had to be canceled because only two schools recommended students. String programs, however, have grown due to the addition of my new school, with 100% participation at Band and Strings Day. I'm afraid, however, that more instrumental music classes will be cut in the future, affecting the growth and opportunities for performance at the high school level.

This year, I wanted the day to be hosted by our school since we have a nice new building with most of the equipment needed for schools to perform. However, teachers wanted it to remain at the high school, even though the daily schedule can be somewhat unpredictable. At 5:30 the night before Band and Strings Day, the high school band teacher called me to tell me he had just been notified of an evacuation drill scheduled right in the middle of our Band and Strings Day. He was so angry because he hadn't been told about the drill beforehand. Because of the evacuation, we were delayed by an hour and half, meaning that groups had to cut the number of pieces they would be playing. High school classes came into the auditorium during our performance and were disruptive. Bathrooms were locked, and the air conditioning non-existent. But we survived! The students performed for each other and got to experience collaboration among the music staff of our district. I hope that next year some of these issues can be resolved (that's thinking very positively).

My response

As a music education student, no one thinks about what teaching would be like without instruments, stands, a functioning copy machine, or books. Yet, even with the newest school in her district, Mrs. Skinner did not have the basic supplies to build a string program. Her story is not atypical among many urban music teachers. "But," you ask, "how is this possible when a budget was submitted and approved the year before?" The answer is: "Assume nothing."

Many schools – suburban, rural, or urban – have felt the economic strain when it comes to resources, field trips, and adequate support staff. However, in most cases, urban schools are the most affected. Low-income families do not have the money to make up for the losses that a PTA or parental donations might remedy in a more affluent district. In Mrs. Skinner's school, for example, teachers are forbidden from asking parents for anything that would cost extra money, such as T-shirts for the band or instrument rentals. Although the desire to help is strong, low-income families who struggle to put food on the table have few options when it comes to renting an instrument or paying for private music lessons.

The most successful urban teachers are those who are resourceful, creative, and flexible. In Mrs. Skinner's case, she called music teacher friends to borrow instruments that were not already in use. With a few borrowed instruments, she was able to start her program with small-group lessons. For her general music class (not reported in her journal), she asked Home Depot to donate plastic buckets so that her students could participate in drumming activities. All of these initiatives helped her begin to teach in a school where supplies were excessively limited.

Unfortunately, many music teachers pay for supplies out of pocket. Clearly, one cannot purchase large items like instruments, but books or rosin or magic markers for the whiteboard or extra strings reflect some of the supplies that music teachers have had to buy to keep their program running. Ms. Sweet remarked, "My first couple years, I was getting a lot of supplies, but the last couple years I'm not getting any. I'm worried that my supplies will run out (e.g. rosin, bows)." Again, this is not unusual – even in some suburban schools – but urban teachers feel it the hardest because they often have the least resources.

How do the economic circumstances of the community affect their schools? It goes without saying that good teachers know the community in which their students live. They understand that the communities are often fraught with poverty and the resulting challenges that low-income families face such as poor medical care, high-price groceries, joblessness, and living from hand to mouth. Such families face decisions that no parent should have to make, for example, keeping an older child home from school to care for a sick sibling so the caretaker won't lose his/

her/their job. Many parents may not be able to attend a school concert because transportation money is rationed for other things.

Poverty is part of the urban context, and urban teachers must understand – not lower their standards – that poverty has an impact on learning, health, well-being, and hopefulness. Whereas economics play a central role in providing resources to run an effective school, perhaps a larger concern lies in the opportunity gap among children from low-income areas as compared to children from middle- or high-income brackets. Family opportunities, such as vacations, trips to museums, community concerts, or simply having a large supply of books to read at home, may have more to do with school achievement than any other factor.

For these reasons, the following chapter will examine poverty, classism, and the opportunity gap as related to how children learn both in and out of the school. While socio-economic forces loom particularly large in urban areas, education remains the key to providing alternatives that lead to a fulfilling life. Teachers, therefore, can become critical advocates for the life skills and experiences that better the human condition. Teachers of the arts can give students the eyes and ears for finding beauty in a world that, at times, seems insurmountable.

Part 2: Narrowing the opportunity gap for urban students

> *I work at regionals and talk with teachers whose schools have it all – and every year I am reminded that those kids are extremely lucky. It's my goal to get my students to that point where they could be in regionals, but that involves grants for private lessons and transportation – all the things that other students don't have to think about.*
>
> – *Mrs. Skinner*

Mrs. Skinner's comments highlight the differences in opportunities for students who come from impoverished or low-income families as compared to those from more affluent homes. We don't often think beyond talent or dedication when supporting students for instrumental ensembles. In many urban school districts, however, there is much more to consider, such as money for instruments (rented or bought), special participation fees, concert clothes, and transportation. What students need in order to have similar music experiences touches on the concept of equity and equality.

Often used interchangeably, "equity" is not the same as "equality." The picture below is a good representation of what it means to have equal versus equitable resources/opportunities.

In the first panel, each child has the same box to stand on. They have been given *equal* resources, yet, despite this, the shortest boy still cannot see over the fence. *Equality* works when everyone starts from the same place. In the second panel, however, one of the boys is tall enough to see over the fence, but the two smaller children are given the number of boxes they need to see. *Equity* recognizes that the children start from different places and, therefore, require different resources and opportunities to level the playing field.

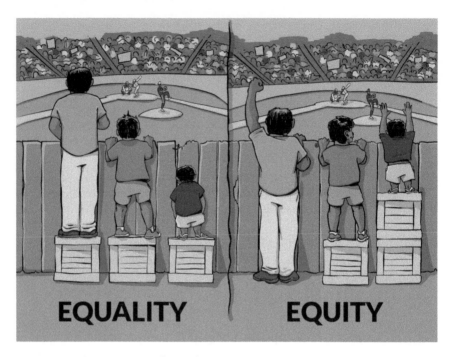

FIGURE 4.1 Comparing equality and equity

Credit: Interaction Institute for Social Change (*interactioninstitute.org*)/Artist Angus Maguire (https://madewithangus.com)

To understand how equity and equality work in music, let's use Mrs. Skinner's school as an example. She teaches in a brand-new school, designed to give gifted and talented students the best education possible. Ironically, financial support for the facility, which may have been equal or even greater than that for other schools in the district, was not enough to start a string program. Hypothetically, Mrs. Skinner's students, in terms of the previous equity/equality image, are most like the small child in the first panel.

The distinction between equal and equitable is an important one not only in terms of financial support but human resources as well. For instance, factors other than money also have an impact on advantage versus disadvantage. Differences in where students live, how they grew up, their parents' level of formal education, with whom they interact, and what opportunities they have beyond the school play a large role in who can see over the fence.[1] In short, there are many variables that affect success in school and in later life in addition to supportive funding.

With the ever-increasing wealth gap in America, though, large numbers of families suffer in poverty. A family in poverty not only lacks the money to maintain a reasonable standard of living but remains excluded from social networks, medical amenities, and social services necessary to sustain health and well-being.[2]

Such problems are deeply embedded in the social structure of our nation. Because schools are inextricably tied to the social conditions that surround them, all teachers stand to benefit from understanding some of the social/economic conditions that create urban poverty.

A comprehensive portrait of how and why poverty exists is beyond the scope of this chapter; however, Jean Anyon provides some historical perspective in her book, *Radical Inequalities*, as a context for thinking about urban poverty.[3] Anyon explains that in the 1960s, a mass migration of Whites and other people of means began to shift from the cities to the suburbs. Consequently, multiple services like banks, medical care, food stores, and shopping areas also moved. This created not only a loss of basic services but also a loss of jobs for adults and youth. Finding work, then, meant traveling outside the city to areas of economic growth, requiring a car or long bus rides. The alternative often resulted in jobs for substandard wages or a dependence on welfare. These were not fair choices but, rather, inevitable circumstances of economic inequity that contributed to financial hardship and, potentially, loss of self-worth. White flight, as some labeled it, left behind concentrations of poor Black and Hispanic families within the largest cities across the United States, a condition that has filtered into smaller communities.[4]

While this is a very small piece of a larger picture concerning urban poverty, it points to the fact that money matters.[5] It matters in the opportunities that parents can afford for their children, and it matters in the resources that schools can provide for their students. It matters in the health and well-being of the child, and it matters in their readiness for school. For instance, according to Robert Ferdman, children from lower socio-economic families enter kindergarten an entire year behind their more affluent counterparts.[6] One-fifth of American children come from impoverished homes, constituting an issue not only of social justice but a national "moral failing" as well.[7] Moreover, "minority group families experience poverty more frequently and in a more severe and persistent form than do Whites."[8] Jonathan Kozol notes, "racial isolation and the concentrated poverty of children in public schools go hand in hand."[9]

Beginning teachers may take for granted that children start school having had rich experiences with story books, nourishing food, family field trips, and medical care. Such conditions, however, characterize the lives of middle class or affluent families rather than those living at the lower rungs of the economic ladder. And, because most teachers come from middle class backgrounds, those assumptions are natural consequences of having lived with multiple opportunities, notwithstanding the fulfillment of basic needs. The first step forward for the beginning teacher, then, is to recognize that urban students have lives that may be very different from that of the teacher. This realization helps music teachers see the world through another lens, which is paramount in developing empathy and understanding the critical need for rigorous schooling that helps disadvantaged students succeed.

Clearly, there is much to be done, within the schools and the society at large, in order to reach equitable conditions where all have an opportunity to "see over the fence." Although families with low socio-economic standing must continually navigate unfair obstacles, it is important to make a distinction between "poor" in terms of opportunities and "poor" in terms of spirit. Being disadvantaged does not equate to a life without meaning.[10] Some of the most economically challenged would affirm that their lives are abundantly rich – whether from a loving family, a network of supportive friends, or a life well lived. Nevertheless, there can be no social equity without active intervention that promotes the freedom to choose opportunities that lead to the well-being and inclusion of all citizens in our democratic society.

Classism and the opportunity gap

A report from the United Nation Development Programme 2016 acknowledges that many conditions contribute to impoverished conditions beyond lack of money. These range from discriminatory actions to natural disasters to lack of education. From a human development perspective, "We want a world where all human beings have the freedom to realize their full potential in life so they can attain what they value."[11]

When neighborhoods are segregated according to socio-economic status, economically disadvantaged children often have very little chance to interact with those from families with strong educational background, rich vocabulary, and professional jobs. Because American schools are typically dependent on local funding, schools in poor neighborhoods with a lower tax base tend to have far fewer resources and opportunities than schools in more affluent neighborhoods. Moreover, because schools mirror the socio-economic status of the community, they reproduce create class divisions as well.

As indicated earlier, the racial composition among schools in affluent neighborhoods as compared to those in economically disadvantaged neighborhoods is strikingly different. Schools in disadvantaged urban communities reflect a predominance of students of color who qualify as low income.[12] In neighboring suburban districts, schools maintain a higher percentage of White children/adolescents from families with middle to high income. This is partly due to White flight from the city, which, in the past, assured families that their children would attend more homogeneous (White) schools – a student body that is rapidly changing with the influx of Latino and other immigrants. From a socio-economic perspective, then, Americans have created a stratified society. According to Jean Anyon:

> One of the most egregious social phenomena, one that undermines urban school reform, continually, is the housing concentration of low-income students into central cities across the country. This housing segregation produces the educational segregation of urban Blacks and Latinos into schools where the vast majority of students are poor. Such schools are notoriously under-resourced and unsuccessful in promoting high achievement.[13]

Take, for example, a school in an economically deprived neighborhood compared with a school in an affluent part of town. The affluent school is likely to be equipped with computer labs, some also providing laptop computers for each student; a large after-school intramural program; music ensembles; advanced placement courses; assemblies that feature successful entrepreneurs; well-equipped science labs; up-to-date textbooks; and – most important – access to peers who have traveled, have parents with college degrees, facility with a large vocabulary, and cultural experiences that place them on equal footing with their friends.

Many urban schools, by contrast, lack similar resources. Textbooks are often outdated and not sufficient to provide enough copies for all the students in the class. Students with parents whose highest level of schooling is middle school or lower often lack the extra boost in vocabulary and world knowledge that leads to success in school. Given the homogeneous grouping of low-income neighborhoods, students only interact with others who have similar backgrounds, resulting in class-based segregated schools.[14] This means that "rich Americans and poor Americans are living, learning, and raising children in increasingly separate and unequal worlds."[15]

These scenarios put students on different life tracks. Anyon reports that socioeconomic status is highly correlated with academic success.[16] In addition, "researchers have found that the single most powerful predictor of racial gaps in educational is the extent to which students attend schools surrounded by other low-income students."[17]

Rather than focus entirely on the economic dimension of poverty, Malcom Gladwell[18] and Robert D. Putnam[19] looked at *opportunities* as the "major factor in driving success" in school and in future life. One leading factor of successful children has to do with the networks they form in their relationships with other families as well as the out-of-school opportunities they experience. Gladwell argues that success is a matter of having social networks and extra-curricular opportunities. The importance of social networks and a range of life experiences cannot be overstated: "Whom you go to school with matters a lot."[20] In addition, "Regardless of their own family background, kids do better in schools where the other kids come from affluent, educated homes."[21] Thus, opportunities to interact with students from different income brackets create an environment that is highly beneficial to disadvantaged students who may not experience the chance to develop a well-rounded perspective otherwise.

Poverty as a matter of social justice

The Human Development Programme 2016 takes a holistic view of poverty as a matter of social justice: "Human development is about enlarging freedoms to that all human beings can pursue the choices they value."[22] Enlarging freedom means that people not only have viable and fulfilling options in life but also have agency to engage in action that can transform their circumstances. The latter part is extremely important because when people are marginalized, isolated, and poorly educated, they have no voice with which to change their situation. Putnam, for instance, found that middle class and affluent adults were far more likely to take an active part in political action than those from the lower class.[23] Hence, the power to make changes that have an impact on one's life resides disproportionately at the higher levels of socio-economic status.

In his provocative article, "Critical Social Class Theory for Music Education," Vincent Bates suggests that a capitalist society involves competition that, by its very nature, has dire consequences for those at the bottom of the hierarchy.[24] As the division between those with wealth and those without continues to increase, impoverished families have little chance to break out of the cycle. Without realistic access to powerful political groups that initiate change, the conditions that create poverty remain the same or worsen.

As stated earlier, there is a strong relationship between poverty and low academic performance. When children enter school, those from poor neighborhoods are typically one year behind their wealthier peers.[25] The cost of remediation and multiple special services such counseling or family services also make urban schools expensive to run. Without more federal backing, urban schools are unable to fund the cost of routine building repairs, textbooks, and other basic necessities. Consequently, some urban schools are dilapidated, dirty, and crowded with lack of access to working bathrooms.[26]

There are two common, but deeply flawed, notions about the impoverished: first, that people in poverty lack the intelligence or work ethic to break the cycle of poverty and second, that the natural evolution of humanity is a sorting process whereby the strongest and most able rise to the top (a call back to Darwin's famous theory "survival of the fittest"). Both notions place the blame for poverty directly at the feet of the disadvantaged. Moreover, "children from poverty are being identified and labeled with grossly overgeneralized, deficit-laden characteristics that put them at risk of being viewed as less capable, less cultured, and less worthy as learners."[27]

Teacher-held beliefs about students from low-income families can influence their expectations and interactions with children/adolescents. For that reason, it is vital that pre-service teachers examine their ideas and biases about poverty. Some of the more common biases include the following: poor people are lazy, poor people are linguistically deficient, and poor people are substance abusers.[28]

Poor people are lazy: Teachers who believe this have lower expectations for student achievement and parent participation regarding homework or school events/parent-teacher conferences.

Poor people are linguistically deficient: When teachers feel that children from disadvantaged families are unable to communicate in what they perceive as standard English, then children are overly corrected and chastised.

Poor people are substance abusers: The misapprehension of drug and alcohol abuse leads teachers to lower their expectations of family support and a family's educational values. In other words, these stereotypes have dangerous consequences. They can create a sense of fear or disregard for low-income students, and they can become the mechanism whereby teachers blame the family for the student's difficulties.

Classism not only projects bias; it also suggests the existence of a "culture of poverty" – that the economically disadvantaged share commonalities such as "predictable beliefs, values, and behaviors."[29] Paul C. Gorski however, argues that there is no common culture of the poor – that families respond to poverty in different ways and do not share common values.[30] For the teacher, this means that each child has his/her/their own story and that, as a sensitive adult, the teacher must unravel that story in order to build upon the child's strengths.

How music education fits in this paradigm

The common mantra "music education for all" suggests a level of access to music that is simply not evident across schools, particularly urban schools. In terms of music instruments alone, educators have come to realize that not all students have access to school lessons due to fees and other resources. This, in turn, unfairly prevents some students from large-scale participation in county and regional ensembles. Initiatives on the part of the individual, school, state, and national organizations have begun to address this problem via scholarships, sliding scale rental fees based on students' applications for free lunch, donated instruments (e.g. the WQXR 105.9 FM instrument drive in New York City, grants (e.g. Mr. Holland's Opus Foundation), and other humanitarian efforts.

From a cursory glance, though, supplying instruments and resources is usually the first area that teachers and policy makers address because it is quantifiable, acutely visible, and easy to justify. Although this is a critical issue, far more concerning are inequitable music teaching practices and values that are not typically associated with financial support.[31] This includes the music and curriculum we choose to teach in the name of a quality music education.

Bates identifies a number of categories in teaching music that keep some students marginalized while giving access to others. According to Bates, these categories involve: musical taste, music performance, and musical experiences.[32] *Musical taste* has to do with the music that music teachers choose as listening models or repertoire. In general, Western art music is predominant in school and college music programs, sending the tacit message that not all music is equal. Thus, Western art music is perceived as a higher form of music than, for instance, popular music or non-Western music. At the college level, audition requirements are designed for Western instruments and Western music theoretical knowledge. Consequently, most college music programs rely on Western art music for teaching music theory, history, solo and ensemble repertoire, and other related classes. Although many music education programs are required to include a course on non-Western music, it is a question of balance – what music is represented the most. As a result, beginning music teachers tend to choose genres for their own students that reflect the bulk of their training: Western art music.

Teaching multiple genres was first formally addressed at the Tanglewood Symposium. Although these views have been in circulation for more than fifty years, the popularity of Western-style repertoire persists, disallowing non-Western or popular music from gaining momentum. For example, current elementary music method-ologies such as Kodaly, Orff, Dalcroze, Suzuki, and Gordon emphasize principles of Western music through Western tonality, harmony, and classical forms. When non-Western music is introduced, it has often been sanitized to fit the particular methodology. At the secondary level, many ensemble directors remain uncomfort-able with music that does not reflect the traditional canon. The larger implications of such repertoire-driven curricular decisions, then, suggests that the music we teach has everything to do with shaping musical taste and constructing a definition of music that does or does not have porous boundaries.

Music performance in public schools typically includes the traditional ensembles: choral, band, jazz, and orchestra. Some schools, fortunately, have begun to offer alternative ensemble experiences like African drumming, steel drum bands, and Mariachi bands. In terms of more popular genres, many secondary schools include guitar programs or popular music programs such as Little Kids Rock. However, these alternative ensemble experiences are scattered. To my knowledge, there are few if any state or regional ensembles for the students in these classes to gain higher recognition. Subsequently, the band, choir, jazz, and orchestra represent the staples of musical achievement. In addition, many music scholars continue to question whether music outside of the Western genre is truly valid in an educational setting. This is marginalizing not only for students who do not come from Western Euro-pean backgrounds but also those for whom popular genres are central to their lives. According to Bates:

> The idea that a classical music education will have a general positive impact
> on students . . . rests on the assumption that the poor are personally, morally,
> and culturally deficient. Rather, it is the music most preferred by the poor –
> for example, country, heavy metal, and rap (in North America at least) . . . that
> holds promise for overcoming oppression.[31]

Musical experiences can also include or marginalize students depending on who makes the music, how one engages with the music, and how the music is culturally contextualized.[32] In Western classical "presentational" music, there is a distinction between the audience and performer(s). In this scenario, performers create or recre-ate the music and listeners participate through active listening engagement, show-ing appreciation by applauding at the end of the piece or during improvisational solos. We teach our students to listen actively and silently as is expected behavior for receiving presentational forms of classical music (i.e. symphonies, sonatas, concerti). There are, however, other ways of engaging with music where the "listeners" have a participatory role, even within Western classical domains (e.g. march, waltz, gigue). This distinguishes "presentational" music from "participatory" music.

Traditional African music, for example, is communal. Everyone from toddlers to the older generation participate in the music making, whether drumming, singing, or dancing.[33] In classical Indian music, the performers represent those of high artis-tic achievement, but the audience often remains involved by counting Tala during performances. Even with popular music, students attend rock concerts where singing, dancing, clapping, and shouting are encouraged. Since music making and music listening should be culturally contextualized, the role of the "audience" would change as well.

Composing, song writing, dancing, singing, and the use of digital formats from Handel to hip hop reflect inclusive curriculums that offer diverse forms of musical participation. Such a curriculum offers access to music on many different levels and cultural contexts. As discussed in Chapter 2, culturally responsive music teachers knows their students, their cultural background, and the community in which they live. Building a program to support these strengths embraces the musical strengths that students bring to the classroom.

The point here is that too often we offer experiences for which urban students, in particular, have no relevance. When traditional instrumental ensembles are the norm, then students can only participate if they play an instrument. When the choir focuses on Western music, then those who come from a culture with a different tonal and tuning system will have difficulty adjusting to Western musical structures. Even song material at the elementary level can highlight class or cultural differences.

Strategies that provide access to music for all

Let's take a step back and think about what all this means in terms of teaching music in urban schools. No doubt, music classes will reflect a large number of low-income, minority students, some of whom have fewer than three meals a day and may have never owned a new piece of clothing or a warm coat. Nevertheless, music plays a significant role in their lives – from church to music of the street or music in the family. Such children deserve nothing less than a high quality of music education. But what does this mean? Playing an instrument? Learning to read music? Participating in traditional ensembles?

In urban schools where injustices are particularly evident, creating music is a powerful medium for giving voice to what may be difficult to express in other ways. Some examples include students composing their own music, writing their own songs, and listening to the music of those who protest social inequities. Hip hop, rap, the blues, spirituals, and gospel are examples of the music for promoting social change. This is also the music of the people – their community, past and present – who express anguish, anger, and hope in a musical form that resonates with urban students. Teaching music for resilience is also a way to help students have some control over chaotic life experiences.

Here are some strategies that may be helpful in the classroom. Lessons on protest music, rap, contemporary popular genres, as well as the blues can examine oppressed people who used music to connect with others. Therefore, it is meaningful to discuss the context of the music. In terms of protest songs, for example, identify the venue – some songs are sung at rallies or sit-ins, while others are composed for a wider audience. What makes a protest song powerful? How can protest songs initiate social change?

The music teacher may want to prompt students with some ideas about incidences or injustices that take place in their own lives. From this discussion emerge words and phrases that can be shaped into a song or rap. If creating a song, how students handle the melody can take several forms. In the younger grades, students can sing a phrase at a time to create a group song that the teacher can notate and harmonize, if desired. In upper grades, students can create a song in groups by either creating an original melody or using an existing melody of their own choosing. At the secondary level, students may want to compose an original song on their own. The music then becomes the vehicle for addressing life issues that affect students deeply.

When urban music teachers have access to school computers, students can choose a song or portions of a speech (e.g. Martin Luther King's speech, "I Have a Dream") and input that episode into iMovie. From there, the project is to choose representative images/pictures that make the music or text more meaningful. Some of these finished projects might even be part of a related assembly or ensemble concert. Another example is to choose selections from poetry or speeches that highlight resilience against oppressive circumstances. In groups, students work on reading the text with musical expression. Then, they pair the reading with a solo instrumental recording (e.g. John Coltrane: "Alabama") to create a moving portrayal of the meaning behind the poetry/speech.

The projects in the previous paragraph were developed by former students. However, these projects and similar activities are successful only when the music teacher integrates meaningful discussion along with the musical process. A follow-up discussion might include places around the world where musicians are engaged in song making to express social injustices that they experience. A good starting place is "Playing for Change" (www.youtube.com/watch?v=oiPzU75P9FA) where musicians collaborate via the internet to create musical pieces of hope.

Another video, "The Landfill Harmonic Orchestra" (www.youtube.com/watch?v=UJrSUHK9Luw), shows disadvantaged children from the village of Catuero who live on a landfill and create instruments with the trash around their homes. Although the instruments and music replicate Western art music, The Landfill Harmonic Orchestra demonstrates how children/adolescents create a musical world solely from the resources in their community. An alternative approach, especially appropriate for students, is to use trash or atypical sound devices from the home to create their own compositions.

In essence, poverty does not equate to musical deprivation.[34] In fact, music class may be the one place where students can collaborate without fighting, learn about others who face similar obstacles, and create music that provides a positive vehicle for change agency in the community. Helping students become aware of classism and poverty may not sound like topics for a music class, but music is not just about the notes on the page. The teacher's skill in addressing issues of social justice through music creates a powerful context for giving disadvantaged students voice and ownership.

How else can we involve all students in deep experiences with music that sensitize them to issues of economic injustice in society? One idea is to choose songs for performance or classroom activities that involve themes of poverty, such as "Blackbird" by the Beatles or "Another Day in Paradise" by Phil Collins, and discuss the meaning of the words in terms of contemporary life. Another example might involve studying a composer or artist who lived much of his/her/their life in poverty yet found inspiration through music. Composers such as Erik Satie, singer Nicki Minaj, and guitarist Jimi Hendrix, as well as rapper Eminem, are some examples of musicians who used music as inspiration despite hardship.

A third example involves familiarizing students with international music projects created to address poverty and hunger. In 1984, Bob Geldof and Midge Uhr created the charity group Band Aid for famine relief in Ethiopia. They wrote and produced the song "Do They Know It's Christmas" that included performing musicians such as Bono, Phil Collins, Boy George, James "J. T." Taylor, David Bowie, and Sting. This single raised 14 million dollars. Inspired by Band Aid, Lionel Richie and Michael Jackson wrote "We Are the World," produced by Quincy Jones in 1985. Proceeds of 60 million dollars were funneled through USA for Africa to provide food and supplies for the famine victims of Ethiopia, Sudan, and other African countries. Additionally, the album, *Metamorphosis*, was an unusual project to fight poverty in that to purchase the album, one had to make a commitment to fighting poverty rather than paying for the album. Sponsored by Global Citizen, fans from around the world were asked to submit poems, stories, or lyrics that prompted songs for the album. Kanye West and Mumford & Sons were some of the many musicians who worked on the project.

Each of these projects might serve as musical models of advocacy for those in need. Music teachers could use the projects as a starting point for discussion about how musicians collaborate to create change. In terms of interdisciplinary work, the music teacher might collaborate with the language arts teacher to have students compose poetry or stories that would serve as inspiration for one or more class compositions. Such compositions could be featured at an instrumental or choral performance with ticket proceeds reserved for organizations to fight hunger or other related causes.

How some urban music teachers created access to music for disadvantaged students

As noted, urban students who come from low-income or impoverished families typically lack the opportunities that more privileged students experience. Therefore, music teachers in urban schools must be particularly cognizant of students "who cannot see over the fence." Whereas these obstacles may sound insurmountable, we also know that there many music teachers have risen to the challenge and created musical opportunities for students to thrive.

Mrs. Gordon-Cartier directs a harp ensemble in a large urban high school. Every year, she fundraises to take students to a harp convention in different parts of the country. This provides many benefits for the students. They have the opportunity to travel beyond their community and visit new places. They meet students and teachers from all parts of the country, and they have the experience of staying in a hotel and eating in restaurants. During one trip, the hotel had a pool, which was an obvious attraction for the students who participated in the conference. When Mrs. Gordon-Cartier's African American students entered the pool area, they were surprised to see a cadre of White students from a different school. The Black students stayed in one part, and the White students stayed in the other. Seeing a teachable moment, Mrs. Cartier called her students together and talked to them about how to start a conversation with someone unfamiliar to them. Soon the pool became a mixed group of students laughing and hanging out together, sharing stories, and making plans to meet during the conference. "It was," as Mrs. Gordon-Cartier said, "one of my happiest moments in teaching."

Not all schools can support fundraising efforts for students to travel, but music teachers can invite professional musicians to do workshops and masterclasses with instrumental/choral students. Mrs. Sweet's school is close to the New Jersey Performing Arts Center in Newark, New Jersey, and she often brings in orchestra members to work with her string players. If there are college music programs nearby, music teachers may be able to develop a partnership where college music students travel to the school to assist with lessons or talk about their experience in college music programs. Some schools rent a bus that transports youth musicians for a side-by-side playing experience with a college ensemble.

My colleague and I have created a summer program at our university for high school urban music students during two weeks in the summer. Those who apply to the camp have free bussing; breakfast and lunch; and a variety of musical experiences ranging from music listening classes that fuse theory, history (including popular and non-Western genres), and technology to private lessons, chamber music, and African drumming. The entire tuition is only $30 per student thanks to financial support from the School of Music. Because the camp takes place on campus, students have a hands-on experience in a college setting where many begin to realize the possibilities of getting a college education.

As another example, Public School 22 on Staten Island serves many disadvantaged children. In 2000, their music teacher formed an elementary chorus that gained much visibility on YouTube. To watch these children sing "Over the Rainbow" is compelling, both visually and musically. With only a piano and an auditorium, the music teacher has an intuitive sense of what songs will captivate his students. His beautiful harmonic arrangements are both emotionally charged and spiritually fulfilling. In fact, several years ago, they were invited to sing for the 83rd Academy Awards.

Conclusion

This chapter addressed poverty in several ways – from an economic perspective, an opportunity perspective, and a music/musical opportunity perspective. As an issue of social justice, poverty, and classism have many layers and complexities that lie well beyond the scope of a single chapter. Yet the impact of poverty on a child's readiness for public school and his/her/their subsequent journey through the school system is so powerful that it would be shortsighted to ignore this critical factor in the schooling process, especially since the plight of the poor lies beyond the experience of most teachers.

Inequitable circumstances pervade America's schools, creating especially difficult teaching and learning situations for students in urban schools. It is well documented that urban schools are underserved, a reprehensible condition for those most vulnerable in our society. Yet money alone cannot equalize the situation. The poor also suffer from segregated housing, lack of important life opportunities, schools that fail to reach national levels of academic achievement, and high-quality teachers. Instead of schools becoming the "great equalizer" for a just and equitable education, the division between urban schools and suburban schools starkly reflects a society that provides advantages for certain people over others. This is an issue of national proportion that requires thoughtful legislation and policy making to close the gap.

Nevertheless, teachers must become bastions of hope for the disadvantaged. Understanding that the roots of poverty and classism are deeply entrenched in our social structure informs the way we think about our students and how music might best serve these children. Nothing about poverty is easy to talk about with students of any age. However, to avoid this issue implies a lack of understanding and compassion for the circumstances that economically disadvantaged students face. They begin school with "both hands tied behind their back." The music teacher can gently untie each arm by empowering students through music making that creates resilience and aspiration. By doing so, music teachers can create a pathway to hope and action that not only challenges difficult circumstances but also generates the confidence to move forward.

Discussion questions

1   How much has local funding supported your music experiences at your home school?
2   What important lessons have you learned by observing in a school that serves low-income families?
3   Why is developing resilience so important for disadvantaged students, and how can you facilitate this in a music classroom?

References

1 Putnam, Robert D. 2015. *Our Kids: The American Dream in Crisis.* New York: Simon & Schuster.
2 Bates, Vincent C. 2012. "Social Class and School Music." *Music Educators Journal, 98* (4): 33–37; Harrison, Anthony Kwame. 2009. *Hip Hop Underground: The Integrity and Ethics of Racial Identification.* Philadelphia: Temple University Press.

3 Anyon, Jean. 2005. *Radical Possibilities*. New York: Routledge.
4 Wade, Oscar S. 2017. "White Flight and The Endless Cycle of Poverty for Urban People of Color in America." *European Journal of Academic Essays, 4* (4): 141–145.
5 Anyon, Jean. *Radical Possibilities*; Bates, Vincent C. 2016. "How Can Music Educators Address Poverty and Inequality?" *Action, Criticism, and Theory for Music Education, 15* (1): 1–9.
6 Ferdman, Roberto A. 2015. "Only in America: Four Years into Life, Poor Kids Are Already an Entire Year Behind." (Wonkblog) *The Washington Post*, December 17.
7 Kristof, Nicholas. 2016. "Growing Up Poor in America." *The New York Times*, October 30: 4.
8 Luthar, Suniya S. 1999. "Poverty and Children's Adjustment." In *Developmental Clinical Psychology and Psychiatry Series* (vol. 41). Thousand Oaks, CA: Sage Publications: 38; Wade. "White Flight."
9 Kozol, Jonathan. 2005. *The Shame of the Nation: The Restoration of Apartheid Schooling in America*. New York: Three Rivers Press: 20.
10 Alter, Adam. 2014. "Do the Poor Have More Meaningful Lives?" *The New Yorker*, January 24.
11 Jahan, Salem. 2016. *Human Development Report 2016: Human Development for Everyone*. Published for the United Nations Development Programme: 169. http://hdr.undp.org/sites/default/files/2016_human_development_report.pdf
12 Boschma, Jane and Ronald Brownstein. 2016. "The Concentration of Poverty in America's Schools." *The Atlantic*, February 29.
13 Anyon. *Radical Possibilities*: 93.
14 Putnam. *Our Kids*.
15 Ibid., 41.
16 Anyon. *Radical Possibilities*.
17 Boschma and Brownstein. "The Concentration of Poverty." 2.
18 Gladwell, Malcom. 2008. *Outliers: The Story of Success*. [Kindle edition]. New York: Little, Brown, and Company.
19 Putnam, Robert D. 2000. *Bowling Alone: The Collapse and Revival of American Community*. New York: Simon & Schuster; Putnam, *Our Kids*.
20 Gladwell. *Outliers*: 166.
21 Ibid., 163.
22 Jahan. *Human Development Report*: 1.
23 Putnam. *Bowling Alone*.
24 Bates, Vincent. 2017. "Critical Social Class Theory for Music Education." *International Journal of Education & the Arts, 18* (7): 1–24.
25 Ferdman. "Only in America."
26 Theoharis, Jeanne. 2009. "Conclusion." In *Our Schools Suck: Students Talk Back to a Segregated Nation on The Failures of Urban Education*, edited by Gaston Alonso, Noel S. Anderson, Celina Su, and Jeanne Theoharis, 177–214. New York: New York University Press.
27 Sato, Mistlina and Timothy J. Lensmire. 2009. "Poverty and Payne: Supporting Teachers to Work with Children of Poverty." *Phi Delta Kappan, 90* (5): 1.
28 Gorski, Paul. 2008. "The Myth of the Culture of Poverty." *Educational Leadership, 65* (7): 32.
29 Ibid.
29 Ibid.
30 Ibid.
31 Bates. "Critical Social Class Theory." 14.

32 Elliott, David J. and Marissa Silverman. 2015. *Music Matters: A Philosophy of Music Education* [2nd ed.]. New York: Oxford University Press; Turino, Thomas. 2016. "Music, Social Change, and Alternate Forms of Artistic Citizenship." In *Artistic Citizenship: Artistry, Social Responsibility, and Ethical Praxis*, edited by David J. Elliott, Marissa Silverman, and Wayne D. Bowman, 297–312, New York: Oxford University Press.

33 Silverman, Marissa. 2017. "I Drum, I Sing, I Dance: An Ethnographic Study of a West African Drum and Dance Ensemble." *Research Studies in Music Education*, *40* (1): 5–27.

34 Bates, Vincent C. 2016. "How Can Music Educators Address Poverty and Inequality? [Forward]."

5

LEARNING TO ROLL WITH THE PUNCHES

Part 1: From the classroom of Mr. Tamburro

Like some of the teachers who contributed to this book, Mr. Tamburro grew up in a White suburban neighborhood. While the town had a fairly substantial population for a rural suburb – around 17,000 – Mr. Tamburro recalls, *by the time I graduated from high school, there were three traffic lights. It was the kind of town where everyone knew each other and called the shopkeepers by name. You couldn't go to the grocery store without seeing familiar faces. The community was small and tight-knit.*

Given this background, teaching general/vocal music in an urban middle school was a stark change for Mr. Tamburro. Whereas his home schooling took place in a small mostly White school, he now taught in a mid-size school that was 99% Black and Latino. This was one of the many learning curves that faced Mr. Tamburro. Although not his very first year of teaching, his other teaching positions did not prepare him for the size of the school, a new level of teaching (middle school), and the daily unexpected happenings that go along with urban teaching.

His school is one of six middle schools. Each middle school houses students for all three years – the district calls this a "looping" model. That means each year, Mr. Tamburro teaches all of one grade level. He started with eighth graders and then began a new rotation with sixth graders. Now, in his fourth year, those sixth graders have become eighth graders, so he's had the same students for three years. This is an unusual division of schools but benefits the students in many ways. Most importantly, teachers have three years with the same students, a scenario that affords teachers and students an opportunity to develop close ties during their adolescence – a particularly important time for students to form relationships with caring adults.

Speaking about his students, Mr. Tamburro recognizes their different home lives: *Home lives are varied. Plenty of kids have very happy homes and great parents. There are neighborhoods that are beautiful. Some kids go home to aunts or grandparents. They love playing music on their phones, playing video games, and dancing. When they consider their future, some want to be doctors or lawyers. Some dream about playing professional sports – football or basketball. Some aspire to sing and rap commercially. And others have no idea at all.* Oscar, one of Mr. Tamburro's students, is just "glad to be alive." Oscar says, "You never know when you get up if it's going to be your last day." While this may seem dark, it is regrettably not unusual for some urban students to feel that life is short, especially in an area with a lot of gang activity.

Mr. Tamburro teaches in a difficult situation, and his journal reflects what it feels like to teach in an environment completely different from his own schooling. Although all teachers experience the "unexpected" – e.g. a fire drill in the middle of a choral rehearsal, a loud lawn mower outside the window, a hot and stuffy room in the late spring – Mr. Tamburro's stories reveal a raw account of his initiation into the urban setting.

Mr. Tamburro's journal, 2015–2016

September 2

It's day one of the school year. Teachers are here, classrooms are bare, and meetings are scheduled. I have to laugh at myself – I'm going into my fourth year in this district, and I'm still surprised when things are not quite as ready as I would have hoped them to have been. It is getting better, though. During my first two years, my classroom was flooded, and the hardwood floors were destroyed three times. Two of the three times coincided with the first day of school, so I spent September and October of those years teaching in the auditorium. My third year, numerous items were removed from my room over the summer and never returned. So off I went on the first day of the school year, scavenging for chairs and tables.

This year I was moved to a new classroom, but the requests I had put in for my materials and equipment in June have yet to be honored. I've done a lot of the moving of furniture myself because I never feel right until my classroom is right. I've only been yelled at a few times so far for scratching floors and being impatient. I'd say that's a win!

I mention this not as a real complaint because I'm an adult and can deal with last-minute stress. However, I remember a realization from my very first year – how much I felt that the students suffered because of the disorganization so early on in the year. No matter how much I placed the issue fairly heavily upon the admin-istration, I now know that there are so many more factors that contribute to this, and much of it is out of the control of those in charge. Everyone is really trying to do his/her/their best. And again, to be fair, I would say this is probably the most prepared the school has been for the students in the four years I've worked here.

We had a lot of administrative and teacher turnover prior to and during the first couple of years I was here. It is typical in this district to lose a bunch of teachers over the summer, but it was, as near as I can tell, an epidemic when I started here. In a school based on a looping model where students are supposed to have the same exact teachers for grades six through eight, teacher and administrator turnover is not a good thing. Luckily, it seems as though we have made it through the most recent transition fairly smoothly. Teachers are excited to be back. Besides a large retiring class, the teachers have all returned and seem to be much more positive about the year. We'll be into our second full year with our current administrators, and we'll be in year three with this batch of students, now eighth graders, who will be promoted to the high school next year. Now . . . if I could just find a few chairs for my students to sit on, we'd be off to the perfect start.

September 21

Week one and two went smoothly, and while we've only been here for a few days, it already feels like we've been at it for months. That's not a bad thing, simply a comment on how quickly things seem to pick right up where they left off and the routine settles in. All is well. My room was ready for the first day. My schedule is amazing. I have many students for the second or third year in a row. They know me, I know them, and things are rolling nicely along. But then there was yesterday. Day 10 . . .

Day 10 was the beginning of my singing test. This is a district requirement that aligns with the state requirements and standards. Everything in our district is now completely tied into data. Data-driven instruction is the big buzzword, or I suppose the buzz phrase. This is not unique to urban schools, but I'm certain it is emphasized to a greater degree in this district because funding and functioning of the district relies heavily upon data that shows evidence of both proficiency and improvement. Of course, as with many policies that are tied into the core courses (math, English language arts, science, and social studies), it doesn't always translate well to the music classroom.

In the music classroom, our district assessment is an individual baseline vocal test. It's simple enough and has a rubric that basically asks if you can sing a song in tune, with a supported sound, with accurate rhythm and a steady beat, and make it musical. The instructions say, "Please do this by yourself in the second week of school. It's a test grade. Good luck!" "Oh, and by the way," I say sarcastically to myself, "you'll do it again in week ten of this cycle and if you don't show a significant amount of improvement, my grade as a teacher will go down." Needless to say, it's a tough sell.

I have found the sixth graders are more apt to do it without hesitation or much fuss. Even my seventh graders have generally just gotten it done. But this year I'm teaching only eighth grade, and as much as they have matured and grown into themselves a bit, they have lost that blissful, childlike fearlessness of getting up and singing a song. The boys' voices are a mess – either changed, changing, or unchanged. So, if they even sing, they either sing in the basement of their range so no one can hear, crack through the three notes of their functional middle range and get laughed at, or sing way up high and immediately get made fun of for being a girl or being gay (as if either of those things were accurate or bad). Then there are the girls who aren't even comfortable in their own skin, let alone comfortable in front of their judging peers. And leading this charge is "mean Mr. Tamburro" making them all do something that makes them more uncomfortable, vulnerable, and terrified than any state test they've ever faced.

To make this task less stressful with more opportunity for success, I've improved the test every year, giving out points for singing, for being a good audience, and (this year for the first time) even for a written response sheet with positive and constructive feedback for each student. The feedback is for my eyes only so that the students will be honest and specific without fear of retribution. With that addition, I think it might have tipped the stress level in the wrong direction because Day 6 was a complete disaster. I know I have some tough classes this first marking period, but many students wouldn't sing, and many others were acting out and resisting every direction I could give. It was a tough day, and one of those days where you go home thinking, *Wow, I'm such a failure.*

Regardless, I still went home and made the nine parent phone calls I needed to make in the one class of twenty-four students. That is almost always a struggle. The telephone numbers in the student information system are often disconnected, out of date, or sometimes flat-out lies. Maybe it's a prepaid mobile phone that hasn't been reloaded with minutes. I've called home phone numbers that turn out to be auto body shops or offices, and never once has the person who answered said, "Oh, so-and-so used to work here, sure, but not anymore." Nope. It's always, "I've never heard of that person before," and I make my apologies for wasting their time. Back to the drawing board.

Happily, however, this time every single number was a working number, and I spoke to nearly every parent in person or left a message that I found out quickly the next day had been received. I did make sure to call a couple parents to let them know their student was doing a great job. I always try to do that. It makes the parent feel great, and it is a helpful reminder to myself that there are a great number of students doing the right thing, just a disproportionate number of students – compared to districts that aren't struggling or failing – that are having significant problems with school for any number of reasons.

Thankfully, Day 11 was a relief as the students knew I was on them and not full of empty threats, but tomorrow is Day 12. From personal experience, those phone calls are usually only good for about a day or two before boundaries are being tested once again. I'm sure it won't be long until I'm back to the phones. But I am optimistic since all the numbers in the system appear updated and functioning. That is a definite advantage that I haven't had in the past. Once again, this year seems to be a big improvement as we are all trying to be the support and consistency our students require and truly want.

October 6

"It's war time! It's war time!" Those were the first words I heard from the first student I saw today while on my morning post. It was loud, it was angry, and it was

7:39 in the morning. I will be honest, usually my mornings are peaceful, but this was also not unusual. When I stopped Megan, the student involved, and allowed the rest of the class to proceed to their lockers, she explained to me that her class-mate (Jayla) had told everyone that she could or did beat her up. When I asked her why that meant "war time" and suggested that those words might not be the best choice, she said I didn't understand. I agreed and asked her to explain it to me, but she flipped out and left while yelling at me. The principal had stopped as well, but that didn't seem to stop Megan from running away. Luckily, the counseling office is down the hall from my post and room, and the counselors diffused the situation. Jayla came through a few minutes later and, as it turns out, Megan had posted some kind of threatening message on KIK, a social media messaging app popular with our students. She had tagged Jayla and some of their friends. The struggles of social media.

It makes me particularly sad to know these students are having problems. This group, as sixth graders, was one of the best classes I've ever had. There was never an issue that couldn't be solved in about ten seconds. Coming from a self-contained, special education class, some have severe developmental delays. But those same students, without hesitation, will stand in front of the class and sing their heart out. I will see all of these students in a couple of hours for class. It sounded like at least Megan will be headed home for the day. Hopefully, we can have some fun singing a bit and learning how to read and write rhythms. Maybe, for forty minutes, music can be their escape.

October 15

The first day of choir is always a crazy stressful day. We are assembling students from three different buildings and three grades who normally aren't together. Because of the way the schools are structured – three schools, each looping a single graduating class through grades six, seven, and eight – the loyalties to the different schools are tight, and there can be some tension or competition among the students. In the past, I have taught chorus in all three schools during the day, but this year the "elec-tives" – which, of course, are not elective at all – were restructured so that I am only teaching in the school that currently has eighth grade (next year they will start the loop again with sixth grade).

I am familiar with some of the seventh graders as I had many of them last year in class or choir, and my counterpart colleague teaches the seventh grade school as well. The only time either of us has interacted with the sixth grade singers was when they came for their auditions last week, so we don't necessarily know about the group dynamics until they show up. Luckily, since choir is after school, audi-tioned, and actually elective, the students we have – even the toughest ones – which I'm a sucker for recruiting – are happy to be there.

When I was hired three years ago, there was no choir program, and my task, along with my colleague, was to build a program. We were both asked to direct a choir. My job was to build the new Boys' Choir, and my colleague's job was the Mixed Choir. We were given three brand-new Wenger riser sections. A former district administrator donated an old Knabe grand piano right from his living room. The rest was up to us. We quickly realized that joining forces was the only way because I could not take boys for my group without severely diminishing (or entirely appropriating) the male singers for the mixed group. By the end of our first year, the Mixed Choir numbered about twenty-five students with eight of them in the Boys' Choir as well.

This year, our fourth year (third full year), we accepted eighty students into our program and probably turned away about twenty. This was huge. Usually, for numbers, anyone who auditioned pretty much made it. This year, I still took on a few weak singers because, like every choir director, I need guys. But the Boys' Choir alone is twenty strong, and nearly all of the eighty students that were accepted showed up at the first rehearsal. But that's the tough part, especially in this area. Attendance is a challenge.

Last year, we started with around fifty-five students. It quickly dropped to a steady thirty-five or forty students and lasted throughout the spring and our all-city festival. After that, we lost a few more and ended up around twenty-five or thirty by our May concert. Some stopped coming. Some we asked to leave due to attendance issues and conflicts with our performances. And some were told they could no longer do it for any number of reasons. The biggest struggle is that even our sixth graders are responsible to babysit or even take on the role of mini-parents. They have to take care of siblings in other schools because their parents (or, in many cases, one parent) aren't home. Even at our first rehearsal today, I had a girl come up to me and hand in her permission slip. She said that she had to go because her mom is out of work and didn't have enough money to put gas in the car. She was going to have to go get her little sister and take her home. Each time you hear these stories, you don't know how to react. For me, this is usually the sequence in my head:

"Oh no, that's terrible."
"Wait, is it true?"
"Is it just that she's unemployed?"
"Am I a jerk (read: stupid, ignorant, spoiled White guy) for questioning it?"
"Ugh, is this going to be all the time?"
"Am I a bigger jerk (read: stupid, spoiled, professional musician) for being upset that it will affect the choir?"
"Can I make an exception?"
"Can I help?"
"How many more are we going to lose?"
"Here we go again. We'll be down to thirty-five by Christmas."
"Wait, you jerk. Remember the part where she can't put gas in the car? Get a grip."

And it kind of continues circling around a bit for a while. We lose a lot of kids to responsibilities for siblings. I can't imagine how many kids we lose because of things they are too afraid or ashamed to tell us. It took a lot of guts for Jenisha to say that to me today.

I emailed her homeroom teacher and guidance counselor to find out the whole story. I also wanted to know what my colleague and I could do for her and her family for Christmas. But after that, how do we throw a $65 trip to Six Flags Great Adventure at her when she's probably already worried about scraping together $50 for the eighth grade promotional activities. And what about Junior Region Chorus, a great way for kids to experience new music, meet other singers their age, and see what it's like to perform for a real crowd? That costs money, too.

I have often talked with my colleagues here and at the main high school we feed about being determined to "bring more color" to events like Music in the Parks and the Region choruses. I want to do it for our kids, mostly, but also for the communities around New Jersey like the one I grew up in that are fairly White-washed and make certain assumptions or generalizations about the place and the students that I now know. I want to tear down those misconceptions. Music, I have always believed and *will* always believe, has that power and brings people from all walks of life together under a common language, culture, and passion. Unfortunately, you still need $65 and a ride to the audition site . . .

November 30

It would be impossible for me to reflect on my teaching over the past four years without talking about two students who have meant a lot to me and have influenced my development as a teacher. I'm sure I'll get to Shakura at some point, but today, as I'm watching him practice his violin, I'm thinking about Travone.

Travone, now an eighth grader, came to me in sixth grade as part of my vocal/general music class. He is a truly fascinating kid. Without any musical training or background, it was pretty obvious to me when I met him – and anyone that meets him – that he was somewhere on the high-functioning end of the autism spectrum (probably in the neighborhood of what used to be called Asperger's Syndrome). He had fine motor issues, was socially unaware or uninterested, could be hyper focused and interested in a couple of distinct and unique areas of study, and had an apparent misunderstanding of jokes and humor. But, as I got to know him, I found out all of those very clear indicators slowly began to reveal themselves as contradictions or inaccuracies.

The first thing I noticed with Travone, of course, was his musical ability. In sixth grade, he could hit a low F (two Fs below middle C) and quickly became my lead bass in my boys' choir. He continues to be my most reliable member, never missing a rehearsal, and always showing up exactly on time. As I got to know him in choir, I was finally able to make him understand and laugh at a joke and even start to understand the nuances of sarcasm. It was a really exciting moment for me. When I spoke to his other teachers, they were just as surprised and excited about me getting him to smile and laugh. Since then, he has started to open up with his other teachers, too. I don't know if it was because of music or because of sixth grade nerves, but I'd like to think it would have at least taken longer without music in his life.

I also noticed he had some unique interests and habits. For instance, he always wore the same hoodie and scarf to school every day, all day. Even on the hottest days. The first time I saw him without it was at our first concert in March. I barely recognized him. This year, in eighth grade, he ditched the scarf and traded it for a pair of work gloves perfectly placed to hang from his pocket and a violin that he purchased online. The only time that violin leaves his shoulder is when he sits in class or gives it to me to tune. "But wait!" you say. "He has fine motor issues!" Good memory. He sure does. I'll get to that in a minute.

Another unique quality of Travone is his encyclopedic knowledge of the animal kingdom, especially fish, reptiles, and insects. Every week he'd have a new plastic container with some sort of organism floating or crawling around in it. He'd carry it everywhere he went, and no matter whether you wanted to or not, you were going to learn everything about it, including its Latin binomial nomenclature. To my surprise, I have never heard one kid tease him about this. He is so confident and knowledgeable that kids simply listen and learn. I mean, let's face it, he's a model teacher.

He is using a living visual aid and knows his content area backward and forward – the first of many contradictions that I expected from my initial evalua-tion of Travone. In any event, I always wondered where he got this stuff. This city is not known for its lush, multi-acre forests, and when he had to pay for a day trip to a music competition at Great Adventure he paid in installments, so I knew his family didn't have much money. As it turned out, he volunteered at a pet store in town, and they paid him in animals.

To this day, he still works there, although he has shifted his focus. And that shift, of course, has been to music. I knew he was interested in singing as he enjoyed participating in the choir and even prepared a solo for a performance in a concert. I initially pegged Travone as a shy person, but I quickly realized he is anything but that. Or he is completely unaware of people around him. It's probably a combi-nation. Another contradiction. A potentially socially awkward child, he somehow navigates the social arena with ease through confidence and, perhaps, lack of aware-ness of social pressures. He just is who he is, and the students truly gravitate toward that. This year, he even gave a very funny speech when running for class office and won! But, once again, I digress . . .

From his interest in singing and music, he was able to rekindle an interest in the violin. Apparently, he had taken lessons when he was at the performing arts elementary school in our district, but he had had a bad experience with some of the students at that school. He opted to switch to my school instead of the nearby arts-centered school (which I'm trying to push him to go back to for high school) and dropped his violin studies. I was concerned because I knew he had some fine motor difficulties. He is, however, a very good artist (drawing) and has decent penmanship even though he holds his pencil in a fist and moves very slowly and deliberately. Nevertheless, it is Travone and once he's into something, he's committed. And this is when it got very interesting for me – and very difficult for us as a student and teacher.

Travone was able to scrape together some cash and buy a cheap used violin. I did some research and knew they might sell for about $200 or so. It was painted white (not stained and varnished), and it came with three strings. He decided to play it "lefty" instead of the traditional way. I'm a vocalist, there is no string program at my school, and I don't really know the folks at the arts magnet school well enough to ask for help. I also don't have a budget. In four years being here, I have only received a music budget once for $700. Even then, I would not have thought to stock up on violin strings. In any case, I suggested to Travone that he look for a store nearby where he could find new strings and I would learn how to string the violin for him. That was actually toward the end of last school year, and we all went home for the summer before it was resolved. I honestly didn't think his pursuits would last the summer. He was struggling, and I thought he might have a new interest in the fall. I should have known better.

He came in this year (eighth grade) with the violin in tow and still only three strings. He couldn't find a place in town that had what he needed, and he and his family, as near as I can tell, are limited to the bus schedule and routes for transportation. I said OK and that I would ask around. He was also still playing lefty and I urged him to stop, but I would ask a couple of string player friends of mine their professional opinion first.

Later that week, I was able to get in touch with my friend who teaches high school orchestra in an affluent suburban district in western New Jersey. I took Travone's violin over to him, and he was able to hook me up with a brand-new set of strings (and showed me how to string the instrument), a lesson book, a shoulder rest, and a proper folder. I brought it back to Travone, and he was elated. He was not so happy to find out, however, that my friend backed up my opinion regarding playing his violin as a lefty. For whatever reason, which he still refuses to tell me, he was and still is 100% determined to play lefty. I told him at that point that he should practice from the book both ways and that I will find out from another professional friend of mine if lefty is possible and, if he is going to commit to lefty, what he should do with the violin. He had all sorts of ideas about changing the strings and the bridge to accommodate his playing position. I really urged him to play righty, but I didn't want to kill his interest in the instrument without sufficient information from qualified professionals.

I talked to another friend of mine who teaches nearby. She also agreed with my suggestion to learn righty. She also advised against doing anything to change the violin externally because the internal structure was not built for that. Needless to say, when I relayed all of this information to Travone, he was disappointed. I thought I finally had him and he'd finally listen. The next day, he had re-rigged the violin to have the bridge turned the other way so that he could play easier. The strings wouldn't tune right and there was so much tension on the E string that you could barely press it to the fingerboard. At this point, we kind of had it out. We argued. A lot. I tried to understand from his perspective what his persistence about playing lefty was and he wouldn't tell me other than he "had to" and that he "made a promise." He also told me that his goal was to be the "King of Violins" and he had to do it lefty.

It was really tough for me. I know I have a lot of credit built up with him, so I can be tough on him, but it was to the point where he was no longer taking my advice and actually going against nearly everything I suggested. Not to mention, he was risking breaking the brand-new strings that I drove out of my way to get and a colleague was generous enough to donate. I told him I'd support him, and he could always use my room as a place to practice, but I might not be the right teacher for him since he wasn't listening to any of the things I was trying to teach him, no matter how much qualified advice or evidence I was able to give him.

I really didn't know what was going to happen. Sure, I took him on his first roller coaster the previous year and listened and laughed as he cursed out loud over every hill but at the end wanted to do it again. Yeah, I joke with him and the other boys in our choir that he is my favorite since he's been in my sixth grade and the rest haven't and that they have to work really hard to beat him and their success is based on the Travone scale. And, yeah, I know he trusts me and looks to me as a role model. I was the first teacher he was really open with. But I was also his mentor and was very hard on him. Maybe even tougher on him than I had been on some of our chronically difficult students. An eighth grader who just loves to play violin. Ugh . . . what did I do?!

Well, lesson learned. Kids are resilient and forgiving. Because even as I am reflecting on this experience now, he's in my room noodling away on his backward violin and smiling as I tease him about it. And now, in a way you can only enjoy by knowing him and hearing him, he's explaining to me how hard it is to have so many girls that like him and how he hopes they don't think he's playing them. As he explained it, "It's frustrating when you have a harem. You have to keep all the girls happy." Yup. Travone is definitely my favorite.

December 7

I don't know how to process today completely. It started off as your typical Monday. I had my first class, and it was fine. Confusion ensued, as it often does, from a scheduled assembly. My second class was supposed to come and then head to the auditorium with me. Instead they went during the prior period with a different teacher and I had to wait for them. Only one of the three self-contained behavior disorder students even came to class. I didn't have a plan and didn't know when/if his classmates would find their way to class, so I let him choose between the computer and keyboard while we waited. His class never came, but a student from one of my first marking period classes did.

Shakura came in with a friend to talk. Shakura is an interesting kid. She loves music and can sing, but she was pulled from my class to have additional support in reading. On top of that, she can be quite a handful with regard to behavior and authority. Luckily she liked music, so I never had an issue with her prior to her leaving for reading support. So, needless to say, when she walked into my room (when she should have been in another class), I was concerned. I don't know why she picked my room of all places, either. I'm completely on the opposite side of the building from everyone (although that would make it a strategic advantage as a hideout), and I am a notorious rule follower and "snitch." Students know I'll shoo them away before they even get a foot inside my room. Especially when they are talkative hall roamers such as Shakura and her friend Amara. But for some reason, today they came to me. And for some reason, today I let them come in and sit. And talk. After a few minutes I knew why.

Shakura needed to get away from her classmates. She explained to me that they were being crazy, loud, energetic, and all "lovey" and she didn't have time for that today. She revealed to me that she lost her father about four days ago and was not in the kind of mood to be around her classmates. Sadly, at first, I wasn't sure if she was telling the truth or not. I had no reason not to trust her, but I have heard some crazy excuses from kids that turned out to be completely fabricated. She seemed to have herself together pretty well, and she was in school only a few days after her father's alleged death, so I felt skeptical. It's a defense mechanism I have developed to protect my usually trusting personality. I'm sure it's not unique to my district, but I have never encountered so much lying – convincing, straight-faced lying – from a group of students. They could give the World Series of Poker champions a run for their money, I'm sure. That said, my skepticism was soon turned around to a completely different kind of disbelief.

I continued to listen and told Shakura I was sorry. She shared that it happened at the end of last week. I asked her if she was close with her father, and she said yes and that she "basically lived with him." She wasn't emotional about it, but she was very reserved compared to her usual disposition. And Amara, who would definitely give her away, was not laughing but just listening carefully. I asked her if she had talked to her guidance counselor and she said she had. Now that it seemed I was hearing a real story from a real kid really hurting, I started paying closer attention. I finally asked Shakura what happened.

> "He was shot," she said.
> No tears, no emotion, just the facts. He was shot.

Three words sent me head (and heart) first into a reality that said, "I have no way to relate to this from personal experience." I asked my next question to try to understand and wrap my head around it, which was: "Oh my God, Shakura, I'm so sorry. What happened? Was it an accident?" *Please, God, let it be an accident.* At least if it were an accident, tragic as it may be, I would be able to be somewhat helpful in offering some support through experience. Never mind for the moment how I was trying to make this easier for *me*.

> "No, it was a setup."
> *A setup?! I have no frame of reference for this. I don't know what to do other than listen . . .*

Shakura explained to me that they were sitting in her father's house and he had gotten a call to go outside. He threw a jacket on and walked out front. A moment or so later, she said, she heard *POP* *POP* *POP* and a car driving away. Amazingly, the drive-by attempt didn't kill her father. However, when a friend came to pick him up to take him to his store, apparently whoever was looking for him found him and finished the job.

Not knowing what to say, once again I offered my condolences. I asked her why she was in school, and she said she had missed too many days already and had to come back. I talked with her for a bit after that. I mentioned she looked like she was dealing with it pretty well (or she was just in complete shock and things hadn't hit her yet, which I did not mention), and she explained she had a very hard time at the funeral on Saturday and her mother was a mess, but her faith brought her peace and gave her hope.

The conversation then strayed tangentially into her project, presenting a "doctoral dissertation" on comparative religions as she eloquently explained the similarities and differences between the Abrahamic religions and the "pagan" religions (I think she meant the occult). She learned about it from her Grandfather originally but did a ton of reading and research to learn more about. It was fascinating. And it was clear that Shakura didn't have a problem reading; she had a problem reading stuff she wasn't interested in.

The bell rang, I once again offered her my condolences, and I told her I'd pray for her and her family. At some point in the conversation, she mentioned how she writes her own songs and even wrote a rap regarding some other family members she had lost recently. I told her I'd love to read or hear anything she'd like to share. She said thanks and left the room, and all I could do was choke back a few tears before my next class arrived two minutes later.

I took my next class to the assembly. Shakura's guidance counselor was there. With the last little bit of doubt I had in my mind, I asked him if he had spoken to Shakura. Of course he had, and he confirmed her story. A quick Google search of her father's name and "shot" also confirmed the story.

I don't know how to wrap up my thoughts on this. It's just another one of those moments as a teacher where you simply do your best to be there, listen, and provide support and stability. As is often the case, I taught Shakura nothing today. She, through her tragedy, taught me something – countless things! When I figure them all out, I'll be a better teacher and a better person. Thanks, Shakura.

February 29

While December (or January if you have your winter concert after the break) is often a crazy time for music teachers, Black History Month comes soon after. In my situation, I teach at one school but help to run an after-school choir that services three schools. So what, you ask? Well, three schools, three administrations, three faculties, and three Black History Month assemblies! This year we got lucky, and only two of the schools asked to include the choir. Well, to be honest, it was us who volunteered our choir for those assemblies because they were both for the schools where we teach.

Assemblies are intimidating here. If you've ever seen the auditorium scene from the movie "Lean On Me," you have a pretty good idea what they can be like. If the moderator doesn't grab and keep the students' attention right away, or if you can't get any more help from other adults in the room, the students have a field day. Sure, it's a dramatized exaggeration, but it's not too far off depending on the group. In fact, a few years ago, we walked off the stage with our choir about four measures into the tune. We went back for the first time this year now that they have a new batch of students (having graduated all of their students last year), and we were able to get through the performance despite their rudeness, but, needless to say, we did not jump when we found they were also doing a Black History Month assembly.

Our middle schools have kids that range from eleven to fifteen years old. They have to be in school at least until sixteen, so dropping out is not even an option. In fact, we have attendance officers that spend their year tracking down parents and students with threats of court appearances and fines to get their kids to attend school regularly. Second, everything is about data. Data, data, data, data, and more data. And guess what? If you are a "focus" or "priority" school, which we are, and you have too many write-ups or suspensions, whether or not they are totally justified, you just can't send kids home. So, when there is a fight in your classroom (and not the wimpy little pushing matches I grew up with in suburban western NJ but a real fist-flying, tackling, weave-pulling brawl), it's a good chance that you'll see those kids back the next day. Sometimes even that afternoon. It's a reality that we have to deal with in a school where funding and complete loss of autonomy are based upon these data points.

Anyway, the assembly I coordinated along with the disciplinarian from our school went incredibly well. The students got a bit antsy here and there, but for an hour-long presentation that went until one minute before the dismissal bell, I'd say it was a huge success. It focused on history as well as today and the future. It included students from the honors classes, as well as the JAG Program (Jobs for America's Graduates), which helps at-risk students stay motivated to stay in school and even go to college. A couple of JAG students were inspired by their own potential through the acting, singing, and even working as stagehands.

The fact is that most of our students have incredible potential and want to learn. They are passionate about life and, when properly motivated, they do amazing work. As I said in my email to thank the faculty the next day, I am so happy and blessed that I can offer students, through music, the chance to have regular success doing something they are good at and work hard at to become better in the face of constant threats and reminders of failure from a misinformed public.

I will never forget the smile on Dameon's face – a boy who came up to me a couple weeks ago and asked to sing the opening solo in our choir's performance of "Glory" from the movie *Selma*. He had never sung in front of an audience before and wasn't even part of the choir. A few notes into his debut, he heard the boisterous applause and hollering of 400 of his peers. Peers who, up until then, only knew him as a class clown, a fighter, and a hall walker. I don't know if that moment changed his life or not, and I may never know, but it changed mine. It always does.

Dameon, and other experiences like that, are the reasons why when I look at other jobs at "better" places, I have a hard time imagining myself anywhere else.

March 29

I realize, as I've been journaling this year, that I have spent a lot of time talking about teaching in urban schools and the stories that surround that, but I haven't focused as much on teaching *music* in an urban school. As I contemplated, I thought it would be beneficial to write down the things that have challenged me as a *music* teacher, especially things that I didn't expect. Since I'm in my fourth year, much of it is still fresh and, even as recently as this past week, I'm still learning.

Before I start rattling off a bunch of things that may sound like I'm frustrated, I will say that my district, generally, is very supportive of the arts. I was hired in an expansion of the arts program, and a choir was established (as an after-school club) for the first time at the school. At a time when so many districts are cutting music, this district is cutting edge with the STEAM (Science, Technology, Engineering, *Arts*, and Math) initiative. They have a beautiful K–5 and 6–12 visual and performing arts magnet school, and the art produced there is amazing. Walking through the building you feel inspired. I do not work at that school. The school I work at, from the outside – and parts of the inside – could easily be mistaken for a correctional facility. And, unfortunately, I think that has a substantial impact on the students and their attitudes. But we still have a growing arts program of which I am very proud to be a part.

So, here was the first big surprise when I walked in for my first day of teaching: No windows; just walls. Well, no windows in most of the classrooms. This is not so unusual for a music room. Often they are big giant boxes with no windows. Converted from a gym or shop or something. In fact, my first room here was a converted auxiliary gym/dance studio. Not only are a vast majority of the rooms essentially in the basement – which is called the first floor, as if it were fooling anyone – but the school building was originally designed as an open classroom, "school without walls" format where multiple classes met in one giant room. It wasn't long before temporary partitions went up and finally more traditional permanent walls and hallways. However, rather than putting the classrooms along the exterior walls and running the hallways in between, they put all the classrooms in the middle and have the hallways running on the perimeter of the building. So nearly every classroom is within the rectangle, and the windows are only in the hallways. Rooms with a view are few and far between and quite a commodity. Talk about thinking inside the box . . .

Next design flaw of my first room: It was a converted gym next to the boiler room. Actually, it was only about a third of the gym, and on the other side of the wall (makeshift drywall construction with absolutely no soundproofing) was another music room. And, oh, by the way, it was right in between the two gymnasiums and the swimming pool. So, constant traffic, hundreds of kids running around, and with no ventilation, I had to keep the doors open to stop the boiler room on the other wall from heating the room up to over 90 degrees.

My room wasn't actually done when I first started. The "first floor" had flooded the previous school year, and they had just finished putting down the new hardwood floor. It took until November for the varnish to dry and fumes to vent to the point where we could bring students in. The one blessing is that my veteran colleague was also in the same predicament and we team taught for my first couple of months in the auditorium. I might not have made it without her for that first bit. It was great.

I was so excited to finally get my room that November. I'm sure you're thinking, "Oh wow, I hope they were able to save all the instruments, desks, chairs, and materials from the room before they got ruined from the flood." Well, yes and no. There were none of those things. My room was an empty box with two small white boards, which, of course, were spared in the flood. When they found out I had two, they took one and replaced it with a bulletin board. Awesome. One tip, never tell anyone what you have.

I had to find all of my furniture. I started out by finding a bunch of mismatched chairs and a table for my electronic keyboard that I brought from home. I had a pair of computer speakers to play music and managed to get a projector from one of the principals. The arts supervisor was able to buy me textbooks and, eventually, a school-issued laptop. I'm not a big music textbook guy, honestly, but they have come in handy on occasion. I taught 250 students per week with those materials for quite some time.

During my time teaching in the auditorium, I was able to rescue an upright piano that had been nearly destroyed. My principal at the time, still excited to have a music teacher, paid for the repairs and tuning, which was amazing. It was well over $600, all said and done. But, as with anything, it took months for approval to go through for the purchase order. I also slowly accumulated things like a teacher desk, storage cabinets, and filing cabinets from throughout the various schools that I serviced. By the spring, the piano had been repaired, and I finally had what I felt to be a fairly respectable classroom. I even got a $700 budget for materials for year two! I bought four keyboards, headphones, stands, and a few posters and solfege cards before my budget was tapped. I struggled through the last bit of the year, barely conscious of what was going on around me, but I was excited because I could start year two the right way.

One flash flood the week before the first day of my second year ruined any chances of the next year starting more smoothly. The room was once again destroyed. This time I had to go "music on a cart" style for the first half of the year. My sixth grade students met with me in the auditorium daily. My eighth graders usually met in the auditorium unless there was a scheduling conflict, at which point we would travel up to the third floor of their section of the building and use a room that almost had enough chairs.

The seventh graders were so terrible at getting from their end of the building to the auditorium that they were banned by the sixth grade principal. I had to travel across all three grades and then up three flights to a science room. Eye wash stations, sinks, computers, and an accordion style divider were in the middle of the room.

All I could move on my cart was a keyboard and laptop speakers (sound familiar?), and I couldn't leave anything in the room for fear it would be destroyed or stolen.

The seventh grade that year was notoriously difficult. On top of that, when seventh grade teachers would walk in and see the mix of students I had (generally because they heard me losing it down the hall and came to check to see if I was OK), they basically laughed and told me good luck. They had essentially hand-picked the toughest kids from each homeroom and put them all in two classes that split ninth period for the week. One group was Monday/Tuesday and the other Thursday/Friday (they alternated having Wednesday every five weeks). I had them for the entire year. Plus, with only two minutes to make a seven-minute trip (including an elevator ride) to the already erupting classroom or hallway or wher-ever they had run off to, the entire semester was doomed to be a mess.

I would love to give you an amazing story of how I reached these kids through music with nothing but a keyboard, guts, and love, but I didn't. It was a struggle. It was painful. It was the hardest thing I've ever done as a teacher and in my top three as a person.

Things got a little bit better when I got my classroom back in January. I found tables for students to sit at instead of using textbooks as writing tablets. I wheeled the choral risers into my room from the auditorium (and wheeled them out for rehearsals after school). And that started to help, but it was still not enough for my toughest two classes. Once their principal observed that it wasn't my fault for being late all the time and the kids were still awful, it was determined that I was just a bad teacher (meanwhile, I was scoring threes and fours on my evaluations from the sixth grade vice principal and district supervisor when they observed me in all of my other classes), and I was given a "co-teacher" to give me some tips and help during the period. She gave me some good advice, which did help, but I essentially had to abandon any of my own style and become your typical state-mandated robot teacher instead of an arts teacher.

I almost didn't make it that year. I felt like a complete failure. My health suffered. My singing voice (another big part of my ability to pay bills and buy food) suffered. And my passion was drained from me every day from 1:30 until 2:10 for 186 days. If my other classes hadn't been so manageable, I might have gone back to paralegal work and packed in the whole teaching thing for good. That's how bad it was. I would almost have taken eight hours in a cube at a computer screen helping banks foreclose on people over another forty minutes each day dealing with students who I couldn't reach no matter what I tried. I knew that teaching had to be better than this and hoped that this was an anomaly, but I had a hard time deciding if I could risk another year like that in the future. One thing I did know was that I had to re-think my approach for the next year and pray to God that they fixed the flood-ing problem.

Year number three. New floor number three. I used to have three cabinets, but now I only have two and no one knows where the other one went. The piano was damaged again – not by the flood but by being moved. However, I would not be deterred. I found tables. Ditched the choir risers, which were problematic for many discipline issues and inconvenient since they really belonged to the auditorium and not to my classroom. I even matched the chairs to stay within shades of blue! I hung all my posters up, got the piano fixed, and started the year in my room for the first time. It was so much easier.

And then, one weekend, it poured. Complete torrential rain. Floods everywhere. Trees down. You name it, it happened. I walked into school that following Monday with a heavy heart assuming the worst, but my fears were unfounded. They had fixed the pump and drain just enough that the flood went to about two feet outside of my door but not in! The custodians had even caught the flood early over the weekend so they were able to set up sandbags and sat outside my door with squeegees until the rain and flooding stopped. Year three was going to be a good year. I finally had a room. It finally stayed dry the entire year. I was finally settled and felt like I had a home. I was finally a real music teacher, and I could concentrate on building my program, getting more things for my room, and settling into a routine.

I got the word in May. I was renewed, but I would not be returning to my room in September. The expletives that rang from my mouth would have made my students and their colorful vocabulary seem like a Disney movie. They let me pick from a handful of rooms on the second floor, all of which were too small. And I was beyond frustrated. But then I saw it. Like an oasis in the desert, I found a room with windows.

April 1

All right. This time I promise, no tangents and stories. I'm even going to stick to a list and keep my bullet points succinct. Urban music education reflections after almost four years . . . GO!

You are the fifth wheel

No matter how supportive your school is, you will never be up there with math, ELA, science, and social studies. You're lucky to have a job, really. If your school is what is currently called a "Focus School" or "Priority School" then you're in even worse luck. Any state funding has to go to certain areas as dictated by your school improvement plan. If you get a budget every year, consider yourself lucky and spend every dime! And anything you buy, show it off whenever possible.

Pros: You will be left alone most of the time and not have to attend a lot of the meetings or do a lot of the ridiculous state-mandated work that your core subject colleagues have to go through. You can really experiment, try new things, and make mistakes without risking your job.

Cons: You might be forgotten. Not being in many of those meetings or not receiving different emails will mean that you're often out of the loop. Not to mention, your evaluator probably won't know what the heck you're doing in your lessons and you'll lose points for not using all the strategies that core teachers are supposed to use (that don't translate to the music room).

Lock it up

Unfortunately, theft and vandalism are big problems. I remember my first week finding it strange that kids would keep their book bags on no matter what, even in the lunch line and sitting in their chairs at their desks. They always had two answers to why when I asked: theft and bedbugs. I could relate to neither of those things. My "locker" in high school was a corner of the music room that my teacher allowed me to dump my stuff because it was more convenient than my hallway locker. As a teacher, I haven't lost too many things to theft or vandalism, but I installed locks on all my cabinets as soon as I had them and have had very strict rules with the instruments I do hand out. Even so, many of my hand percussion instruments were destroyed only after a few uses. Partly because they were cheap but partly because they became projectiles or, despite my numerous warnings, were pounded on with no regard for their condition.

The person you need is not nearby

If you need funding or a key or a room or anything, the person you need is probably at least two buildings and three forms away. My district has over 1,100 teachers and over 20 schools, and it is run like a corporation. The amount of red tape will strangle you in some cases. My first few years I had six bosses. I worked for three schools (so three principals), and my evaluator of record was the vice principal of my reporting school. Plus, I had my district supervisor and my superintendent. I didn't really have to deal with the superintendent at all, but all the others, yes. I was lucky to have a Visual and Performing Arts supervisor who used to be a music teacher, so she was (and still is) my biggest advocate and support. The tricky part was asking for instruments, tunings, or other materials. The concern from my reporting school principal was always: "Will the students from the other schools be using it?" And then it was a matter of getting two other principals to split the costs. It made things much more difficult.

Students in the audience will not sit for a choir and band concert

My initial year was the first year we had choir and band in the building. Our first concert for students was a major disappointment. We did it for all three grades, each separately. The band was able to more or less play over the noise, but we had to stop a couple of times to wait for the audiences to be quiet and stop heckling our groups. The seventh grade did a great job, the eighth grade got it together eventually, but the sixth grade (the same group that was the seventh grade the year I almost quit) was a mess. The next concert we did for the schools, we pulled our kids off the stage for the really challenging group and vowed to not return. After that, our daytime concerts were offered as rewards for students whose teachers believed they could behave themselves for a twenty-five-minute concert. We would get about 50 to 100 students out of 1,200 across the three schools.

Some things that help: Good music. Lots of amplification. Invited guests only. Smaller groups. I also spend a lot of time in my general music classes teaching students how to listen and be an audience.

You will pay for stuff

I'm looking at my classroom set up right now. We have been learning some basic piano skills. Three of the six pianos are mine from home. The sound system is my personal home theater system. The class binders were my purchase. We get one ream of paper per month from our principal. Everything over that is on our dime. The giant box of staples copy paper in the corner is mine. I even get paper for Christmas from my family. Extension cords, computer cables, printer, and toner. Mine, mine, mine. The list goes on. I don't know how much I've spent over the years, but I know it's more than the $250 the government allows to be deducted from my taxes every year.

Note: The end of the year was so busy that Mr. Tamburro's journal ends here.

My response

A hallmark of a good teacher is *not* that they don't make mistakes but that they are reflective and thoughtful about their craft and the students who they teach. Mr. Tamburro is particularly honest about the ups and downs in his journey with urban students. As a teacher in the beginning of his career, his eloquent writing gives pre-service students a raw, unabridged story of the joys and challenges in the first few years of teaching. On one hand, you could read this journal and focus only on the inadequate facilities or the difficult encounters with some students. On the other hand, you could read this journal and recognize that, among the rough spots, were powerful breakthroughs with troubled students and the realization that sheer tenacity may mean more to students who come to expect instability as the norm than students of privilege for whom schooling is part of the vivid landscape in which they live. Of the many stories from this journal, perhaps the stories of two students, one whose father was murdered and the other who became obsessed with learning everything he could about the violin, provide the most nuanced portrait of what a music teacher might encounter in the daily life of an urban school. For certain, nothing is routine.

Although his students may seem wary or unpredictable, "the fact is that most of our students have incredible potential and want to learn." This is often overlooked by pre-service teachers who tend to think about urban students as confrontational and out of control. It is these very students, however, who are the most vulnerable and in need of teachers who understand their learning needs as well as the challenges that they face on a daily basis. As Mr. Tamburro remarks in his journal, the students are used to teachers who abandon them for more comfortable jobs in suburban schools. It is true that the teacher turnover rate is highest in urban schools. This is one reason why students develop thick skins when it comes to school. They not only know that teachers, especially beginning teachers, may leave at the end of the year but also that urban schools house some of the weakest teachers in the schooling system who tend to teach from prescribed lesson plans or an abundance of seat work.

Additionally, in most schools throughout the nation, testing and data collection has put even the best teachers in a straightjacket. Knowing that test scores are tied to their evaluation as teachers, there is tremendous pressure to teach to the test rather than the development of creative, innovative thought processes. It seems that these pressures are particularly strong in urban schools where many are fighting to maintain their credibility. Mr. Tamburro talks about the tests that the music program has developed to assure that learning has taken place. Unfortunately, as he describes, the singing tests are both inadequate and counterproductive to the development of a safe community of learning; yet, he is bound by the curriculum to administer these tests all the while realizing the ludicrous nature of these standardized measures in a music class.

Fortunately, "kids are resilient," and there is much more to teaching than a week or two of testing. His description of the students gives a far better picture of urban teaching than state imposed mandates. Clearly, there are heartfelt reasons why Mr. Tamburro continues to teach in his position. Like the other contributors to this book, the students' need for good teachers and the relationships that they develop with their music teachers counts for a lot.

All students deserve an education that promises excellence in teaching. Urban students, especially, need continuity, stability, and good teachers. Although they do not need to be "saved," they do need strong adults who believe in their capabilities and hold them to the high standards that develop confidence in their ability to succeed. The journey, Mr. Tamburro writes, is tough: "It was a struggle. It was painful. It was the hardest thing I've ever done as a teacher and in my top three as a person." The difficulty is navigating a system where so much seems to work against progress. However, the rewards often lead to an unparalleled feeling of caring, satisfaction, and hope. As all the contributing writers in this book assert, "It's the kids that make urban teaching so rewarding."

Music, when taught well, has the transformative power to change lives, and music teachers can do wonderful things to give students a voice when they usually have none.

Part 2: Learning to roll with the punches

> *Things change all the time. Schedules change, kids change, everything changes all the time. There is so little continuity. There is a constant stream of change.*
>
> — *Mr. Tamburro*

Adapting to a shifting and changing environment is not exclusive to urban schools, but somehow the unpredictability of flooded classrooms, loudspeaker interruptions, students coming and going (in terms of enrollment), administrative promises that fall through, or the death of a family member or child seems more frequent and severe in the urban school. All of the contributing writers in this book mention flexibility as a key attribute to successful teaching. Flexibility, in this case, is not only the ability to roll with the punches but also intrinsic to teacher success in an urban school setting. Ironically, it appears that change is the one thing urban teachers can count on.

Mrs. Sweet talks about flexibility as "being able to move with the kids." For instance, *if there were a shooting in the neighborhood, you have to be flexible and have the strength to listen to these stories even if it hasn't been your experience. You can't feel helpless because you need to help them cope with this every day.* During a summer music camp for urban teens at my university, a student was uncharacteristically absent one day. Her mother called to explain that there had been a drive-by shooting and, although no one was physically hurt, several bullets tore through the house while they had been sleeping. One of the bullets hit the student's guitar. Fortunately, she could still play the instrument, but the bullet hole was a blunt reminder that urban students often live under conditions that many pre-service teachers have never experienced.

There are countless incidences that call upon the teacher's strength, emotional maturity, and leadership in the face of difficult circumstances. In most college teacher education programs, however, pre-service teachers learn how to carefully plan instructional content with accommodations for students who may have unique learning needs. Rarely do teacher education students talk about experiences in dealing with unpredictable events, whether student initiated, administrator initiated, or things that are simply out of the teacher's control. Moreover, these issues often happen at the beginning of the year when first-year teachers are the most vulnerable and inexperienced. My first day in an urban school was no different:

> From the time the doors opened to the end of the school day, our energy focused entirely on averting crises, rather than setting a tone for compelling learning activities. What teachers can learn from days where nothing seems to go right is that another day is always coming. . . . Perhaps the very best thing we can do for our pre-service teachers is to convey the fact that many events in teaching are caused by things beyond the individual teacher's control.[1]

For novice music teachers, just walking into an urban school can create culture shock. The school students may all be a different color; there are often security guards at the door; and, in some cases, the teachers may have to walk through a scanning device before heading off to their classrooms. According to Joe Kincheloe, teacher educators must understand that "urban schools are thorny and complicated places for teachers."[2] Because most pre-service teachers live lives so "culturally distant from their students, these teachers need to understand both the communities in which poor urban students live and the nature of their daily lives."[3]

It is critical, therefore, that pre-service teachers seek out every opportunity to experience the urban school setting and working with urban students. All pre-service teachers are required to do fieldwork in the schools. Every student should have an opportunity to experience an urban school – if not required, it is strongly recommended that pre-service teachers request such a placement through the university. Before arriving at the field site, go online and read everything about the school, such as the mission and the events. Find out as much as you can about the music program and the names of the different music specialists who teach at the school. Know the name of the principal as well as the arts supervisor.

One-on-one experience with a child or adolescent who attends an urban school can be very illuminating. Such experiences might involve tutoring, assisting the mentor teacher, or giving private lessons. It is much better to work continuously with a student (every week, etc.) rather than once in a while. Developing trust takes time and continuity. Another idea is to volunteer with a community organization that serves economically disadvantaged people. Some places include soup kitchens, after-school programs, or other community organizations.

Because the college teacher education program can never prepare pre-service teachers for everything they may experience as a teacher, it is incumbent upon the pre-service teacher to seek out these opportunities. This is especially vital for urban teaching given the following reasons. First, few colleges adequately prepare pre-service teachers for urban teaching positions. And, second, without any experience in the urban setting, pre-service teachers tend to maintain their misperceptions about urban teaching and never have a chance to counter those assumptions.

Familiarity with the urban environment and dynamics of urban students gives new teachers some grounding for responding to incidences that occur outside of the teacher's own experiences. Unpredictability, however, is always unsettling. It can create inner panic on the part of the teacher and self-doubt in one's ability to handle the multi-dimensional aspects of urban teaching. As Anna Ershler Richert acknowledges,

> Teaching is hard work. So hard, in fact, that it takes a lifetime to learn to do it well. One reason it's so hard is because of the uncertainty of the work. Every day – all the time – teachers encounter problems that are not easily solvable.[4]

Reichert notes that new teachers must distinguish between problems and dilemmas. Problems are situations that, despite the aggravation or inconvenience, have standard solutions. A good example of a "problem" is Mr. Tamburro's unfortunate experiences with a flooded classroom: *During my first two years, my classroom was flooded, and the hardwood floors were destroyed three times.* This problem created a host of difficult issues, including having to teach in another space that was not conducive to an active music class, searching for chairs and other equipment that were taken from the classroom, and adjusting lessons that required music equipment or supplies not available in the new space. Yet, all these problems were solvable, albeit not quickly enough, by installing new hardwood floors and finding the necessary equipment.

A dilemma, however, has no "right" solution and requires some type of decision that involves a myriad of factors that have to do with the teacher's values; prior experience; and, most importantly, the context of the situation.[5] Both Mrs. Sweet and Mr. Tamburro were confronted with dilemmas involving death. For Mrs. Sweet, the dilemma was highly personal because it involved the death of her student. Mrs. Sweet confronted the very difficult task of dealing with her own feelings of loss in addition to those of her other students. What to say? How to move on with a "vacant seat" in the orchestra? How to best honor the memory of her student?

Mr. Tamburro faced the dilemma of how to comfort his student in light of her father's murder. The dilemma involved a multitude of decisions – was she telling the truth? If so, should he ask how it happened? What could he say that would support the student without sounding trite? Mr. Tamburro writes, *I have no way to relate to this from personal experience.* Yet, this dilemma required action and empathy on his part as her mentor.

Dilemmas characterize the kinds of issues that teachers face most of the time – having to weigh alternatives to determine what is best for the student(s). John Goodlad, an internationally recognized author and educator, wrote passionately about the moral dimensions of teaching.[6] From Goodlad's perspective, there is a moral component to all aspects of teaching, including how we nurture students, define curriculum, work toward the good of the learning community, and engage in democratic practice. A moral dilemma essentially poses the question, "What is the right thing to do?" among a host of competing values, contextual factors, and short-term versus long-term goals.

Although this chapter began with the assertion that constant change in the learning environment is a normal part of the urban teaching experience, there are a number of "predictable" dilemmas that merit discussion. Several sections of this chapter will identify some of the dilemmas that music teachers may face when teaching in an urban school. Again, it is important to recognize that dilemmas have no easy answers and depend heavily upon the context of the situation. Nevertheless, it is my feeling that such dilemmas need to be addressed for the purpose of practicing how to think through difficult situations. According to Richert:

> If teachers can sort through and separate problems from the dilemmas, they will have accomplished the first step in managing them both. Knowing that dilemmas do not have easy, foolproof, "right" answers can help teachers begin the process ... of considering possible ways to respond to their students' needs and line those needs up with their purposes and the possible consequences of any action they might take.[7]

Dealing with grief and loss

At some point in their teaching career, most teachers will deal with grief and loss in the classroom. The death of a teacher, family member, or friend is particularly traumatic, especially when it is sudden and unexpected such as an accident, shooting, terrorist attack, or suicide. The student's grief, however, is no less significant when the loss occurs from a long-term illness. The Amelia Center (www.childrensal.org/

amelia-center), an online service for grieving students and parents, explains that teachers are trusted adults and, though they are not trained counselors, they can still provide healthy settings for the grieving child and students in the classroom. Although the teacher may have his/her/their own grief to manage, this section focuses primarily on how to help students with their grief process.

It is important to note that students have different ways of grieving and that teachers should not have expectations about how students express their grief. Moreover, different cultures have their own customs, rites, and beliefs about death that must be honored when dealing with grief. Age is also a factor in understanding how to respond to students. For example, elementary students below age eight sometimes engage in magical thinking where they have trouble understanding the finality of death. Middle and high school students understand the finality of death but may harbor guilt over what they could have done to prevent the death.[8]

Teachers may see the following behaviors from students: crying, withdrawal, anger, depression, inability to concentrate, somatic complaints (stomachaches or headaches), high-risk behaviors, substance abuse, and suicidal thoughts. The greatest dilemma for teachers is how to respond in such situations. Because of the sensitivity of the issue, teachers often have much anxiety about what to do and how to talk about it with students. A good online resource for how to talk to students about grief is *After a Loved One Dies: How Children Grieve and How Parents and Other Adults Can Support Them* (http://www1.newyorklife.com/newyorklife.com/General/FileLink/Static%20Files/Bereavement-bklet-English.pdf). In addition, teachers may need to adjust their ways of talking to students according to whether the loss affects a single member of the class, an entire class, the school community, or a family member.

Generally, there are some important things to keep in mind. Talking with children/adolescents is important. "School personnel are often concerned about the possibility that they will upset children by raising the topic of death. They may worry that they will make matters worse. They may choose the say nothing."[9] Not talking about it suggests that you are insensitive to their struggles, incapable of helping students develop coping mechanisms, or disapproving of discussions about death. These messages, while often unintended, can deepen the grieving process and deprive students of the support that they need from a caring adult.

In our culture, it is not easy to talk about death. However, teachers must take an active role in initiating discussion (especially when a class has lost one of their own) and helping students process their grief. The Coalition to Support Grieving Students (see Appendix A) and The Amelia Center offer suggestions for how teachers might engage the class in a discussion: Begin the discussion with facts such as how the death occurred, funeral arrangements, and any other appropriate details; validate students' emotions in a gentle way using a normal tone of voice; and, if appropriate, have an activity ready for students such as singing a song that may have been a favorite of the deceased student, composing a vocal or instrumental piece memorializing the student, or learning a special song/instrumental piece in honor of the student to perform at a school assembly.

There are also things to avoid such as talking too much, trying to cheer up the student(s), and or telling students to be strong when they express different emotions. Table 5.1 is a helpful resource for learning how to phrase sentences and questions that facilitate conversation with a student who has experienced loss.

TABLE 5.1 What to say (or not to say) to grieving students

Don't say this	Say this instead
"I know just what you're going through." You cannot know this. Everyone's experience of grief is unique.	"Can you tell me more about what this has been like for you?"
"You must be incredibly angry." It is not helpful to tell people how they are feeling or ought to feel. It is better to ask. People in grief often feel many different things at different times.	"Most people have strong feelings when something like this happens to them. What has this been like for you?"
"This is hard. But it's important to remember the good things in life, too." This kind of statement is likely to quiet down true expressions of grief. When people are grieving, it's important they be allowed to experience and express whatever feelings, memories, or wishes they're having.	"What kinds of memories do you have about the person who died?"
"At least he's no longer in pain." Efforts to "focus on the good things" are more likely to minimize the student or family's experience (see above). Any statement that begins with the words "at least" should probably be reconsidered.	"What sorts of things have you been thinking about since your loved one died?"
"I lost both my parents when I was your age." Avoid comparing your losses with those of students or their families. These types of statements may leave children feeling that their loss is not as profound or important.	"Tell me more about what this has been like for you."
"You'll need to be strong now for your family. It's important to get a grip on your feelings." Grieving children are often told they shouldn't express their feelings. This holds children back from expressing their grief and learning to cope with these difficult feelings.	"How is your family doing? What kinds of concerns do you have about them?"
"My dog last week. I know how you must be feeling." It is not useful to compare losses. Keep the focus on grieving children and their families.	"I know how I've felt when someone I loved died, but I don't really know how you're feeling. Can you tell me something about what this has been like for you?"

Credit Line: The Coalition to Support Grieving Students (Grievingstudents.org)

Showing care and concern for students is particularly vital when students have lost a significant person in their lives. Even if children or adolescents do not know the deceased person personally, they may feel sad and scared about the finality of death. The teacher's compassion in times like this are of deep support to the student(s). We can also learn a lot from students who have faced such tragedy in their own lives. In one instance, two high school girls from Lexington, Kentucky, lost a good friend to street crossfire. To cope with this loss, they spoke at a national conference in Colorado on the effects of gun violence. They also brought this message to their school and community, hoping to improve response to gun violence. Their words are valuable information for teachers:

> Listen to us. Be there with us. Hug us. Check back in. Ask us how we feel. You don't know what's going on in people's lives and what they go through. . . . For teachers, start the bond the first day of school and love them. Then if they lose someone, you're there for them. This can help students get their emotions out and actually talk about what they're feeling.[10]

Creating a safe space for LGBTQ students

LGBTQ is an acronym for members of the Lesbian, Gay, Bisexual, Transgender, and Queer community. Sometimes a second "Q" is added (LGBTQQ) for people who are in the process of questioning their gender or sexual identity. Unfortunately, schools can be hostile environments for LGBTQ youth.[11] According to the 2015 National School Climate Survey, 82.5% of LGBTQQ students experienced verbal harassment at school. Physical harassment (e.g. pushing and shoving) occurred with 27% of students where half of these students were physical assaulted (e.g. punched, kicked, injured with a weapon).[12] Not surprisingly, cyberbullying constituted a significant part of the harassment. This frightening and threatening environment correlates with a high rate of absenteeism and the reluctance to join extra-curricular activities.

All students, however, deserve a school where they can feel safe. When a teacher shows a commitment to creating a safe place for learning, every student benefits. Providing a welcoming and inclusive environment lets students know that peer behavior that oppresses others is not ok. It also models an intrinsic form of care that says, "This is a place where you are valued for your unique gifts as a human being." According to Bruce Carter,

> When students observe teachers making a stand against bullying and harassment, they recognize your intention for a safe classroom. When students feel safe, they are more likely to ask questions and engage in your class in dynamic and meaningful ways – both musically and non-musically. Only when students feel safe can they learn.[13]

Music teachers are in a strong position to become allies of the LGBTQ community. An ally is a person who not only supports LGBTQ students but also educates for respecting the rights of LGBTQ in the classroom.[14] Allies often put a special "Safe Space" triangular seal on their door that indicates support for LGBTQ youth for both students and faculty.[15] Because music teachers often see students over a period of time, they can develop a trusting relationship that reflects their willingness to talk about sensitive issues. For many LGBTQ students, the music classroom serves as a refuge where they have a voice through music making and a community that honors diversity. One important sign of respect for transgender students is to use a pronoun, such as he/she/they, that the student prefers.

Music teachers can be of greatest help when they are familiar with key terminology (e.g. What is the difference between "transgender" and "gay?" What does "gender fluid" mean? What is queer theory?) and the history behind the LGBTQ movement. Names like Harvey Milk and George Moscone are well known as the first political figures who brought the rights of LGBTQ people to national prominence. The shooting death of these brave advocates became the impetus for the formation of the San Francisco Gay Men's Chorus. This ensemble paved the way for many other LGBTQ adult and youth choirs throughout the nation today.[16]

National issues, such as the rights of transgender students to use school bathrooms that honor their preference, have created heated arguments across the country. Political legislation under Obama's presidency provided transgender students the right to use gender-segregated bathrooms according to their gender identity.[17] Arguments against this legislation, however, pervade the current political climate.

Teaching music advances the cause of safe classrooms when teachers educate students not only as musicians but also as respectful human beings who understand that oppression of any group disrespects everyone. This means that music teachers must model openness to diversity and intervene when behavior is derogatory and hurtful. Students who use words like "fag" and "dyke," for instance, do so intentionally to degrade students whom they perceive as LGBTQ. As with any hurtful language, the music teacher must take immediate action by letting all students know that such language is hurtful and not welcome in the classroom.

Another oft-heard phrase is "that's so gay." Surprisingly, many students use this phrase unintentionally to mean "that was ridiculous," or "that was so off the mark." When called to their attention, students may protest that the phrase is common usage and not meant to be inflammatory. A savvy teacher will see this as a teachable moment to help students recognize the power of language. The Gay, Lesbian, and Straight Network (GLSEN), a national education organization focused on ensuring safe and affirming schools for all students, suggests that teachers might say any of the following: "What do you mean by that?" "How do you think a gay person might feel?" "Did you say that as a compliment?" "So, the connotations are negative? Maybe that's not a good thing."[18]

The importance is that music teachers address the behavior directly with the intention of helping students understand *why* this language is inappropriate rather than just scolding the offending student. Herein lies a major dilemma: How does the teacher educate for respect and understanding without putting the targeted student on the spot? There are no prescribed answers for this question but in the context where the behavior takes place, the teacher must immediately stop the behavior and make a decision whether to address the class about hurtful language or talk to the offending student privately. At a later time, the music teacher may want to design a lesson around the music of musicians who had to keep their sexual orientation a secret or have openly declared their sexual orientation. The discussion might start as simply as a question: "Does a person's sexual orientation or gender validate music as a worthy piece of art?" Other starting points could include themes of diversity, acceptance, human rights, or what it means to struggle against societal norms.

Creating a safe space for LGBTQ students involves an environment of acceptance and respect for all students. Music teachers can model this through their own behavior, their expectations of students in the class (and hallways), and activities that encourage inclusion. Some of these activities might include having same sex parents assist with a concert; playing recordings and YouTube clips of LGBTQ composers/performers along with an accompanying discussion; devoting a bulletin board to musicians who represent diverse life-styles; or celebrating LGBTQ events such as LGBTQ Pride Month.

There are numerous resources online for reading about LGBTQ issues and how to support students who may need such affirmation. The "Space Kit," (see Appendix A), created by GLSEN, includes information directly related to teachers. In terms of choral music, the international Gay and Lesbian Association of Choruses (GALA) and youth choral groups such as the Diverse Harmony Chorus (Seattle, WA), Youth Pride Chorus (New York City) and Diverse City Youth Chorus (Cincinnati, OH) provide a resource for titles of choral repertoire as well as an opportunity to view performances on YouTube. In addition, music teachers can find much information regarding repertoire and other musical resources through The Center (see Appendix A).

The themes in music performed by GALA choruses are universal – societal pressures, love, acceptance, anti-bullying, and harrassment.[19] Such themes provide grounding for many forms of music that provide pathways into meaningful discussions about diversity. Only in a safe place can students begin to grapple with complex social issues and thoughtful exploration of the human condition. According to Casey Hayes, "Music has the ability to reach all students regardless of gender identity/sexual orientation or any form of marginalization. A music classroom has the ability to transform all students, including those who find themselves questioning their sexual identity and/or expression."[20]

In essence, students make music courageously when their music teachers take a stand for the rights of all individuals. Teacher education programs must specifically address LGBTQ students' special needs and intervention techniques for eliminating oppressive comments or behavior.[21] Likewise, teacher education programs can help pre-service teachers discuss scenarios that involve LGBTQ students, such as what to do on a school overnight trip when a "straight" student asks to have a room that does not include an LGBTQ student. These and other scenarios are dilemmas that pre-service teachers may face in their teaching. Consequently, it is extremely helpful to discuss these issues so that students have had some experience thinking through how to create a safe classroom.

Dealing with bureaucracy and unsupportive administration

If teaching were just about teaching, life would be considerably easier. With urban school districts, especially large urban districts, however, the layers of bureaucracy can make teaching much more difficult.[22] Part of the problem with large urban districts is the sheer size and number of schools to oversee. This, as well as state department mandates, often leads to decisions made for teachers instead of *by teachers* and standardization of policies that may not be in the best interest of the program or students. In the most unfortunate instances, administrators prioritize time and resources to disciplines where test scores are published and used as an evaluation measure for the teacher or school itself. While "the idea that some students need more math, reading, and science but less art, music, and beauty in their lives than other students do is condescending and demeaning,"[23] the music teacher must find ways of coping with the multiple demands of administrators without sacrificing the integrity of the music program.

Some of the demands require additional paperwork and approval signatures, which is doable but requires a longer time frame than other types of requests. For instance, the time frame for arranging bus transportation to a music concert, if field trips are supported in the district, often takes months for an approval to go through. Other demands may include curriculum mandates that are written with disciplines other than music in mind. Equally frustrating are demands on the music teacher to cover classes for other teachers when they are late, having to take two classes at once, or last-minute requests for an ensemble to perform at a board meeting.

Teacher evaluation as related to standardized test scores is a hotly contested topic in education. Part of a teacher's overall evaluation also includes observations by the arts supervisor and/or principal. When the observer is neither schooled in best practices for teaching music nor particularly supportive of the arts, a music teacher's evaluation may be reduced to areas of classroom management and proper bulletin boards rather than a thoughtful assessment of the teaching itself. There is nothing more frustrating than receiving an evaluation based on non-teaching measures, even if the evaluation is stellar. In this case, it helps to sit down and talk about the evaluation with the evaluator.

Educating administrators about music teaching is not as unreasonable as it might initially sound. Many have not had meaningful experience with the arts in their own schooling or are so overwhelmed with the monstrous amount of detail that accompanies such a position that the intricacies of teaching music may fall off their radar. Their problems are real and understandable. It is important that the music teacher take this into consideration when planning a meeting with an administrator.

Sometimes it is better to be pro-active. Depending on the administrator's accessibility and openness to conversation, a music teacher might make an appointment at the beginning of the year to explain his/her/their program, advocate for the arts, and talk about what good music teaching looks like. Another idea is to invite a principal or supervisor to participate in an ensemble rehearsal or to find a way for them to participate in a seasonal concert (whether musically or not). Having the principal read a short, related children's book or poem at an elementary school concert or inviting the principal to conduct a march (with a very strong ensemble) at the secondary level are two of many ideas for getting administrators involved in your program.

There are times, however, when the demands or wavering support from the administrator do not respond to reasonable intervention on the part of the teacher. In addition, there is high turnover of administration from year to year. It is not unusual for an urban teacher to have a different principal/superintendent every other year or find that the arts supervisor's position has been cut from the budget. In those cases, other teachers in the school can be the greatest allies. It helps to cultivate friendships with trusted faculty members, especially because teaching music can be so isolating. The more experienced teachers have been around for a while and have a sense of history that may help reframe troublesome issues in a different light. A veteran high school music teacher, Ms. Gopal, who taught in a nearby urban district, told me:

> When you go into an urban school the most important thing to find out is who are the most successful teachers and why. Get to know them and observe their classrooms. You can't live in the bubble. I had an opportunity to observe the best teachers in science, language arts, and math.

Each school is different, and there are many urban administrators who are proud and supportive of the music program. Take the time to thank the administrator for his/her/their support and be specific about those comments or resources that help you build your program. Look for ways to advocate for music in the schools. Also, build a strong parent/caregiver base who can rally for the music program when necessary.

Insufficient contact information for reaching parents

In previous chapters, I emphasized the importance of getting to know the students and their families. A phone call to a parent or guardian may not be so easy, as Mr. Tamburro explained in his journal. Families move unexpectantly, give a phone number of another relative, or have their phone service shut off. In her book, *Teaching While Black: A New Voice on Race and Education in New York City*, Pamela Lewis describes her dilemma in contacting a parent:

> A teacher may have every intention of spending most of her prep period writing a daily lesson plan, expecting to need only five of those minutes to call a child's mother. But to make that call the teacher may find herself going through every single number on the child's blue emergency card before she

finds one that is still in service, and that number may be the child's best friend's mother's brother, who may give the teacher his sister's number in hope that the sister may actually have the number of the person with whom the teacher wanted to speak. After a wild-goose chase that has caused the teacher to lose her entire prep period, the number provided may be the same number she had called to begin with, a number that was out of service because the mother hadn't paid her phone bill or had changed her number without informing the school.[24]

In my urban school teaching, I experienced similar problems. Although it may take time to track down a parent, open communication with families remains an integral part of building trust in the community. Hopefully, the calls will be as much about successes and proud moments in the classroom as they are in seeking help for problem behavior. Because urban parents are used to the latter, the music teacher should look for moments to celebrate a student's work and accomplishments in the music class.

Conclusion

New teachers are particularly "thrown" by change in the school setting. Veteran teachers, however, understand that change is a normal part of the school day and come to expect the unexpected. Having weathered many changes in their career, they have a much better handle on what to do, who to call, and when to take a stand toward resolution. In a previous book, I wrote:

> Teachers often face situations that are not of their making but they are still held accountable. A fire drill might interrupt a discussion just as it starts to take off, the maintenance man shows up unannounced to fix a leaky radiator, unpredictable announcements crackle over a high-volume intercom system, and so on. While such episodes become familiar interruptions for novice and experienced teachers alike, they still create a jolt in the teacher's plans and the students' learning.[25]

These are irritating problems that might have created an interruption to an important moment in the lesson, but they have workable solutions. It is the dilemmas that arise from tragic events, students struggling with their identity, political dimensions of teaching, and the moral dimensions of teaching that create the most stress. We are not trained as counselors or health care professionals nor are we trained to deal with the politics of teaching. Yet, there are countless situations that call these skills into play.

Fortunately, there are many good resources online, some of which have been included in this chapter. Also, there are many online support groups for music teachers in all specializations. Consider starting a "new teacher" network among the graduates of your college/university. Every teacher has questions and dilemmas that pop up and it's comforting to share these with others in similar situations.

No one ever said that teaching was easy. There are moments when you say just the right thing to a struggling student and other times when you are at a loss for words. There are times when you are rewarded for a job well done and times when nothing you do seems to satisfy a cantankerous principal. Consequently, new teachers must learn how to take care of themselves first so that they are in a better position to take thoughtful action. Ms. Gopal advises new teachers:

> *Take care of yourself first. Take care of your mental health, exercise, eat well. Some teachers meditate, do yoga, or listen to positive thinking mantra. To prepare myself for this year I listened to Tony Roberts for hours. It's easy to dwell on negative thoughts and harder to see the positive. As a society we are trained to gravitate toward the negative. I had to train myself to turn that off and cut off people that were bad energy. You have to learn how to shut that off.*

Change is not always negative; change can also bring about new administrators who support the arts, curriculum initiatives that advance a music program, and new students who bring a breath of fresh air into the classroom. As Ms. Gopal explains, *it's easy to dwell on negative thoughts and harder to see the positive.* That is not to diminish the difficult problems/dilemmas that urban teachers face but rather to remind us that difficult situations can often have positive outcomes. Even in the most heart-wrenching moments, such as the death of a student, music teachers can help others find the inner strength to move forward. In doing so, there is a new level of closeness between teacher and student, opening doors that were previously shut.

> Beginning teachers enter the profession believing that teaching is a straight-forward line toward that symphonic spot where everything falls into place and one has finally arrived. But teaching is not linear and never really arrives at a point where you finally feel like you know exactly how to do it.[26]

For new teachers, this ambiguity is both frightening and unsettling. But it *is* the reality of teaching, whether in a suburban, rural, or urban school. The best preparation, then, is to understand that when you are caught unaware by that powerful wave, riding the current will eventually lead you to shore. In other words, your leadership instincts and your sensitivity for others in distress will guide you until you are able to put your feet on the sand and walk confidently on your own.

Discussion questions

1   What are some important things to remember when talking to a student or class in the wake of a tragedy?
2   How can you build an inclusive classroom for students who are part of the LGBTQ community in which students support each other regardless of their diverse backgrounds?
3   As a new teacher, how can you build support among the parents of your community, especially if some of them do not speak English?

References

1 DeLorenzo, Lisa C. 2012. *Sketches in Democracy: Notes from An Urban Classroom.* Lanham, MD: Rowman & Littlefield: 9.
2 Kincheloe, Joe. 2007. "Why a Book on Urban Education?" In *19 Urban Questions: Teaching in the City*, edited by Shirley R. Steinberg and Joe Kincheloe, 1–27. New York: Peter Lang: 12.
3 Ibid.
4 Richert, Anna Ershler. 2012. *What Should I Do? Confronting Dilemmas of Teaching in Urban Schools.* New York: Teachers College Press: 4.
5 Ibid.
6 Goodlad, John I. 1994. *Educational Renewal: Better Teacher, Better Schools.* San Francisco: Jossey-Bass.
7 Richert. *What Should I Do?*: 104.
8 Schonfeld, David J. and Marcia Quackenbush. 2014. *After A Loved One Dies: How Children Grieve and How Parents and Other Adults Can Support Them.* New York: New York Life Foundation. www1.newyorklife.com/newyorklife.com/General/FileLink/Static%20Files/Bereavement-bklet-English.pdf
9 Coalition to Support Grieving Children. 2018. "Talking with Children." USC National Center for School Crisis and Bereavement.
10 Spears, Valerie Honeycutt. 2017, November 25. *Girls Who Lost Friend Trinity Gay in Shooting Now Find Voice.* Lexington, KY: Herald-Leader.
11 Bergonzi, Louis S. 2015. "Gender and Sexual Diversity Challenges (For Socially Just) Music Education." In *The Oxford Handbook of Social Justice in Music Education*, edited by Cathy Benedict, Patrick Schmidt, Gary Spruce, and Paul Woodford, 221–237. New York: Oxford University Press.
12 The National School Climate Survey. 2015. *LGBTQ Students Experience Pervasive Harassment and Discrimination, But School-Based Supports Can Make a Difference.* Executive Summary. Washington, DC: GLSEN: 4. https:// www.glsen.org/nscs
13 Carter, Bruce. 2011. "A Safe Education for All: Recognizing and Stemming Harassment in Music Classes and Ensembles." *Music Educators Journal, 97* (4): 32. doi: 10:1177/0027432111405342
14 Safe Space Kit. *Guide to Being an Ally to LGBTQ Students.* 2003–2018. New York: GLSEN. www.glsen.org/sites/default/files/Safe%20Space%20Kit.pdf
15 Ibid.
16 Hayes, Casey J. 2016. "Safe Classrooms: A Fundamental Principle of Democratic Practice." In *Giving Voice to Democracy in Music Education*, edited by Lisa C. DeLorenzo. New York: Routledge: 87–101.
17 Arenas, Alberto, Kristin L. Gunckel, and William J. Smith. 2016. "7 Reasons for Accommodating Transgender Students at School." *Phi Delta Kappan, 98* (1): 20–24.
18 Safe Space Kit. *Guide to Being an Ally.* https://www.glsen.org/sites/default/files/GLSEN%20Safe%20Space%20Kit.pdf
19 Hayes. "Safe Classrooms."
20 Ibid., 100.
21 Gorsky, Paul C. 2013. "An Examination of the (In)visibility of Sexual Orientation, Heterosexism, Homophobia, and Other LGBT Concerns in the U.S. Multicultural Teacher Education Coursework." *Journal of LGBTQ Youth, 10*: 224–248. doi: 10.1080/19361653.2013.798986
22 Kopetz, Patricia, Anthony J. Lease, and Bonnie Z Warren-Kring. 2006. *Comprehensive Urban Education.* Boston: Pearson.

23 Fitzpatrick-Harnish, Kate. 2015. *Urban Music Education: A Practical Guide for Teachers*. New York: Oxford University Press: 5.
24 Lewis, Pamela. 2016. *Teaching While Black: A New Voice on Race and Education in New York City*. New York: Empire State Editions: 120–121.
25 DeLorenzo. *Sketches in Democracy*: 5.
26 Ibid.

6

WHEN WHITE TEACHERS TEACH STUDENTS OF COLOR

As a White teacher, I've always wondered whether my color puts me at a disadvantage with Brown and Black students. Does my skin color make me an outsider in their world? Will they question my instruction as something that works for White students but not for them? How much does race matter in schooling?

Mr. Tamburro, a White teacher, writes:

> *It's definitely there* [racial awareness among students] – *and important for them to have Black teachers. Most of them don't care much but they notice. Sometimes, they forget you are White and will say something like, "Just another group of White people" – then they see me and say, "Oh sorry, Mr. Tamburro. You've been here so long you're Black anyway."*

Patricia Lewis, a Black teacher in New York City states,

> Rarely do people consider how the race of one's teacher can affect a child's psyche, or how detrimental it can be to a child's belief in the ability and intelligence of his own people to have mostly white teachers throughout his school career.[1]

Through her eyes, Black students often develop trust more quickly with teachers who look like them. There is an unspoken understanding that Black teachers have a lived experience similar to their students.[2]

On the other hand, Black, Latino, and White teachers, are educated to teach all children. Although race may play an initial role in gaining trust, students do respond to teachers who show care from both a personal perspective and an academic perspective. This speaks to the hard work that White teachers must do in order to know the student and where he/she/they comes from, as well as to understand that

Black and Brown students have unique learning needs rooted in their culture and their identities.

Each of us has an identity through which we view the world. Our identities are formed through our families, our activities, our beliefs, how we perceive that others see us, sexual identity, nationality, social class, gender, etc.[3] Race (which includes White) has a particularly strong impact on shaping identity and perspective and influencing how we interpret an issue, idea, or practice. This doesn't mean that people of any one race think and respond the same way. It does, however, point to the importance of recognizing, valuing, and affirming racial differences in the children we teach.

Why spend an entire chapter on race? As Lewis suggests, race affects us in more ways than we realize. When working with students of color, all teachers hold positions of power and need to think about issues of racism regardless of their own racial/ethnic background. According to Joshua L. Miller and Marie Garran, "Ultimately racism hurts and degrades us all, even those from white skin privilege."[4] Although many music teachers have students from numerous races and ethnicities, this chapter will focus on Black/African American and Latino/Hispanic students because these are the two largest minority groups in the United States.

Historical context of race in the public schools

From the 1900s to the Civil Rights Movement, the approach to race in the public schools went through three transformations: "race as a nation, race as color, and race as culture."[5] Zoë Burkholder's compelling book, *Color in The Classroom: How American Schools Taught Race, 1900–1954*, chronicles the long history of race and education in America.[6] Because public schools are charged with the democratic education of young people, schools have a major influence on how people understand race and respond to racism.

In early discussions of race, the term "minorities" referred to national differences such as Polish, Italian, and German. Note that Africa, Asia, Middle East, and other non-European nations are not mentioned. This is because the perceived function of schools, at that time, was to Americanize immigrants from Europe into idealized citizens for the United States. Consequently, teachers, along with the public, believed that minorities needed to be assimilated into the American culture. In 1913, teachers were encouraged to Americanize foreigners while still maintaining an appreciation for the culture that these people brought from their own countries. This reflected a notable shift from a deficit-perspective approach to a celebration of cultural gifts. Teachers taught units on different cultures including songs, dances, and costumes for the purpose of familiarizing children with their "neighbors." Termed as "tolerance education," however, this theory continued to hold Anglo-Saxons at the top of the hierarchy.

During this time in America, Black students attended public schools segregated from White schools. These schools were staffed by Black teachers – "educators who shared their racial and ethnic background and knew firsthand the identity stories that were being told at home and in the neighborhood."[7] The segregated nature of these schools, especially in the South, contributed to the invisibility of Black persons in conversations of race at that time. In other words, Black students were not even considered part of the minority in public school discussions on race.

Latino students, too, attended segregated schools or separate classrooms within the schools. The buildings were dilapidated and school equipment substandard; teachers were inexperienced and sometimes without credentials.[8] Most egregious, large numbers of Latino children were classified as "retarded" because they failed to meet the grade level expectations of White students.

With the advent of World War II, skin color took on new meaning as a primary definer of racial categories.[9] It was a political imperative that America be seen as a racially tolerant country, given the horrendous racism and genocide in Europe. Racism was viewed as a threat to democracy. During this era, some teachers began to teach racial tolerance for Black and Asian students.

Once the war ended, the political impetus for these lessons declined. In the rising Cold War era, teachers could lose their jobs if they addressed race or racism in the classroom. Discussions on race, then, were silenced despite the fact that blatant racism continued around the nation. Instead of diversity-oriented instruction, students learned about how to be good neighbors, as reflected in this student's poem: "I've never met these neighbors/ And whether they're short or tall/ Or black, brown, white or yellow/ Doesn't matter much at all."[10]

After the end of the war, the term "culture" became the favored terminology in school instruction. Teachers were encouraged to promote a "color-blind" pedagogy. This type of pedagogy stressed the commonality of human beings regardless of skin color. Because teachers refused to openly discuss race, racial difference, and racial minorities in the postwar era, the dominant educational discourse on race stagnated in American schools.[11] In effect, color-blind teaching denied the unique needs of Black and Brown children, affirming the "melting pot" image of American society.

The Civil Rights Movement in 1954–1968 quickly brought race to the forefront of public scrutiny as Blacks demanded equity and equality of privileges to become fully sanctioned citizens of the United States. The demand to integrate schools was one of many issues associated with the Civil Rights Movement. In 1954, the Supreme Court ruled against segregated schools in the landmark case Brown v Board of Education in Topeka, Kansas. The decision sparked riots and white supremacist violence around the country. Clearly, this decision was the beginning of contentious nationwide dialogue regarding identity and equity in education.

In the ensuing years, conflicts regarding race and ethnicity persisted in America. Whereas school integration was the civil rights issue of the 1960s, the achievement gap among Black, Brown, and White students became the issue in the following decades. In an effort to study equality of educational opportunity, Congress commissioned a task force in 1964, headed by James Coleman, to survey students in more than 3,000 schools across the country.

The results were surprising: the *Equality of Educational Opportunity Report*, known as the "Coleman Report," found that family background (e.g. parents' level of education, socio-economic level) had a much stronger relationship to student achievement than other aspects such as lower class size or expenditures per student. The results were so contrary to what politicians wanted to hear that they actually hid the results by distorting this message to the public.[12] As a result, federal funding became the cure all for inequality in education. "Compensatory education," then, directed attention away from the social problems that the Coleman Report highlighted so strongly. Although contemporary research found flaws in the study, many of the findings are still relevant.[13]

The achievement gap persists today. Recent research identifies elements of poverty that exacerbate achievement such as low access to quality health care, housing instability, and stress from parental unemployment.[14] Geographically, low-income minority families tend to live in concentrated urban areas. Consequently, students in poor urban areas go to schools that are nearly 100% students of color.

For all intents and purposes, then, the nation continues to support a segregated system of schooling.[15] According to Richard Rothstein, "The low achievement of children in racially isolated urban ghettos is, indeed, the civil rights issue of our time but it is unlikely to be meaningfully addressed by school reformers' policies."[16] In other words, schools cannot make significant headway in providing an equitable education if inequality persists in the framework of society.

Why history of race in schools is so important

With a strong grasp of history, we can better understand the roots of racial inequities that exist in education today. Clearly, issues of inequity in college graduation rates, performance on standardized tests, and day-to-day learning progress do not happen in isolation. A look at the history of race and education illustrates the longevity of racial issues before and since the Civil Rights Movement. These inequities have not gone unnoticed. Today, organizations like Black Lives Matter, committed to justice for Black Americans, have spurred national conversations about race that are unprecedented in the years since the Civil Rights Movement. While the tipping point for Black Lives Matter focused on police brutality, awareness of racial inequities in the schools has also played a role in discussions on race.

There still remain, however, many who deny that racism exists in America. Recently, a former student and respected, congenial African American music teacher posted the following remark on Facebook:

> *The amount of times I've been called the "N" word in my tuxedo, playing cello for a wedding, has now crossed into the double digits.*
>
> *May 2016*

This comment angers me and is not unlike other stories from African American and Latino students with whom I've taught. Although the cellist's post is a flagrant example of racist talk, racism is not always about one-on-one interactions. The more insidious effects of racism are those that fly under the radar. In other words, racism is so embedded in the fabric of daily living that White people are often unaware of its existence.[17] For teachers, an awareness of institutional racism, in society and education, is critical. Such awareness undergirds culturally responsive teaching and advocating for equal access to school opportunities. According to Gary Howard, "Our responsibility as White educators is to understand the past and present dynamics of dominance in order that we might more effectively contribute to the creation of a better future for all of our students."[18]

Preparing White teachers for race-based issues

To prepare teachers for meeting the needs of students of color, many college/ university teacher education programs are taking a more pro-active role. Some universities provide space in courses or offer a workshop in order to address issues of racial identity. Although such efforts are limited with respect to helping White pre-service teachers reshape their mindset, they are an important first step.[19] When no opportunities are available, some additional experiences might include listening carefully to the stories and accounts of people of color, reading novels or non-fiction by persons of color, watching first-person video accounts of racism, or comparing a news story reported from a White person's perspective as compared with the same story presented in a newspaper that is directed toward people of color.

In conversations about race, it is necessary to acknowledge Whiteness as a race. This acknowledgment runs counter to "otherness" thinking about race, i.e. "There is me and then there are all the others." According to Tatum, "When White adults have not thought about their own racial identity, it is difficult for them to respond to the identity-development needs of either White children or children of color."[20]

Learning to think of one's self as "raced" is a new way of thinking for many White students.[21] When thinking about identity, "White is seen as the default, the absence of race."[22] White teachers tend to filter their experiences through a White lens because that is what they know.[23] Consequently, it is difficult to step out of one's skin and imagine the world from the perspective of a non-White person. Racism is not a problem for people simply because they are White; the problem stems from Whites growing up in an environment that normalizes Whiteness, which ultimately suggests that "Whiteness is superior."[24]

Not surprisingly, many White pre-service students and teachers experience profound difficulties when talking about race.[25] Some take a color-blind approach: "I don't see color; I only see children." This, writes Valerie Hill-Jackson, is the "unconscious stage" in teacher/pre-service students' beginning discussions on race.[26] Sometimes White teacher education students exonerate themselves from participating, saying, "Some of my best friends are Black or Brown." For these students, encounters with persons of a different race/ethnicity may have been positive and even inspiring. Other students have gone their entire life without talking to or having a friend of color. In both situations, it is common to deny institutionalized racism because the word racism is perceived solely as individual acts of malice toward other human beings of a different skin color. According to Christine Sleeter,

"Pre-service teachers tend to see racism as a matter of interpersonal interactions and not as participants in social institutions that systematically deny opportunities to people of color."[27]

Facilitating critical discussion about race makes many teachers so uncomfortable that they avoid this topic entirely. Although the intent is to embrace a pluralistic world, avoiding issues of race denies equitable treatment of all children.[28] When White teachers continue to deny themselves as raced, or hold on to the belief that racism is not a significant problem in our schools or society, they will continue to reject the need for culturally responsive teaching.

When one begins to examine the historical and social roots of racism, though, the role of White people as oppressors begins to surface. This realization is shocking to many pre-service teachers, and a common reaction involves guilt or anger – guilt that, despite efforts to treat people of color with dignity, racism continues to exist in our society and anger that Whites are active participants in creating a racist society.[29] It is, consequently, a challenge in discussions about racism to acknowledge the privileges associated with Whiteness.

If we think about racism as a system of advantages, then we can begin to explore the privileges that White persons have in comparison to those of color. For example, Blacks, whether poor or affluent, often experience "poor service, surveillance in stores, being ignored at retail stores selling expensive commodities, receiving the worst accommodations in restaurants or hotels, and being constantly confused with menial workers."[30] White persons, in contrast, don't need to think about getting pulled over just because they may be driving in an affluent neighborhood. They can be assured of being among those that look like them in most public places.[31] Thinking about the range of advantages that White persons hold reveal the institutional nature of racial inequality that pervades much of American culture.

How are racist remarks and institutionalized racism different? Music teachers might overhear a student saying, "Well, he's Latino. That explains why he is so lazy." This is an unkind, uninformed remark that requires corrective attention. Such a remark has racial implications but doesn't necessarily mean that the offending student is a racist. Students unwittingly stereotype students of color based on unfounded assumptions or talk they hear from other people. As a teacher, though, it is an opportunity to teach, *not scold*, the student about the ramifications of a comment, whether intentionally or unintentionally meant to harm.

Institutionalized racism, however, silently condones inequitable treatment of persons based on color. These actions are so embedded in the fabric of traditional practice that they often go unnoticed. In schools, for example, the unequal assignment of Black students to special needs classes is one example of institutionalized racism.[32] Another example often cited is the achievement gap between Black students and White students.[33] Regarding the achievement gap, Gloria Ladson-Billings, a highly respected author on race and education, uses an alternate term for achievement gap: "education debt."[34] She believes that the "achievement gap" holds the individual student accountable for performance on tests whereas the term "education debt" shifts attention toward the structural barriers that make it difficult for Black and Latino students to succeed. The shift is not merely one of semantics but rather refocusing attention on the institutional nature of achievement.

Getting stuck in deficit thinking

Rethinking one's identity is a lifelong process. But, in terms of supporting students of color, it is a necessary process – important not just for selecting culturally responsive content but for also recognizing inequities that affect students in the school. For instance, Black students are punished more often and more severely than White students.[35] Historically, Black and Latino students have scored lower on standardized tests than their White counterparts. The unfortunate outcome of this information leads to a deficit-oriented pattern of thinking about Black and Latino students. Deficit thinking has to do with seeing only the problems and deficiencies of Black and Latino students rather than the rich background that they bring to school. It also leads to the kind of stereotypical ideas that Blacks and Latinos are less intelligent than Whites, do not care about school, and are more likely to engage in disruptive behaviors.

Tim Wise, in his provocative book, *Letter to White Americans*, describes four commonly held *myths* about racism[36]:

> *First*, it isn't racism that holds back persons of color – especially blacks – but that these people have dysfunctional values. The evidence stated includes high rates of out-of-wedlock childbirth, reliance on public assistance, and lack of interest in educational achievement.
>
> *Second*, Black people simply don't work hard enough. This remark is followed by, "Plenty of other groups (like the Irish, Italians, and Jews) have pulled themselves up, and even Asians, a non-European group, have done so as well. If they can do it, anyone can, with sufficient effort."[37]
>
> *Third*, putting so much emphasis on racism (if it really exists) actually harms people of color, suggesting that they adopt a victim mentality.
>
> *Fourth*, it is unfair to criticize the United States for racism in the past or present; after all, every nation has had its problems with discrimination and inequality. If anything, America has done more than other places to make things right and to create an equal opportunity society. Black and Brown folks are better off here than anywhere else on earth.[38]

Deficit thinking, based on the myths described above, is particularly dangerous, especially in the schools. It places undue responsibility on the students of color to continually prove their value. When teachers engage in deficit thinking, they have lower expectations for students of color in assignments, class participation, and in-class projects. Students of color have to work harder than White students to overcome this barrier. Some Black and Latino students perceive this challenge as insurmountable and stop trying. This, then, reinforces the teacher's prejudice that students of color have deficits, thus supporting a toxic cycle of behavior that teachers with this perspective perpetuate.

Racism in music education

Where are the intersections of racism and music education? There are at least three areas that music teachers should consider: racism embedded in the curriculum or lessons we teach, how we address issues of race/ethnicity in the classroom, and interpersonal remarks about race/ethnicity. Unquestionably, racism is sometimes difficult to spot as music teachers have engaged in certain music teaching practices so long that racism does not seem evident. Consider this quotation as a starting point: "People will tell you they are fans of Black or Latino music, but few will claim they love White music."[39] Here, the term "White music" is jarring as most do not think of music as raced.

Racism embedded in the curriculum or lessons

In college, music education pre-service teachers spend most of their time analyzing, performing, listening, composing, and studying music from a Eurocentric perspective. The emphasis is usually on music as an aesthetic – the harmonic structure, the melodic line, the moment of climax, the rhythmic drive – all woven together in an intricate sonic whole. These are important skills for understanding and deconstructing the musical experience. However, when music teachers focus exclusively on the aesthetics or elements of music, issues of race or any other aspect of its social context are far removed from the conversation. According to Deborah Bradley, "The belief that music's sonorous qualities have meaning without reference to the historical and cultural contexts . . . lulls educators into misguided pedagogies focused on performance where attention to notes and rhythms take priority."[40] That is, by focusing primarily on the theoretical structure of music, the social/ historical context, which gives music meaning, is lost in the process.

One might argue that spirituals, for instance, have a meaningful place in the choral curriculum. Without talking about the context of the music, however, the spiritual remains just another concert piece. How might the meaning of the music change if, during a rehearsal, teachers engaged students in conversation about the text and the role of songs in providing slaves with a means to express hope, despair, or praise? Further, what if the teacher asked, "Do these songs have relevance in the American landscape today?" There are many possibilities for addressing race on a past-present continuum.

Some directors protest that there isn't enough time for these discussions or that rehearsals should concentrate on the music itself. Ironically, when students have a personal connection to the music, through understanding its context, performance takes on a whole new meaning. Such conversations humanize the music, bringing its meaning home to the student. This is not to say that all music teachers avoid such conversations, but I speculate that this is the exception rather than the norm.

What about the music we use choose for the classroom? The choice and prioritization of music literature reflects what music teachers value and deem important in the lives of their students. It also tends to reflect how teachers have been trained as music educators. As noted in Chapter 4, Western art music is a mainstay of most university music education programs. A reliance on classical Western art music for listening, performance, theory classes, music history, etc. suggests the primacy of Western music in preparing music education students to teach.

Several music educators have questioned the predominance of classical Western art music not only in teaching but in audition requirements for college music programs as well.[41] This practice prompts questions like: "Who defines music?" "How do our musical choices represent music of the world?" and "Why is Western music presented as the dominant musical art form?" With the exception of jazz, music listening choices typically foster the Western classical canon, focusing on White male composers. While this may change during Black History Month or Cinco de Mayo, when Black or Latin music is relegated to a specific month or celebration, it suggests that this music is secondary to what students study on a routine basis.

Since most higher education music programs focus on Western art music, music education students (often taught by White professors) tend to reproduce this model in their teaching. For music teachers in training, this is especially troublesome because they usually don't have the experience or range of musical repertoire for teaching music any other way. Some might ask, "Why should we teach music that students already know; isn't it our job to introduce students to what they don't know?" The problem in teaching from a purely classical music perspective, though, is the implication that other musics are less worthy of consideration.[42]

In examining the overall music curriculum, Ruth Iana Gustafson states, "Curriculum and pedagogy derive from a broad array of racialist ideas and aesthetic tenets in music teaching."[43] For instance, the way we teach singing skills, whether for children or adolescents, is generally based on a Western European tradition. Yet, the vocal traditions of other ethnicities/cultures sound very different, for example, music of the Balkan regions, Chinese opera, or gospel music. The point is *not* that vocal teachers should abandon the pure, head-voice approach to singing, common in American ensembles, but avoid presenting this vocal tradition as the only, correct approach to achieving a "good" vocal sound.

In terms of music education, teachers need to carefully examine curricular and ensemble opportunities that render students of color invisible. Initiating steel drum ensembles, African drum ensembles, and Balinese or Javanese gamelan ensembles provide musical experiences with diverse musics. By doing so, White teachers can become "allies" rather than silent bystanders.

Reshaping our mindset where racial/ethnic context is as important as the notes on the page is a conscious, deliberate act and one for which most of us have not been prepared. When we say that music is for all children, we mean that our teaching practice must remain inclusive of the lives, histories, stories, and cultures from which music emerges. Although complex as it may seem, music teachers who bring these dimensions into their classroom do a great service to students of color as well as White students. Consequently, race *does* matter in terms of curriculum development and music listening choices.

Addressing race in the music classroom

When addressing race as part of a lesson, students first need a safe space to talk. Secondly, discussing racism requires sensitive facilitation on the part of the teacher. Encouraging conversations about race in the classroom or ensemble rehearsal has as much to do with the teacher's comfort level as it does in establishing the context of the music. Such discussions need not be negative or contentious but might, instead, focus on the resilience and courage of those oppressed.

Juliet Hess makes a strong argument for using direct rather than neutral or euphemistic language. Instead of terms like "diversity," "at-risk," or "urban," she suggests a more direct reference to oppression that "prevents us from moving forward."[44] It stands to reason that, to talk frankly about oppression and power relationships, the classroom must be a safe space. Students need to trust that the teacher respects them and their peers – that the teacher will listen without judgment and help students consider different ways of looking at things. It is impossible, though, to gain much headway with students (in any type of school) who have not yet developed habits of citizenship in the classroom.[45] While it may sound like an understatement, classroom management is critical in creating a safe place. Sensitive discussion cannot take place when students make unkind judgments about others' comments or interrupt the speaker.

In facilitating conversations about race for the purpose of illuminating a musical experience, there is no substitute for first-hand knowledge about your students (see Chapter 2). Knowing the community, favorite spots for students to hang out, and what music they listen to lets students know that you care about them more than just coming to school and doing your job.[46] Urban cities and towns each have a culture of their own. The music teacher, who often resides in a suburb outside the city, particularly needs to learn about Black and Latino culture, attend community activities, eat lunch at local cafés, and familiarize him/herself with the musical culture that families bring to the school. White teachers can teach students of color, but they have to work harder at integrating this culture into their teaching style.

When asked "what it means to be a White teacher with students of color," Mrs. Skinner replied:

> *It puts an immediate stigma on what the students perceive that I know or don't know: "Oh, Mrs. Skinner doesn't know Spanish." When they come to know me they find that I love culture. However, I've been in this town for 4 years and do not know very much about the culture. I've made it my mission to know more. I try to get to know people at places where I eat lunch and I'm interested in going to their church. This is a very closely connected city. If you've grown up, gone to school, and live here everyone knows you.*
>
> *My students don't listen to classical music, but much of what we play is classically based. Regarding Latin music (most of my students are Hispanic), we don't play this style because a lot of it is my discomfort with the music . . . rhythmic difficulties with*

beginning strings . . . reading issues. Much of what is out there is too difficult for begin-
ning strings or nonexistent. There is a big disconnect between reading music and what
they hear in their culture. But parents really want their kids involved. I have to find a
better connection for them.

Some music teachers may be reticent about trespassing into political terrain.[47] Teachers might worry about repercussions from parents or the principal. These are not trivial concerns but, in practice, most schools do include instruction on sensitive issues such as slavery in America, the Holocaust, and the establishment of internment camps for Japanese American citizens during World War II. No doubt history and language arts teachers in the school grapple with similar issues when teaching these themes. Because each school is different, it may be helpful to talk to a seasoned history or language arts specialist to find out if and how they address race/ethnicity in the classroom.

What if White teachers have a classroom without any students of color? How important, then, are conversations of race to the overall program? The answer is "very important." Music has a social and political context. Although some children/adolescents may go through school without significant contact with a person of color, they see issues of race on television, and they hear adults as well as peers talking about race – all of which shapes the students' perspective about race. Some of the messages are positive, and some are negative. Consequently, a perceptive teacher can help eliminate the "otherness" categorization ("it's us White folks and then there are the others") that dominates the thinking of many White students.

It may very well happen that a productive conversation on race arises during the lesson. In one urban classroom (100% Black), for example, I played "The Entertainer." The students responded with great excitement – not so much about the music but the fact that it was a tune of the local ice cream truck. Because I wanted them to know a Black composer wrote this music, I talked about Scott Joplin and his life as a Black musician. Discussion then moved to what it was like for Black composers to have their music performed in his era, let alone published. This opened the door for questioning the kinds of challenges that today's Black artists may face. In the students' minds, "The Entertainer" gradually transformed from an ice cream truck jingle to a remarkable human achievement and that this music was composed by someone who looked like them.

Discussion such as these may last no more than two minutes or go on for much of the period. It generally depends on the relevance of the material, the class's tolerance for discussion (e.g. listening to other points of view), and the teacher's comfort level in facilitating conversation. As indicated earlier, discussions of this nature require trust between the teacher and the students, often asking the teacher to take a road that isn't well defined. Unquestionably, it takes courage to launch a conversation that has the possibility of moving in several directions.

Interpersonal remarks about race/ethnicity

Racial slurs or unkind remarks regarding race are not unusual. Students are highly aware of race and not inhibited when it comes to verbalizing their thoughts. When I was teaching in an urban school, for example, I had a very sweet and shy student from Nigeria. I noticed that she had few friends and was often ignored by the other students. When I asked one of the more mature students about it, she told me, "Oh, she's too Black," meaning that her skin color was darker than the others in the class. It was my first encounter with interracial discrimination.

Besides giving the Nigerian student some discreet extra attention, I might have found more ways to use this as a teaching opportunity for discussing how discrimination hurts and diminishes a person. It would have been a conversation that did not in any way bring my student's plight to the foreground but could have created a foundation for dealing with racial insults in the future. I wish I had been brave enough to follow through with this, but, at the time, I didn't know what I know now – that part of a teacher's responsibility is to educate beyond the music.

Many students have no problems talking about race in their own interactions with other peers.[48] Think back to the opening excerpt from Mr. Tamburro, whose students talked about their image of White people. Such conversations can be benign or hurtful depending on the purpose or intent of the dialogue. When students engage in "race talk," the teacher needs to decide whether someone or some group is intentionally or unintentionally targeted. Even when students deny their intention to harm someone, the teacher can use the opportunity to teach how those remarks might be "heard" from another person's perspective. Although situations regarding race talk may feel uncomfortable, music teachers should defer to their role as an educator rather than a disciplinarian. In essence, music teachers must see their role as educators of music *and* of people.

Multiculturalism versus anti-racism

Music educators have made a conscious effort to honor people of different cultures in textbook series, workshops, and other professional development activities. Publications abound with songs, activities, and listening examples of global significance. In this multicultural approach, the intent is to not only to learn about persons from different cultures but also to bring a broad palette of music to their students.

The term "multiculturalism" is an umbrella term for music of the world and focuses on the celebration of diversity through music activities usually derived from holidays or other relevant cultural events. For instance, many general elementary social studies units have a section on Native Americans. The music teacher might enhance this instruction by teaching some authentic Native American songs and games. Lessons generally focus on learning the music and its context in the lives of Native Americans.

There are, however, a core of researchers who feel that emphasizing the celebratory aspects of diversity sidesteps issues of oppression and unequal power structures that play a role in the lives of the people. Currently, "anti-racism" is the term that scholar-teachers use because it directly addresses inequities as a system of power. According to George J. Sefa Dei and Agnes Calliste, "Anti-racism shifts the talk away from tolerance of diversity to the pointed notion of difference and power."[49]

Anti-racism is more than a philosophical position. It examines institutional power used to "deny or grant people and groups of people rights, respect, representation and resources based on their skin color."[50] Also, it involves action by consciously initiating change to address discriminatory practice.[51] Music teachers who teach from an anti-racist perspective constantly examine their teaching and related practice for evidence of inequality based on race.

Thinking back to the Native Americans example, an anti-racist teacher might go beyond the function of the Native American song (e.g. work song, war song, harvest song) to a discussion about how some of these songs were forbidden under colonist rule. This might also include talk about Native American children who were forced to go to schools that specifically denied their language and aspects of their culture in order to assimilate them into American culture. Today, Native Americans continue their struggle to preserve their heritage so that songs and other aspects of their culture are not lost forever.

Here are some questions (in no particular order) that a music teacher might ask to interrogate teaching and practice from an anti-racist perspective:

1   What is the complexion of the school ensemble or a youth ensemble outside of the school? If it is not representative of the student population, then what are the actions needed to diversify the ensemble?
2   Are required solo/ensemble pieces inclusive of Blacks, Hispanics, Indigenous People, women, and LGBTQ?[52]
3   What is the implicit message when we only present the music of African Americans during Black History Month or Latinos during Cinco de Mayo?
4   What do students know about the social and political factors of the music we teach?
5   What are ways that the students could become involved in social justice issues through music?
6   Is the curriculum accessible to children of color?
7   How could members of the Black or Latino community share their music and stories with the students?

In response to the first question, this might mean providing scholarships as well as transportation so that low-income urban students have access to regional band/ orchestra/choir auditions. In other instances, anti-racist action could mean initiating one or more sessions at a NAfME conference that bring teachers of color together with White teachers for the purpose of identifying racial bias in music education. According to Tatum, "It is not just about what pictures are hanging on the wall, or what content is included in the curriculum, though these things are important. It is about recognizing students' lives – and helping them make connections to them."[53] Koza writes:

> I invite all music educators, especially those who identify as White, to continue to listen carefully for Whiteness, *not to affirm it*, but to recognize its institutional presence, understand its technologies and thereby work toward defunding it. Not only is it important that music educators talk substantively about race in discussions of school music, but also that we explore multiple ways of thinking and talking about music, learning, teaching, and quality.[54]

Conclusion

Although a White person can never fully understand what it feels like to be of color, there is much that one can do to become a more sensitive music teacher. Learning to teach and care for students of color requires introspection about one's racial identity, beliefs, and values, as well as an understanding of the challenges that students of color face in a racialized society. Such introspection lends itself to the broader picture of what it means to teach and care for students of color. This is an intensive and effort-laden journey but necessary for affirming students of color.[55]

The prevalence of Whiteness is present in many aspects of music education, from a focus on the Western-European canon to teaching a head-voice singing model as the "right way" of singing to selecting music repertoire that is primarily representative of White composers. Although schools acknowledge the importance of multiculturalism in affirming the differences between cultures, an anti-racist approach examines power and oppression in a social context and calls for action to address these inequities. Students and teachers take responsibility for racism by carefully examining their practice and that of the school in terms of equity and personal interactions with students of color.

Issues of racism may be acts of individual discrimination, but it is especially important to recognize racism as systemic throughout America, including education. Patricia Collins and others talk about racism as a system of power. By acknowledging this, a framework is established for "catalyzing change."[56] The difficulty of addressing race in music programs is not that teachers are inherently racist but that they don't often see musical experiences or content as raced. For this reason, substantive discussions about race and teaching students of color are particularly integral to a comprehensive teacher education program.

It was noted that talking about race is not only uncomfortable but can create a strong sense of guilt or anger. The underlying impetus for this is fear – fear of rethinking ones' own identity as a White person, fear of saying the wrong thing, and fear of sounding angry or racist.[57] In terms of educating teachers, such conversations cannot happen in a one-time session, but require many opportunities to examine one's life in relation to people of color. "Because the ideology of White racial superiority is so deeply embedded in our culture, the process of 'unlearning racism' is a journey we need to continue throughout our lives."[58] Critical thought about racism and coming to terms with the fact that skin color does make a difference in people's lives is the mark of a courageous teacher.

Although individual teachers cannot undo the effects of racial inequities in society,[59] they can make changes in teaching practice that acknowledge the lives and culture of students of color. On one hand, this requires conscious recognition of the responsibilities that address diversity in the classroom or school. On the other hand, this requires action on our part to counter inequities in the music education profession. "Equity does not mean treating everyone in the same way. It means doing whatever it takes to get everyone to the same place."[60]

In her groundbreaking book, *Other People's Children*, Lisa Delpit states "There can be no doubt that issues of diversity form the crux of what may be one of the biggest challenges yet to face those of us whose business it is to educate teachers."[61] Indeed, there is much work to be done in examining the music curriculum and teaching practice for racial bias. Bradley reminds us, "If we can overcome the taboo about naming race in discussion, and begin to talk more knowledgeably and confidently about racial issues, we can begin to make our music education praxes more racially equitable and socially just."[62]

Discussion questions

1   Have you ever witnessed an episode of racial/ethnic insensitivity? Describe what happened.

2   Vivian Paley[63] asks, "How much does it matter if a child cannot identify ethnically or racially with a teacher? Does it matter at all? If the teacher accepts him and likes him as he really is, isn't that enough?" Although this is a rhetorical question, many teachers feel strongly about this point. How would you respond to these questions?

3   If you are White, what is one thing that you can work on to be a more effective teacher for students of color? If you are a teacher or student of color, what is something that you think is important for a White teacher to know when working with students of a different race/ethnicity?

4   If you see a racial incident in school, no matter how small, how could you use this incident to *teach* your student(s) about sensitivity to people other than their own color?

References

1   Collins, Patricia. 2009. *Another Kind of Public Education: Race, Schools, the Media, and Democratic Possibilities*. Boston: Beacon Press: xii.
2   Griffin, Ashley and Hilary Tackie. 2016. *Through Our Eyes: Perspectives and Reflections from Black Teachers*. Washington, DC: The Education Trust: 1–16.
3   Miller, Joshua L. and Marie Garran. 2017. *Racism in the United States: Implications for the Helping Professions*. New York: Springer: 1.

4 Ibid.

5 Burkholder, Zoë. 2011. *Color in The Classroom: How American Schools Taught Race, 1900–1954*. New York: Oxford University Press: 11.

6 Ibid.

7 Tatum, Beverly Daniel. 2007. *Can We Talk About Race? And Other Conversations in An Era of School Resegregation*. Boston: Beacon: 24.

8 San Miguel, Guadalupe, Jr. 2010, June 15. "Mexican Americans and Education." *The Handbook of Texas Online*. San Antonio: Texas State Historical Association. https://tshaonline.org/handbook/online/articles/khmmx

9 Burkholder. *Color in the Classroom*.

10 Ibid., 158.

11 Ibid., 11.

12 Rothstein, Richard. 2013. "For Public Schools, Segregation Then, Segregation Since: Education and The Unfinished March. Report." *Economic Policy Institute*, August 27: 1–24. www.epi.org/publication/unfinished-march-public-school-segregation/

13 Hanushek, Eric A. 2016. "What Matters for Student Achievement: Updating Coleman on The Influence of Families and Schools." *Education Next, 16* (2): 18–26. http://education next.org/what-matters-for-student-achievement

14 Rothstein. "For Public Schools."

15 Alonso, Gaston, Noel S. Anderson, Celina Su, and Jeanne Theoharis. 2009. *Our Schools Suck*. New York: New York University Press; Collins. *Another Kind of Public Education*; Kozol, Jonathan. 2005. *The Shame of the Nation: The Restoration of Apartheid Schooling in America*. New York: Three Rivers Press.

16 Rothstein. "For Public Schools." 13.

17 Miller. *Racism in the United States.*

18 Howard, Gary. 1999. *We Can't Teach What We Don't Know: White Teachers, Multiracial Schools*. New York: Teachers College Press: 64.

19 Sleeter, Christine. 2016. "Critical Race Theory and The Whiteness of Teacher Education." *Urban Education, 52* (2): 1–15. doi: 10.1177/0042085916668957

20 Tatum. *Can We Talk?*: 37.

21 Bell, Lee Ann. 2002. "Sincere Fictions: The Pedagogical Challenges of Preparing White Teachers for Multicultural Classrooms." *Equity & Excellence in Education, 35* (3): 236–234. doi: 10.1080/10665680290175248; Bell, Lee Ann. 2008. "Expanding Definitions of 'Good Teaching.'" In *Everyday Antiracism: Getting Real About Race in School*, edited by Mica Pollock, 287–290. New York: The New Press.

22 Lalami, Laila. 2016. "The Identity Politics of Whiteness." *The New York Times Magazine*, November 27. www.nytimes.com/2016/11/27/magazine/the-identity-politics-of-whiteness.html

23 Sleeter, Christine E. 2008. "Preparing White Teachers for Diverse Students." In *Handbook of Research on Teacher Education: Enduring Issues in Changing Contexts* [3rd ed.], edited by Marilyn Cochran-Smith, Sharon Feiman-Nemser, and D. John McIntyre, 559–582. New York: Routledge.

24 Hyland, Nora E. 2005. "Being a Good Teacher of Black Students? White Teachers and Unintentional Racism." *Curriculum Inquiry, 35* (4): 432.

25 Garrett, H. James and Avner Segail. 2013. "(Re)Considerations of Ignorance and Resistance in Teacher Education." *Journal of Teacher Education, 64* (4): 294–304. doi: 10.1177/0022487113487752; Hill-Jackson, Valerie. 2007. "Wrestling Whiteness: Three Stages of Shifting Multicultural Perspectives among White Pre-Service Teachers." *Multicultural Perspectives, 9* (2): 29–35. doi: 10.1080/15210960701386285

26 Hill-Jackson. "Wrestling Whiteness."

27 Sleeter. "Preparing White Teachers." 560.

28 Fergus, Edward. 2017. "Confronting Colorblindness." *Phi Delta Kappan, 98* (5): 30–35; Mitchell, Derek, Jesse Hinueber, and Brian Edwards. 2017. "Looking Race in the Face." *Phi Delta Kappan, 98* (5): 24–29.

29 Hill-Jackson. "Wrestling Whiteness."

30 Bonilla-Silva, Eduardo. 2003. "New Racism, Color-blind Racism, and the Future of Whiteness in America." In *White Out: The Continuing Significance of Racism*, edited by Ashley W. Doane and Eduardo Bonilla-Silva, 271–284. New York: Routledge: 274.

31 Collins. *Another Kind of Public Education;* McIntosh, Peggy. 1989, July/August. "White Privilege: Unpacking the Invisible Knapsack." *Peace and Freedom Magazine*, a publication of the Women's International League for Peace and Freedom. Philadelphia, PA: 10–12.

32 Noguera, Pedro A. 2008. *The Trouble with Black Boys: And Other Reflections on Race, Equity and the Future of Public Education.* San Francisco: Jossey-Bass.

33 *School Composition and The Black – White Achievement Gap.* 2015. (NCES 2015–018). U.S. Department of Education. Washington, DC: National Center for Education Statistics. http://nces.ed.gov/pubsearch

34 Ladson-Billings, Gloria. 2013. "The Stakes Is High: Educating New Century Students." *The Journal of Negro Education, 88* (2): 105–110.

35 Delpit, Lisa. 2012. *Multiplication is for White People: Raising Expectations for Other People's Children.* New York: The New Press; Noguera. *The Trouble with Black Boys.*

36 Wise, Tim. 2012. *Dear White America: Letter to a New Minority.* San Francisco: City Lights Books: 40–41.

37 Ibid., 40.

38 Ibid., 41.

39 Lalami. "The Identity Politics of Whiteness."

40 Bradley, Deborah. 2012. "Avoiding the 'P' Word: Political Contexts and Multicultural Music Education." *Theory into Practice, 51*: 193. doi: 10.1080/00405841.2012.690296

41 Bradley, Deborah. 2007. "The Sounds of Silence: Talking Race in Music Education." *Action, Criticism, and Theory of Music Education, 6* (4): 132–162; Koza, Julia E. 2008. "Listening for Whiteness: Hearing Racial Politics in Undergraduate School Music." *Philosophy of Music Education Review, 16* (2): 145–155; Palmer, C. Michael. 2011. "Challenges of Access to Post-Secondary Music Education Programs for People of Color." *Visions of Research in Music Education, 18*: 1–22. http://www-usr.rider.edu/~vrme/v18n1/index.html

42 Gaztambide-Fernandez, Ruben A. 2011. "Musiking in The City: Reconceptualizing Urban Music Education as Cultural Practice." *Action, Criticism, and Theory for Music Education, 10* (1): 15–46.

43 Gustafson, Ruth Iana. 2009. *Race and Curriculum: Music in Childhood Education.* New York: Palgrave Macmillan: xii.

44 Hess, Juliet. 2017. "Equity and Music Education: Euphemisms, Terminal Naivety, and Whiteness." *Action for Change in Music Education, 16* (3): 4.

45 Michelli, Nicholas M. 2005. "Education for Democracy: What Can It Be?" In *Teacher Education for Democracy and Social Justice*, edited by Nicholas M. Michelli and David Lee Keiser, 3–30. New York: Routledge.

46 Mitchell, Hinueber, and Edwards. "Looking Race in The Face."

47 Bradley. "Avoiding the 'P' Word."

48 DeLorenzo, Lisa C. 2012. *Sketches in Democracy: Notes from an Urban Classroom.* Lanham, MD: Rowman & Littlefield.

49 Dei, George J. Sefa and Agnes Calliste. 2000. "Mapping the Terrain: Power, Knowledge and Anti-racism Education." In *Power, Knowledge and Anti-Racism Education: A Critical*

Reader, edited by George J. Sefa Dei and Agnes Calliste, 11–22. Halifax, Nova Scotia: Fernwood Publishing: 21.

50 Lee, Enid. 1998. "Anti-Racist Education: Pulling Together to Close the Gaps." In *Beyond Heroes and Holidays: A Practical Guide to K-12 Anti-Racist, Multicultural Education and Staff Development*, edited by Enid Lee, Deborah Menkart, and Margo Okazawa-Rey, 26–34. Washington, DC: Network of Educators on the Americas: 27.

51 Dei and Calliste. *Power, Knowledge, and Anti-Racism Education*: 13.

52 Robinson, Mitchell. 2016. "It's Not About You: More Adventures in Institutional Privilege, Music Education Edition." *Eclectica Blog*, October 31. www.eclectablog.com/2016/10/its-not-about-you-more-adventures-in-institutional-privilege-music-education-edition.html

53 Tatum. *Can We Talk?*: 31.

54 Koza. "Listening for Whiteness." 162.

55 Tatum. *Can We Talk?*

56 Collins. *Another Kind of Public Education*: 44.

57 Singleton, Glenn E. and Cyndie Hayes. 2008. "Beginning Courageous Conversations About Race." In *Everyday Antiracism: Getting Real About Race in School*, edited by Mica Pollock, 18–23. New York: The New Press.

58 Lawrence, Sandra M. and Beverly Daniel Tatum. 1998. "White Racial Identity and Anti-Racist Education: A Catalyst for Change." In *Beyond Heroes and Holidays: A Practical Guide to K-12 Anti-Racist, Multicultural Education and Staff Development*, edited by Enid Lee, Deborah Menkart, and Margo Okazawa-Rey, 45–51. Washington, DC: Network of Educators on the Americas: 46.

59 Coates, Ta-Nehisi. 2015. *Between the World and Me* [Kindle ed.]. New York: Spiegel & Grau.

60 Lee. *Anti-Racist Education*: 33.

61 Delpit, Lisa. 2006. *Other People's Children: Cultural Conflict in The Classroom*. New York: The New Press: 105

62 Bradley. "The Sounds of Silence." 135.

63 Paley, Vivian. G. 1979. White Teacher. Cambridge, MA: Harvard University Press: 35.

7

DEMOCRACY, SOCIAL JUSTICE, AND HIP HOP

What do democracy and social justice have to do with teaching music? Actually, quite a lot. Throughout this book, we have encountered terms like equity; equality; fairness; culturally responsive teaching; and the right to a rigorous, meaningful education. These are all dimensions of democracy and social justice that apply not only to the music we choose to teach but the learning environment that we cultivate for and with our students.

The connection between education and democracy

In order to understand urban schools, you must recognize the connection between schools and the broader social context. If schools are a microcosm of American society, then schools have an obligation to enculturate students as participants in a democracy.[1] Consequently, questions of fairness, equity, and justice are not only central to teacher-student relationships but to the institution of schooling as well. All teachers, then, have a greater responsibility than just teaching their content area.

However, most college teacher education programs (including music education) focus exclusively on what and how to teach. As music education students, we are taught how to direct ensembles, how to choose appropriate repertoire, how to teach music to young children, how to play traditional band and orchestra instruments, etc. Although these are necessary skills in the pedagogy of teaching music, how often do we talk about issues of fairness such as providing all students with access to instrument lessons despite family income or teaching about power relationships when learning a spiritual? What about cutting back on music instruction to give more time for testing preparation? Do we stop to ask why regional and all-state ensembles are overwhelmingly White? Have we considered the ramifications of young children who attend preschool programs rich with arts experiences versus those whose parents can't afford preschool?

These are important issues to contemplate because they broaden our perspective about the purpose of art in our nation. As music educators, we believe that music is the right of every child – that music is an avenue for a kind of knowing that is different from that in science, math, or language arts. For this reason, making music while engaging in critical/creative thinking leads to a visceral experience that is unique to the arts and, therefore, distinct from other disciplines. Dennis Creedon states:

> To deny urban children arts education is societal child abuse. For those who feel that we can't afford arts education, we must remind them about the cost of a child who drops out of school or becomes incarcerated. A full education that includes the arts is the insurance we pay for our nation's democracy.[2]

Note that Creedon makes two connected statements: Arts education is essential for all students, and the arts insure our nation's democracy. This suggests that teaching music as democratic practice involves not only the skills and understandings needed to participate fully in music activity but an attentiveness to justice as well. However, because artists often create works that reflect social commentary, their work in non-democratic societies can be threatening and subject to severe repercussions. For instance, Stalin and Mao would only tolerate music that had a "positive" political message. The Taliban destroyed musical instruments in an attempt to disallow music of the people. Other historical instances abound and raise provocative questions about the very essence of art within a social/political context. Such questions are valuable prompts for helping students recognize the power of music beyond a school concert.

What, then, does a democratic music program look like? At the classroom level, for example, the teacher might examine his/her/their curriculum for kinds of music that present substantial inclusion of non-Western genres, women composers, popular musics, and other genres often neglected in favor of Western art music. At the school level, a music teacher might approach the principal with a well-articulated argument for eliminating the practice of taking away a student's music class for remedial work or as punishment for some infraction. At the regional level, the music teacher might question whether select state-sponsored ensembles are truly accessible to all who qualify. According to Vincent Bates:

> On an even playing field, all students would have access to high-quality musical instruments, private instruction from highly qualified teachers, no fees for assigned uniforms or other concert attire, adequate funds to participate fully in music-related trips, reliable transportation to and from lessons and before- and after-school practices or performances, and anything else that either is required or will significantly increase the likelihood of success in the music program. [3]

The examples given in the previous paragraph could easily relate to any school district. In the urban school, however, questions of fairness and equity are even more critical because so many instances of inequality already exist. When we stop to think about these questions and consider the ramifications that these issues have in society, we acknowledge that music teaching has social implications in addition to the art and craft of making music. For instance, it also involves sensitivity to inequities in schooling that urban students face when compared to their more affluent counterparts.

Consider the following scenario: Black History Month is an opportunity for music teachers to place special emphasis on the music and lives of Black composers. Some teachers might ask students to choose a favorite black artist, either contemporary or from the past, and write a report. Other teachers might arrange an assembly for students to sing some Civil Rights songs with the entire school. However, simply engaging in these activities without addressing the challenges that Black artists faced both in the past and present sidesteps the intent of reflecting on the Black experience.

What if a middle school general music teacher engaged students in a discussion about the role of music in racial struggles as a starting point for introducing a song of the Civil Rights era or a contemporary Black artist? Further, suppose that same teacher asked students to record the song on GarageBand. Then, that teacher or students could choose excerpts from speeches of Martin Luther King, Malcolm X, or Sojourner Truth to create a digital piece by interpolating spoken excerpts as an introduction or insertion at poignant places in the music (a successful project for urban middle school students designed by a student teacher from my university).

This helps students delve into the meaning and purpose of the music rather than simply writing a report or singing a song. It directly addresses the marginalization of Blacks in historical and contemporary times that, in turn, sets into motion the critical thinking necessary to connect the arts with matters of social justice. Patricia Collins writes, "In essence, depending on where you stand, American democracy constitutes a reality, a promise, a possibility, or a problem."[4] Projects, such as the example described above, bring to light how different people envision democracy depending on their experiences, the history, and the context in which they live.

Democracy and artistic citizenship

A democracy depends on the ability of people to work together toward a humane and purposeful life for all citizens. A democracy, then, is more than casting a ballot but rather the good sense to build communities that are inclusive, respectful of different perspectives, and socially responsible for the welfare of others.[5] Given that most children receive their formal education through public schools, developing democratic habits of mind and justice serve an important mission in sustaining a healthy, vibrant democracy.[6]

Talking about citizenship and civic responsibility, however, seems so distant from what is traditionally conceived as music education. Yet, Paul Woodford argues against music teachers who solely identify themselves as performers with the responsibility of replicating traditional Western music practices. He advocates, instead, for music teachers who are "politically aware and disposed to question and challenge the professional status quo."[7] In addition, "maximum individual development" and "full participation in the human conversation" have everything to do with arts, for it is through the arts that one experiences the human condition.

David Elliot, Marissa Silverman, and Wayne Bowman offer the term "artistic citizenship."[8] By this, Elliot explains that music making is not the exclusive province of the performer on stage, the composer working on a score, or the cantor in a synagogue. Artistic citizenship refers to "music makers of *all* ages and abilities who *put their music making to work* to facilitate and create positive social and cultural transformations – including, of course, advances in democracy and social justice."[9]

The concept of artistic citizenship, then, involves two key factors. First, music making is inclusive of everyone, whether five years old or ninety-five years old, and, second, music making has a role in furthering ideals of democracy and social justice. For example, teaching children to respectfully listen to their peers and engage in thoughtful discourse in response to a music listening lesson helps them learn a basic tenant of tenant of democracy: appreciating other points of view and respecting the right of every person to participate. Middle school adolescents who organize a concert to raise money for a student who needs costly surgery learn about the power of like-minded individuals in helping one of their own. High school music students who create a musical-digital piece, after studying Beethoven's life, recognize the achievements of persons with disabilities and celebrate the human spirit despite life's challenges.

Achieving the transformation that students experience when musicing in a socially responsible way need not be a huge undertaking – it can be as simple as using music to help students create a kinder, more peaceful classroom. The intent, however, is *not* one of classroom management but rather to facilitate habits of coexistence reflective of an emerging and evolving democracy. Likewise, efforts to connect music making with social themes such as alienation, hope, or oppression help students widen their perspective of the world in which they live.

What does a democratically based music classroom look like?

The first indication of a democratic classroom involves the role of the teacher and the student. When entering a music class, one would see a music teacher who encourages students to make sense of what they are learning, whether in a rehearsal or general music setting. The kinds of questions that engage students in constructing their own ideas about music generally involve question that start with "why," "how," "when," "suppose," "what," etc. For example, *Why do national anthems have similar musical features? How does culture play a role in African music? When would you breathe to achieve a long musical line in this song? Suppose you got to choose one piece of music to send into outer space; what would it be? What might you consider when deciding the order of music for our program?*

Second, music making is central to the learning process and is characterized by thinking critically and creatively about musical choices. Such activities include performing, composing, improvising, and listening to a variety of genres ranging from popular music to non-western to Western art music. Along with active listening, the teacher makes students aware that every musical artifact has a story, not necessarily a narrative, but something that belongs to a certain time, place, and cultural context.

Third, there is a general sense of well-being among the students. They value what others say whether or not they are in agreement. There is mutual respect between the teacher and students as well as among the students themselves. In addition, there is respect for materials in the classroom such as instruments, stands, or electronic devises. Materials are handled with care and returned to their space in the classroom.

Fourth, the teacher and students continually engage in community building. Music class is a time to celebrate each student's contribution. It is a place for making music together and uniting in that single purpose. Differences in race/ethnicity, gender, religion, sexual orientation, gender, or musical talent are honored as basic human rights via whose music is represented, whose culture is woven into the fabric of the lesson, and who participates in the music making experience.

Fifth, music teachers recognizes that teaching is inherently a political act and strives to contemporize their teaching by relating instruction to the social climate in which students live. There is a conscious effort to make connections between art and themes of social justice. When, for example, 9/11 took place, many teachers sought ways to help their students find ways of coping with loss, fear, and confusion. Some music teachers helped students compose songs in dedication to the lives lost. Others had students create digital stories of peace and hope to a related piece of music. In short, artists bring a perspective to social themes in a way that other disciplines cannot.

What is social justice?

Although democracy and social justice are often used interchangeably, social justice implies action, transformation, and change agency in the pursuit of a more just democratic nation. Social justice has its roots in valuing humanity and human life.[10] Those who engage in social justice seek to disempower inequity and oppression for the purpose of enlarging human freedoms, such as the freedom to shape one's life and environment.[11] Because education involves actions that affect human beings, issues of social justice such as curriculum, policy mandates, and cultural responsiveness are always present.

Teaching in and for a democracy, with sensitivity to issues of social justice, may at first seem overwhelming. Without question, good music teachers are among the busiest teachers in the field and often stretched way too thin. Some worry that democratic practice is yet another "add-on" to everything else they have on their plate.[12] On the contrary, teaching for democratic practice and social justice are not things that you "do" but rather a philosophical grounding for everything that takes place in the music class. The persistence of asking open-ended questions that help students make sense of what they are learning and the building of a community in which students listen to each other enhance the curriculum. Maintaining a peaceable classroom and providing substantive problem-solving music activities enrich the music making experience for all involved. These are not separate, disjointed activities in the music curriculum. It is an *approach* to music teaching based on the premise that dispositions of creative, critical thinking; social consciousness; and getting along with others prepare students for sustaining a healthy democracy.

Social justice requires students and teachers to not only recognize issues of inequity and injustice but also take action to address the situation.[13] This suggests that part of teaching music is helping students become autonomous through relevant and meaningful decision-making. According to Gary Spruce,

> One of the defining characteristics of a socially just approach to music education is taken to be the opportunity for students not only to 'participate' in music education, but also be 'included' in it as their voices being heard in decisions about curriculum and pedagogy and in the construction of musical knowledge, understanding, and *value*.[14]

Organizing instruction so that students have a voice teaches students to weigh options and consider criteria in order to come to a decision. With the tragic mass shooting at Marjory Stoneman Douglas High School in Parkland, Florida (2018), it was the groundswell of students, not legislators, who organized protest rallies in Washington and in schools across the country. The message – "Schools are no longer safe places for us. What are you going to do to preserve the sanctity of our educational institutions?" – captured national attention. Like many other protest rallies in history, it was the young people – those very same students in our classrooms – who galvanized the call for unity and justice.

Along the same lines, the music of youth has always been responsive to social injustice. Woodstock, for instance, represented a large-scale youth-inspired movement in support of civil rights and ending the Vietnam War. Billed as a three-day festival for peace and music, many iconic songs, bands, and artists emerged from this event and remain classics in popular music today. Learning about the role of music in a political context reiterates how people turned to music to bring about change.

According to David Elliott, "We need to enable our students to develop *musical replies* to the social, cultural, moral, and political dilemmas of today and tomorrow by creating musical (or hybrid musical, bodily, and visual) expressions of social problems."[15] Such teaching acknowledges the relevancy of social and political events in students' lives, while providing music experiences that teach about resistance and resilience.[16] In doing so, we are furthering the development of artistic citizens who gradually acquire the tools and habits of mind for full participation in a democracy.

Teaching music for democratic practice and social justice

As stated earlier, democratic classrooms have a different look and feel from other types of learning spaces. Most importantly, the role of the teacher and the student differs considerably from a traditional teaching model, which Paolo Freire describes as the "banking model."[17] In this model, the teacher exhibits full responsibility for the instruction process with the student as the passive recipient of information. In a democratic model, the teacher constantly poses questions and problem-solving activities that encourage students to construct their own understanding of concepts and content. It is the difference, for instance, between a music listening activity where students follow a chart that indicates what elements of music to hear versus a listening lesson in which students engage in discussion that focuses not only on the musical content but the meaning of the music within its cultural context as well.

In essence, teaching music for democratic practice involves a sharing of knowledge between the teacher and the student with mutual respect for what each brings to the learning environment. Sometimes, music teachers worry that a facilitative approach to learning means less control over the curriculum or a "ban" on direct teaching, such as demonstrating skills toward technical proficiency on an instrument. A democratic approach to teaching music, however, does not diminish the expertise that the music teacher brings to the lesson. Rather, it is a fine balance between knowing when to intercede for the purpose of demonstrating important techniques/concepts and when to give students just enough information for them to solve musical problems independently. Teaching music reading, for instance, can be fairly straightforward in terms of teaching note values and pitches on a staff. In a democratic classroom, the music teacher might take this a step further and, at a later time, share different methods for notating music such as tablature, Gregorian chant, or contemporary graphic notation for the purpose of helping students understand that standard Western notation is useful for certain kinds of music.

Teaching for democratic practice also involves the development of social and collaborative skills toward a community of learners. Knowing students' names, who they are as "people," and the strengths they bring to the classroom is one part of building a community. The other part involves teaching students to socialize respectfully with one another. This includes listening to others without judgment and understanding that everyone has a right to share his/her/their opinion, including the teacher. Such behaviors are not necessarily automatic. They require a lot of modeling, direct teaching, and positive reinforcement so that every student feels safe and valued. Some might argue that teaching the students social skills takes away from teaching music. I submit, however, that unless students support each other and work as a team rather than a collection of individuals, music learning is minimal at best. In the long run, taking the time to develop a peaceful classroom environment contributes exponentially to music learning in the future.

In terms of social justice, Chris Philpott and Jason Kubilius talk about two levels of discourse in the music classroom. Democratic discourse assures that "all students are able to take part . . . in a wide variety of musical knowledge and perspectives."[18] This speaks to the effort that the teacher takes to plan inclusive lessons that present many musical genres, as well as the students' participation in a supportive, non-judgmental environment.

The second level of discourse has to do with helping students recognize issues of inequality and inequity in music and in society. As stated earlier, protest songs from various eras of history provide a good starting point for talking about musical responses to injustices. Learning to sing the various protest songs, discussing the social context of the songs, comparing protest songs, and composing a protest song that addresses a contemporary issue – these activities engage students in thinking about music as a relevant art form in unifying people for a common cause.

Because social justice implies action, sharing student compositions with or performing for others makes the message public. Such action could be as simple as performing for another class with an explanation of why the issue is important to "us." Or, action might be as complex as planning a concert of student works for the school and community. Performance alone, though, is not sufficient in educating the public. Program notes, narratives by the students, or visual or digital displays from the art class give the music purpose and meaning for all participants.

Teaching music through themes of social justice

We often associate social justice with specific political events such as the terrorist attack on the World Trade Towers (9/11) or the fight for LGBTQ rights. There are, however, other ways of bringing social justice themes into the classroom. Issues such as the fragility of our planet or oppression of immigrants illustrate open-ended themes that have relevance to music in many social contexts. The music teacher can build an entire unit of lessons around a social justice theme that provides a framework for the study of music from its artistic, historical, and social implications. Listed below are some starting places for such a unit:

- *Freedom*: Beethoven's *Ninth Symphony*
- *Heroism*: Mussorgsky's "Great Gate of Kiev"
- *Resilience*: "We Shall Overcome"
- *War*: U2's "Sunday Bloody Sunday"
- *Peace*: John Lennon's "Imagine"

What would a justice-themed music unit look like? During a summer music camp with urban teenagers, my colleague and I focused on Beethoven's *Fifth Symphony* as the anchor piece for dealing with themes of heroism and resilience. From a musical standpoint, students learned terms such as sonata-allegro form, motivic development, exposition, development, recapitulation, etc. They learned to sing/play the first and second themes. This provided musical material for a small-group composition project that involved the development of the first motive (using accents, changing the rhythm, changing the tempo, etc.) and the beginning of the second theme. Along with the music making, students discussed aspects of romanticism and historical events, such as the French Revolution, that influenced Beethoven's thinking. They also discussed the heroic aspects of Beethoven's life, including how he shaped the music for generations to come as well as his continued composing despite his gradual descent into deafness.

Over the eight two-hour sessions, students had comprehensive experiences with music, its history, Beethoven's life, and the social context in which the symphony was composed. For the final project, they recorded their earlier composition on Garage Band and added loops with images on iMovie that captured their perspective of heroism/resilience. These short videos became the opening for a public recital featuring works of Beethoven. Thus, the students deconstructed a legendary work of art to reconstruct their own music from an informed, socially conscious perspective while gaining immense appreciation for Beethoven as a composer and a person.

Themes of social justice have as much relevance in the elementary music class as they do in secondary education. Deejay Robinson taught in the Boston Public schools prior to his current position an early childhood general music teacher at an independent school in Cambridge, Massachusetts.[19] As a Black music educator, Robinson is steeped in American history of Black oppression. His lived experiences with stereotyping, discrimination, and the marginalization of Black and Latino voices in music education deepened his resolve to design a curriculum for elementary general music that focuses on issues of social justice:

> I argue that any music education curriculum – studio, classroom, lecture hall, and the board room – that holds itself oblivious to race disparities in American (music) society is denying students learning experiences that are essential to building a diverse field and a better world.[20]

Robinson's second grade curriculum includes both traditional goals in vocal development, rhythmic acuity, and composition/improvisation as well as themes in social justice such as specific cultural/political activities that provide a counter-narrative to White privilege in music and in American society. Over the duration of a year, Robinson addresses identity ("Who am I in relationship to myself and others?"); community ("How is music the same and different in our community/world?"); conscious and unconscious biases in music education ("Why are some musicians forgotten and others known?"); music as a social ritual ("How and to what extent is music used in social settings?"); and the making of a better world ("How has music been used to create a more just and equal world?").[21]

I describe the work of Robinson to illustrate that social justice can be taught in some form at any grade level. In fifth grade, for example, Robinson teaches a special lesson on "The Death of a President." The reference is to John F. Kennedy, who was assassinated on November 22, 1963. As I discussed in Chapter 5, grief and loss are difficult topics yet worthy to address with children/adolescents. Although Kennedy's assassination took place years before Robinson wrote the lesson plan, he crafted a music listening lesson that tied the students' experiences with death or tragedy to this important event in American history.

How did he do this? The lesson began with a discussion about personal experiences with tragedy leading up to an explanation of the November 1963 event. He then showed a video of a performance that the Boston Symphony Orchestra gave the afternoon of the assassination; before Maestro Erich Leinsdorf began to conduct, he announced to the audience that the president had been shot. At that point in the program, Leinsdorf led the orchestra in the funeral march from Beethoven's *Eroica Symphony*. After listening to the music, students were directed to write a short reflection about their response to the music. These responses became the impetus for a longer conversation on music and its role in affecting the human spirit.

Robinson is an educator who takes seriously teaching for democratic practice. He sees the paradoxes and ironies of the ideals of democracy versus the lived realities of those in the margins. As a music teacher, he regards his role in helping students analyze and question these paradoxes through music as a moral obligation. The final paragraph in his article, "A Labor of Love: A Rationale and Second Grade Music Curriculum for a More Just and Equitable World," bears repeating:

> Empowering students to interrogate inequalities in American society and its music education is tedious; but, very, very joyous work. If the field of music education is to end the racial abyss, then, music teachers must be willing to rethink hegemonic curriculums and design a new model of teaching that seeks to empower students to build a better world not only for themselves, but for all who come after.[22]

Hip hop, punk, and social justice

No chapter on democracy and social justice would be complete without the inclusion of the hip hop and punk movement. From a democratic standpoint, this powerful music is rooted in the protest of youth against race/ethnicity, culture, and identity.[23] Its relevance notwithstanding, hip hop, in particular, represents a musical form that has captured the rapt attention of youth throughout the world. According to Collins, "It is important to remember that youth have been on the front line of important questions of envisioning democratic possibilities in a U.S. and a global context."[24] To avoid the acknowledgment of hip hop and punk as music worthy of study for all students leaves a gaping hole when teaching music as democratic practice.

As a cultural phenomenon, I have chosen to focus on hip hop and its close cousin punk because of their impact on the social consciousness of youth. Hip hop began in the streets of South Bronx, New York, where poor Black youth gave voice to condemnation of their lived experience with poverty, race, gangs, death, marginalization, joblessness, and street violence. "Hip hop music, no matter how widely accepted in the mainstream," states Bakari Kitwana "isn't entertainment alone; it's a voice of the voiceless."[25] Punk music, on the other hand, originated in White suburbia in the 1970s, protesting the ills of capitalism and the dominant class. Both hip hop and punk were born of youth culture and characterized resistance, rebellion, and anti-establishment.[26]

Hip hop, as an art form, includes five key elements: tagging (graffiti art), b-boying (break-dancing), DJ-ing (spinning and scratching records), MC-ing or rapping, and fashion.[27] "So, today, when we speak of hip-hop culture, we are also referencing a hip-hop-specific language, body language, fashion, style, sensibility and worldview."[28] Although there are non-musical elements of hip hop, this chapter will use the terms "hip hop music" and "rap music" interchangeably.

DIY Punk or Do It Yourself Punk formed a new wave of anarchy against the dominant and established order.[29] The punk movement was characterized by loud, fast, angry music along with drugs and alcohol, destruction of property, and spiked clothing. Although hip hop and punk originated from different social groups, the message was similar as "a form of overt rebellion and transgression" against the dominant class.[30]

Beth Ballliro states, "The street and hip-hop stylistic roots of young, urban, self-actualized artists deserve to be nourished as assets, and must inform the pedagogy and advocacy for access in art education."[31] Music teachers, however, often have reservations about rap and hip hop in the classroom. Some are concerned about the misogynistic and often violent text, believing that rap/hip hop is inappropriate for school settings. Others feel that students are saturated with music of today's culture and need to broaden their repertoire of musical genres. Still others feel that rap and hip hop are not a viable form of music. The following list responds to some of the primary concerns:

1   *The language is too explicit for school*: Unquestionably, the cursing and misogynistic lyrics are sometimes so overbearing that they divert the listener's attention from the real message of the song. It should also be noted that much of what students hear on the radio or other musical devices today has been greatly influenced by "what sells." The beginnings of hip hop had much more focus on themes of social justice; but as hip hop became corporatized, it's original intent was lost, so much so that Tricia Rose, in her book *The Hip Hop Wars: What We Talk About and When We Talk About Hip Hop – and Why It Matters*, defines this as the "crisis of hip hop."[32] Consequently, much of the commercial hip hop has messages and language counter to the earlier roots of hip hop and is not as useful for teaching. Some rap artists, however, such as Mos Def and Common, are making socially conscious music.

There are several considerations to keep in mind when choosing hip hop music: First, there are classic examples of hip hop music from the

1970s–1980s, as well as some contemporary artists (e.g. MF Doom, Kid Cudi, Common, and Lupe Fiasco), that present lyrics with no or a minimum of explicit language. Second, some explicit language is part of the street talk that gives the hip hop and punk its authenticity – which is why it makes little sense to play a "clean" version as the students already know the original version.

2 *The content, including pimps, drugs, and violence, is inappropriate for discussion:* To acknowledge this important concern, one must be clear about the distinction between socially conscious hip hop and commercial hip hop. When advances in technology and mass marketing began in the 1990s, hip hop themes about the serious conditions that shaped the black ghetto (e.g. joblessness, marginalization, race, economic instability) dissolved into themes that the market proliferated – themes about gangstas, pimps, and sexual exploitation, which created biased views that reinforced stereotypes of the black ghetto. Although not all rappers recede into this type of denigration, much of it is unfortunately accessible to children/adolescents via technological devices and not representative of the forces that birthed hip hop.

Hip hop in its earlier days and that which has gone "underground," however, is closer to the ideals of hip hop as a socially progressive, creative art form from which students have much to learn. "Hip hop was born and grew up under extreme social and economic pressure; its powerful tales of fun, affirmation, and suffering should be honored but also recognized as reflections of the stress under which it was bought into creation."[33] The themes represent youth protest against social problems that plague the inner cities. These themes, especially for urban students, reflect their lived experiences. Using hip hop as a teaching tool provides a safe space for reflecting on relevant issues and exploring reasonable mechanisms for developing resistance and resilience.

3 *Young students are not old enough to deal with issues of poverty, broken relationships, or gang activity:* Because young children from the urban settings often grow up under these conditions, it makes sense to address these issues on a level that is age-appropriate. Jerome Bruner said, "the foundations of any subject may be taught to anybody at any age in some form."[34] Some entry points might include bullying or missing someone that was a part of their life (e.g. the death or incarceration of a family member).

4 *Teachers should be teaching music that students don't know, e.g. classical, rather than working with music that they listen to all the time:* There is no reason why any genre of music should supplant another. Hip hop is valuable because it has particular relevance to the urban student. In fact, hip hop is so globalized in the current times that most students are familiar and committed to this music. However, classical, pop, non-Western, and jazz deserve recognition as well. It is not unusual to start with a hip hop song and branch into other relevant musics *without implying* that one has more value than the other.

5   *I don't know enough about hip hop to include it into my curriculum:* Here is an opportune moment for students to switch roles with the teacher. Having students share their favorite (approved) hip hop song, artist, or band gives students not only a chance to show what they know about music that means something important to them but also places the music teacher in the role as a learner. Teachers cannot know everything and, by taking an active interest in "new" music, models the kind of behavior one expects from the students.

6   *What about meeting the state/national standards and assessment plans?* If you are teaching well, then you are teaching through the standards. Hip hop and punk music are artistic tools in the same light as other musics. Hip hop is relevant to analysis, theoretical content, discussion about lyrics, and history. Its form is often stylistically similar to many vocal pieces throughout different genres of music. In addition, hip hop has its roots in African music and the music of African Americans. Its social relevance depends not only on the music selected but, for the most part, represents culturally responsive teaching for many different races and ethnicities as well. In terms of assessment, hip hop and punk music are as viable forms of music as jazz, classical, and non-Western musics. Consequently, any type of music need not alter assessment plans.

Why hip hop and punk in music class?

Today, rap and hip hop are too enmeshed in students' lives to ignore this very rich material in music teaching. In fact, most of our students have lived their whole lives with this music. For several decades, hip hop and punk have provided a musical form that gives critical insight into the lives and messages of those overlooked in society. Although rap/hip hop started with African Americans, it is now a worldwide phenomenon.

Contemporary urban musicians use the richness of hip hop, punk, and other popular musics to take a political stand on issues of inequality. There is a rawness and beauty to this music that provides authentic entre to the urban students' personal stories and experiences. According to Roymieco Carter, "The teaching of aesthetics in urban education is better understood if tied to lived experiences within the urban environment."[35] For that reason, music teachers who teach in urban schools have a potent platform for acknowledging the important role that music plays in giving voice to those who are disenfranchised. Hip hop, rap, soul, R&B, and punk represent music that shapes the aesthetic culture of urban students and requires teachers to reframe their idea of what music is and what music is valued.

In short, the messages of punk and hip hop music reflect important issues of social concern, especially for urban students. Because they originated from urban youth, this music is particularly relevant in providing strong examples of resistance to oppression. Although the language and imagery of hip hop and punk may push the boundaries of what is appropriate in a school setting, I have tried to identify songs, in the next section, that have social themes and a minimum of explicit

language. At the same time, offensive language can also become a unique opportunity for older adolescents to think about questions such as, "What purpose does
questionable language serve in rap?" "Does the inclusion of this language enhance
or detract from the message of rap?" "What is the message about women and why
would rappers so often degrade women in their music?" "Could this piece of rap
convey the same message without explicit language?" In the past, I have consulted
with my supervisor before having some of these conversations so that he/she is
aware of the dialogue to take place and might offer important suggestions for navigating such a conversation.

I am not suggesting that punk and hip hop comprise the entire music curriculum but rather that the social context of punk and hip hop can be a significant
venue for discussing issues relevant to youth. Race, poverty, alienation, homeless-
ness, and other oppressive conditions underlie the conditions for many youths in
American society today. For this reason, carefully selected examples of punk and
hip hop provide an avenue that has a decided impact on students from the urban
schools. For teachers, Ladson-Billings states:

> The decision to introduce hip-hop as a form of protest and social justice art
> requires a serious of pedagogical decisions. Work on culturally relevant peda-
> gogy suggests that teacher who focus on student learning, cultural compe-
> tence, and critical consciousness are more likely to be successful with students
> of color who have struggled to experience school-based excellence.[36]

Three songs and one album for teaching themes of social justice

The book, *Rebel Music: Resistance Through Hip Hop and Punk*,[37] deserves a place
on every music teacher's shelf who is committed to popular music that highlights
themes of social justice. This book is divided into social justice themes, e.g. oppression, resistance, marginalization, respect, and community. Each section highlights
two songs (hip hop and punk) that represent classic examples of the music from
different eras in hip hop/punk history. For music teachers who want to include
hip hop and punk but feel somewhat lacking in their personal repertoire, this is an
accessible and substantive collections of essays on selected classic pieces from The
Game and Lil Wayne to Tupac to Green Day.

One of the early punk songs, "Petroleum Distillation" by Fifteen, is a good
example of a song that protests capitalism, pollution of the Earth, and autonomy as
freedom from oppression.[38] A particularly relevant part of the song addresses emis-
sions from cars, toxic waste, and other forms of pollution.[39] Because many schools
celebrate Earth Day, "Petroleum Distillation" provides much food for thought
about man's "assault" on the Earth as well as other themes about oppression. True
to punk form, the song provokes our thinking about how to *take it upon ourselves* to
address these oppressive conditions (personal autonomy).

Zach Furnass warns that the lyrics alone are not sufficient in grasping a song without listening carefully to the music:

> We can't really learn anything significant about a piece of music by extract-
> ing it from the larger social, cultural, and political contexts . . . it's like trying
> to learn something interesting about a person without knowing where she's
> from, how she spends her time, what her family is like, and what kinds of
> things make her curious, passionate, depressed, or delighted.[40]

For that reason, any serious study of punk or hip hop requires examination of both lyrics and music.

Between 1987 and 1992, "no act in the history of hip hop *felt* more important than Public Enemy."[41] The impact of this band's radical music projected new sonic landscapes and inventive lyrics that paved the way for hip hop artists to come. When Spike Lee produced his provocative movie *Do the Right Thing*, he asked Public Enemy to create the theme song. The song, "Fight the Power" became a rallying cry for disparities in race, housing, sexuality, gender, employment, and police brutality. As David Stovall reflects on his own experience hearing "Fight the Power," "I was affirmed by the suggestion of taking power rather than asking for it."[42]

Although this song was released in 1989, these themes are as relevant today as they were during that time period. Because urban students often confront home-lessness, joblessness, violence, and gang activity, the theme of resistance is particu-larly compelling in helping students consider non-violent forms of holding their ground. Writing songs with strong lyrics, creating music videos, holding protest marches, and composing letters to politicians help students learn strategies of resist-ance with issues that are critical to their life space. Teachers must help subvert the urge for students to engage in physical violence by considering more democratic acts of civil disobedience. According to Stovall, "We must use this context to create thoughtful, clear, justice-oriented curriculum that works to develop the skills of our students to navigate and change the current reality."[43]

Hip hop as a form of socio-political philosophy has been included in many disciplines including music, language arts, and philosophy. In its early days, as well as today, hip hop was (is) dominated by men of color, thus rhyming through the lens of the male rapper.[44] Often, women are represented as sexual objects for misogynistic commentary. Gradually women MC's and rappers emerged, bringing a fresh view to issues of male dominance. Queen Latifah was one of those rappers who spoke out for the marginalized women in her song, "Ladies First," released on the album, *All Hail the Queen*, in 1989. According to Noell Chaadock,

> Queen Latifah gave us a unique perspective through a Black feminist philos-
> ophy. Women of color who produce Hip Hop philosophy and Black femi-
> nism are not only responding to race and poverty; they are also responding to
> male dominance and oppression within Hip Hop.[45]

"From the start, Latifah was a phenomenon: her natural charisma, warmth, and sense of dignity appealed to round-the-way kids and suburban rap fans alike."[46] Fortunately, hip hop provided a vehicle where Queen Latifah could express her philosophical views, which foreshadowed the beginning of Black feminism. Her song exalts women without criticizing men.[47] Free of offensive lyrics, it is a song that is accessible for school students as a prompt for talking about inclusion in music, women composers, and women artists.

Often referred to as the "greatest rapper alive" and the "voice of Black America," Kendrick Lamar was a street kid living with poverty and gang violence. He is currently (at time of this writing) one of the biggest rap stars in America. In 2018, his album, *Damn*, won the Pulitzer Prize for music. This astounding accomplishment earned Lamar the first Pulitzer ever awarded to a rap artist. Since 1943, the prize had been traditionally awarded to classical artists and, more recently, three jazz musicians: Wynton Marsalis, Ornette Coleman, and Henry Threadgill. That *Damn* won the Pulitzer Prize in a popular music genre, among more traditional musics, insures hip hop not only as a recognized form of music but an elegant statement about the music itself.[48] Dorian Lynsky wrote, "His combination of technical virtuosity, moral complexity, political acuity, wit, empathy, and musical depth and breadth makes him the only MC who can unite teenage hip hop fans, Golden Age aficionados and people who barely follow the genre."[49]

Lamar's artistry has been called "unapologetically Black" – that his music honors Black culture while avoiding the lens of a "White gaze."[50] His album is listed in the top 10 albums of 2017 in *The Atlantic* and other publications, where he is broadly known as the King of Hip Hop.[51] According to Lynsky, "The award says less about hip-hop at large than it does about Lamar's exceptional place in American culture." Moreover, "Lamar's latest album, *Damn*, speaks about the condemnation of black Americans in this country and calls for individuals to re-evaluate themselves and seek out the change that they can create."[52] Consequently, Kendrick Lamar deserves a hard look when examining hip hop music and social justice.

Other rappers include Grammy Award winner Chance the Rapper, who made his first EP *10 Day* when he was suspended from his public school for ten days in West Chatham, Chicago. Jessica Finkelstein (email message to author, April 8, 2018) writes, "Not only is Chance an example of success without corporate influence, experience, or money, but he is an example of an upstanding citizen who works towards social justice in a city whose public education has been declining for several years." Jamila Woods, another hip hop artist, raps about social justice for Black women who are among the most underserved citizens in this country. Both Chance the Rapper and Jamila Woods have written lyrics that are especially poignant and relevant to students in the urban schools.

Conclusion

This chapter brings together critical themes throughout the book, such as cultural responsiveness, pedagogical nurturing, access to knowledge, and the purpose of schools. The importance of democracy and social justice in the music teacher's lexicon cannot be over-emphasized. Estelle Jorgensen adds, "Music educators *ought* to be concerned with matters of justice among other things."[53] Such concerns include *whose* music is taught, *what counts* as musical knowledge, *who* participates in music experiences, and *how* assessments are implemented.[54] According to Ruth Wright, "Students are very well aware that certain subjects, such as music, as it is delivered in many traditional pedagogic models, are more accessible to 'elite' students." And further, "Students who exclude themselves from participation in music because they recognize themselves as 'non-elite' are therefore acknowledging that they know the rules of this particular game and recognize that they are unlikely to win it."[55]

Teachers take on a dual role when teaching for democratic practice and social justice. On one hand, teachers need to think about and plan curriculum that is inclusive, culturally responsive, and musically challenging. On the other hand, teachers must recognize inequities and oppression within the classroom or school and take non-confrontational positions to address these issues. Music teachers may recognize these inequities but not know the appropriate avenues for taking up the cause.

Although this book encourages teachers to speak out, one must realize that not all teachers/administrators will value this effort. According to Collins, "They see politics as somehow lying outside the classroom door and the ivory tower. But ... inequalities are produced within the educational system, just as schools are essential to inequality's survival."[56] Making changes in a deeply entrenched system is not only difficult for one person but may have negative implications for non-tenured teachers. Knowing the political landscape is always the first step in working toward change. Forming a committee of like-minded teachers with the inclusion of an interested administrator, as a second step, may have more strength in facilitating change.

As music teachers, there are plenty of issues of democracy and social justice to take under our wing. From a curricular point of view, take a look at the music presented throughout the year. Does your curriculum include genres such as non-Western music, women composers, contemporary composers, musicians of color, and popular music in equal emphasis with Western art music? Are these forms of music a prompt for meaningful discussions about oppression, marginalization, and the role of music in its historical context, etc.? Do programmatic decisions for ensemble performances include education beyond the notes on the page? Do all students have access to music activities that honor the music of their culture? Have students interrogated avenues of resistance for making the music program more socially just?

In current times, it seems that the terms "democracy" and "social justice" are used indiscriminately to describe anything from a simply singing a freedom song from South Africa to defining classroom rules of conduct. Although these activities might lead to more socially just experiences, by themselves they do not engage students in the full participation of democratic practice. The arts are a powerful means of expression. It takes a courageous teacher to design lessons that not only develop musical competence but social consciousness as well. As Woodford states, "If nothing else, the pursuit of a democratic aim or purpose through music education should motivate children to care more about, and thus to become more involved in, the wider musical and social world around them."[57]

Discussion questions

1   Think about your own school experiences. Did you have any role models that exemplified teaching as democratic practice? Describe how these teachers created a democratic classroom.
2   Identify a current issue of oppression or disadvantaged people. How could you create a music learning experience based on this issue that includes both musical and social justice objectives?
3   List some hip hop songs or artists that could form the basis of a socially conscious music lesson. How would you defend your musical choices to a principal or parent?

References

1   DeLorenzo, Lisa C. 2016. "Introduction." In *Giving Voice to Democracy in Music Education*, edited by Lisa C. DeLorenzo, 1–9. New York: Routledge; Sodor, Roger. 2001. "Education for Democracy: The Foundation for Democratic Character." In *Developing Democratic Character in the Young*, edited by Roger Sodor, John I. Goodlad, and Timothy J. McMannon, 185–205. San Francisco: Jossey-Bass.
2   Creedon, Dennis W. 2011. "Fight the Stress of Urban Education with the Arts." *Phi Delta Kappan, 96* (6): 36.
3   Bates, Vincent C. 2012. "Social Class and School Music." *Music Educators Journal, 98* (4): 5. doi: 10.1177/0027432112442944
4   Collins, Patricia C. 2009. *Another Kind of Public Education: Race, Schools, the Media, and Democratic Possibilities*. Boston: Beacon Press: 7.
5   Darling-Hammond, Linda. 1977. "Education, Equity, and the Right to Learn." In *The Public Purpose of Education and Schooling*, edited by John I. Goodlad and Timothy J. McMannon, 41–54. San Francisco: Jossey-Bass: 4; Dewey, John. 2007. *Democracy and Education*. Middlesex: Echo Library; Richard Neumann. 2008. "American Democracy at Risk." *Phi Delta Kappan, 89* (5): 328–338.
6   Sodor, Roger. 1996. "Teaching the Teachers of the People." in *Democracy, Education, and the Schools*, edited by Roger Sodor, 244–274. San Francisco: Jossey-Bass.
7   Woodford, Paul G. 2005. *Democracy and Music Education*. Bloomington, IN: Indiana University Press: 23.
8   Elliott, David J., Marissa Silverman, and Wayne D. Bowman. 2016. "Artistic Citizenship: Introduction, Aims, and Overview." In *Artistic Citizenship: Artistry, Social Responsibility, and Ethical Praxis*, edited by David J. Elliot, Marissa Silverman, and Wayne D. Bowman, 3–21. New York: Oxford University Press.
9   Elliott, David J. 2016. "Artistic Citizenship, Personhood, and Music Education." In *Giving Voice to Democracy in Music Education*, edited by Lisa C. DeLorenzo. New York: Routledge.
10 Jorgensen, Estelle R. 2015. "Intersecting Social Justices and Music Education." In *The Oxford Handbook of Social Justice in Music Education*, edited by Cathy Benedict, Patrick Schmidt, Gary Spruce, and Paul Woodford, 7–28. New York: Oxford University Press.

11 Jahan, Selim. 2016. *Human Development Report 2016: Human Development for Everyone.* New York: United Nations Development Programme.

12 Sapon-Shevin, Mara. 2008. "Teachable Moments for Social Justice." *Independent School,* 67 (3): 44–47.

13 Lucas, Tamara. 2005. "Fostering a Commitment to Social Justice Through Service Learning in a Teacher Education Course." In *Teacher Education for Democracy and Social Justice,* edited by Nicholas M. Michelli and David Lee Keiser, 167–188. New York: Routledge.

14 Spruce, Gary. 2015. "Music Education, Social Justice, and the 'Student Voice'." In *The Oxford Handbook of Social Justice in Music Education,* edited by Cathy Benedict, Patrick Schmidt, Gary Spruce, and Paul Woodford, 287–301. New York: Oxford University Press: 288.

15 Elliott. "Artistic Citizenship, Personhood, and Music Education." 30.

16 Dylan Smith, Gareth. 2016. "Neoliberalism and Symbolic Violence in Higher Music Education." In *Giving Voice to Democracy in Music Education,* edited by Lisa C. DeLorenzo, 65–84. New York: Routledge.

17 Freire, Paulo. 1990. *Pedagogy of the Oppressed.* Translated by Myra Bergman Ramos. New York: Continuum.

18 Philpott, Chris and Jason Kubilius. 2015. "Social Justice in the English Secondary Music Classroom." In *The Oxford Handbook of Social Justice in Music Education,* edited by Cathy Benedict, Patrick Schmidt, Gary Spruce, and Paul Woodford, 426–445. New York: Oxford University Press: 427.

19 Robinson, DeeJay. 2017. "A Labor of Love: A Rationale and Second Grade Music Curriculum for a More Just and Equitable World." *Topics,* 3: 75–116.

20 Ibid., 97.

21 Ibid., 108.

22 Ibid., 99.

23 Pulido, Isaura. 2009. "Music Fit for Us Minorities: Latina/os Use of Hip Hop as Pedagogy and Interpretive Framework to Negotiate and Challenge Racism." *Equity & Excellence in Education,* 42 (1): 67–85. doi: 10.1080/10665680802631253

24 Collins. *Another Kind of Public Education*: 51.

25 Kitwana, Bakari. 2005. *Why White Kids Love Hip Hop: Wankstas, Wiggers, Wannabees, and the New Reality of Race in America.* New York: Basic Books: xiii.

26 Parmar, Priya, Anthony J Nocella II, Scott Robertson, and Martha Diaz. 2015. "Introduction." In *Rebel Music: Resistance through Hip Hop and Punk,* edited by Priya Parmar, Anthony J Nocella II, Scott Robertson, and Martha Diaz, xix–xviii. Charlotte, NC: Information Age Publishing.

27 Ladson-Billings, Gloria. 2015. "You Gotta Fight the Power: The Place of Music in Social Justice Education." In *The Oxford Handbook of Social Justice in Music Education,* edited by Cathy Benedict, Patrick Schmidt, Gary Spruce, and Paul Woodford, 406–419. New York: Oxford University Press.

28 Kitwana. *Why White Kids Love Hip Hop*: xxii.

29 Parmar, Nocella, Robertson, and Diaz. *Rebel Music.*

30 Anyon, Jean. 2015. *Radical Possibilities.* New York: Routledge: 169.

31 Balliro, Beth. 2015. "Access and Failure." *Journal of Social Theory in Art Education,* 35: 4.

32 Rose, Tricia. 2008. *Hip Hop Wars: What We Talk About When We Talk About Hip Hop -and Why It Matters.* New York: Basic Books.

33 Parmar, Nocella, Robertson, and Diaz. *Rebel Music*: xxi.

34 Bruner, Jerome. 1960/1977. *The Process of Education.* Cambridge, MA: Harvard University Press: 12.

35 Carter, Roymieco A. 2007. "Can Aesthetics Be Taught in Urban Education?" In *19 Urban Questions: Teaching in the City*, edited by Shirley R. Steinberg and Joe L. Kincheloe, 229–244. New York: Peter Lang: 243.

36 Ladson-Billing. "You Gotta Fight the Power." 415.

37 Parmar. *Rebel Music.*

38 Furness, Zach. 2015. "Petroleum Distillation by Fifteen." In *Rebel Music: Resistance Through Hip Hop and Funk*, edited by Priya Parmar, Anthony J Nocella II, Scott Robertson, and Martha Diaz, 13–18. Charlotte, NC: Information Age Publishing.

39 Ibid.

40 Ibid., 15.

41 Light, Alan. 1999. "Public Enemy." In *The Vibe History of Hip Hop*, edited by Alan Light, 165–175. New York: Three Rivers Press: 165.

42 Stovall, David. 2015. "'Fight the Power' by Public Enemy." In *Rebel Music: Resistance Through Hip Hop and Funk*, edited by Priya Parmar, Anthony J Nocella II, Scott Robertson, and Martha Diaz, 43–51. Charlotte, NC: Information Age Publishing: 47.

43 Ibid., 44.

44 Jamison, Laura. 1999. "Ladies First." In *The Vibe History of Hip Hop*, edited by Alan Light, 177–185. New York: Three Rivers Press.

45 Chaddock. Noelle. 2015. "Ladies First by Queen Latifah." In *Rebel Music: Resistance through Hip Hop and Funk*, edited by Priya Parmar, Anthony J Nocella II, Scott Robertson, and Martha Diaz, 21–27. Charlotte, NC: Information Age Publishing: 22.

46 Jamison. "Ladies First." 183.

47 Ibid., 183.

48 Coscarelli, Joe. 2018. "Kendrick Lamar Wins Pulitzer in 'Big Moment for Hip-Hop.'" *New York Times*, April 16. www.nytimes.com/2018/04/16/arts/music/kendrick-lamar-pulitzer-prize-damn.html

49 Lynskey, Dorian. 2018. "From Street Kid to Pulitzer: Why Kendrick Lamar Deserves the Prize." *The Guardian*, April 22: 2. www.theguardian.com/music/2018/apr/22/kendrick-lamar-wins-pulitzer-prize-damn-album?CMP=share_btn_link

50 Blake, John. 2018. "Beyoncé and Lamar Show What It Means to Be Unapologetically Black." *CNN*, April 21. www.cnn.com/2018/04/21/us/beyonce-lamar-unapologeti cally-black/index.html

51 Kornhaber, Spencer. 2017. "The 10 Best Albums of 2017." *The Atlantic*, December 12. www.theatlantic.com/entertainment/archive/2017/12/best-albums-2017/547451/

52 Lynskey. "From Street Kid." 2.

53 Jorgenson, Estelle. 2007. "Concerning Justice and Music Education." *Music Education Research*, *9* (2): 173.

54 Matthews, Richard. 2015. "Beyond Toleration – Facing the Other." In *The Oxford Handbook of Social Justice in Music Education*, edited by Cathy Benedict, Patrick Schmidt, Gary Spruce, and Paul Woodford, 238–249. New York: Oxford University Press.

55 Wright, Ruth. 2015. "Music Education and Social Reproduction." In *The Oxford Handbook of Social Justice in Music Education,* edited by Cathy Benedict, Patrick Schmidt, Gary Spruce, and Paul Woodford, 340–356. New York: Oxford University Press: 345.

56 Collins. *Another Kind of Public Education*: 134.

57 Woodford. *Democracy and Music Education*: 58.

8

THE GOOD TEACHER

Part 1: From the Wisdom of Mrs. Gordon-Cartier

Mrs. Gordon-Cartier has taught music in the urban schools for twenty-five years. Of all the contributing writers for this book, Mrs. Cartier (as her students call her) has the longest record of teaching. Her wisdom as a veteran teacher is particularly enriching in terms of what it means to be a good urban teacher. She began her teaching at the elementary level, then taught two years as a harp/piano/gospel choir teacher at a high school, and now teaches harp at a fine and performing arts middle/high school that is part of the public school system. She is one of the few public school teachers in the nation to develop a thriving harp program in the public schools.

Although students audition for admission to the school, Mrs. Cartier points out that these students have never played harp, so she tends to have a typical cross-section of neighborhood students in her classes. Her students cannot practice outside of school because they do not have harps; however, Mrs. Cartier has worked hard, through grants and connections in the "harp world," to acquire donated harps. She loans these harps to students she knows will "put in the time and practice at home."

The mission of Mrs. Cartier's school is "dedicated to creating a learning environment and educational opportunities utilizing the New Jersey Common Core State Standards to ensure that our students become competitive and well-minded." She imagines the district is well-meaning in its mission but,

> like most of the other public *schools* we are now all about whatever new program and standardized test comes along. We have become a place that not only teaches to the test, we also have become a place of stressed out teachers who are evaluated by this standardized method.

Despite its title, "Performing and Fine Arts," this school seems to incur the same challenges as many other public schools around the country.

Mrs. Cartier grew up in the same town where she now teaches. This is an important advantage because Mrs. Cartier knows the community, the families, and the backgrounds of many students. Research states that living in the same town where one teaches (e.g. Ms. Foreman) gives the teacher a sense of credibility right from the start. As an African American teacher who teaches primarily African American students, she is a good role model for students, not only as a professional but also as a superb musician.

Regarding musicianship, Mrs. Cartier is a nationally recognized harpist and performs regularly in concert venues throughout the United States. She is a sought-after motivational speaker who often combines these presentations with her harp performances. In 2015, Mrs. Cartier won one of the few national grants, the National Artist Teacher Fellowship, for her excellence and leadership in teaching. This fellowship was sponsored by the Center for the Arts in Education at Boston Arts Academy. Clearly, she has much to tell us about teaching music in the urban school.

Interviews with Mrs. Cartier, 2015–2016

Because Mrs. Cartier (as her students call her) has taught for so long, won so many awards, and inspired so many students, I decided to change the format for this section of the book. Instead of a journal, I asked Mrs. Cartier to talk about the joy in her life as an urban music teacher. She read me this quote:

"Not all storms come to disrupt your life, some come to clear your path." This quotation beautifully articulates the journey of an urban teacher. Although there are rocky days ahead and times when you wonder why you became a teacher at all, another day is coming. To teach urban students and to make a difference don't always happen in the moment. As the teacher, making a difference in the lives of the students you teach happens gradually. Many times, the rewards come later – after a particularly difficult confrontation or even after the students have graduated and return to give thanks for your patience, care, and willingness to hang with the student through difficult times.

Below are some stories from Mrs. Cartier's experience that make music teaching worth all the effort:

> *The best stories are those that happen after the fact. It's after the students leave that you get a reminder why you're here. Sometimes I wonder, "Is it going to matter? Are you going to be a better person because of what you've learned in my class?" Teaching is more than music. You try very hard to make good people – citizens. Because it's the kids who might stand up and bring attention to issues in our world that need to be fixed. You forget sometimes that they have power, and you need to encourage this.*

> • *LaToya wasn't one of my top players, but she was a really good student. When I see a student who is invested in his/her music and schooling, I tell*

them, "If you get your college degree and are engaged to be married with no children (Mrs. Cartier loves children but wants the students to have time to develop without the extra attention needed to raise a child), I will play for your wedding as a gift." This is no small gesture as Mrs. Cartier is in high demand for weddings and earns a substantial amount of money for these gigs. However, in doing so, she is encouraging her students to work hard and lets them know that they are capable of better things. Happily, she has played at many weddings.

- *Precious told me she wanted to be a physical therapist. I said, "Hey, why don't you get your doctorate." She took this advice seriously and is now a licensed physical therapist with a doctorate.* True to Mrs. Cartier's promise, she played for Precious' wedding. The wedding was on New Year's Eve day in Delaware. *Although I have a standing engagement to play a concert on New Year's Eve, this time I went to Delaware after the concert to honor my student's special day.*

- *Iman went to college as a music education major with harp as her applied instrument. She was not a conservatory harpist but was good enough to make a living from her playing. She was doing really well but couldn't pass music history. Many history professors have no time or patience for students who don't already know the music historical periods and related information. Iman failed the course three times and, according to departmental regulations, was dismissed from the program. She knew, however, that she wanted to teach, so she changed her major to elementary education with, ironically, a major in history. She is now teaching in an urban community in New Jersey. The point is, here's a kid who grew up in a poor neighborhood, and the harp helped her get into college. I'm so thrilled that she is a teacher.*

- *Lauren won the New Jersey Governor's Award in Arts Education. She also competed in the Afro-Academic Cultural Technological and Scientific Olympics (ACT-SO). ACT-SO operates under the aegis of the NAACP. Its mission is worth reading to understand the importance of this competition for African American students:*

> The mission of NAACP New York City Academic, Cultural, Technological, & Scientific Olympics (NAACP NYC ACT-SO) is to overcome the vicious cycle of low scholastic expectations and achievement that plagues Black underserved minority youth throughout New York City; to strengthen Black high school students' academic skills and inspire the confidence they will need to succeed as adults; and to offer individualized academic mentorship and diverse enrichment activities, of which there is short supply in the New York City public high schools.
>
> Lauren competed as a harpist and won the ACT-SO at the local division for three years in a row. That allowed her to compete at the national level. She's traveled to Las Vegas, Philadelphia, and Florida. Although she didn't win at the national level, she gained a lot by being

around high-achieving students who looked like her. It raised her hori-
zons. Even though she attends a school with kids who often don't work
hard or have little commitment to school, she can see beyond this. Lauren
is now a sophomore at a college in New Jersey where she was awarded a
substantial scholarship for her talent on the harp.

I take my kids to an annual harp conference in New Jersey. They stay for three nights. It is a special trip because many of them have never been outside their own town, let alone staying in a hotel. I take my younger kids (middle school) so they can experience a conference environment and hear other students in their age group perform. During the day, they go to harp classes. I allow them find their way on their own. This gives them confidence to figure out how to navigate a hotel and take classes with other harp students. In the meantime, I am presenting, giving concerts, and assisting with the conference details. This is good because they see me in another light. Suddenly they see me as a leader in the field and someone who performs at important events.

At the last conference, a group of students came to me with concerned looks on their face. I asked them, "What's the matter?" The students were discouraged by one of the harp teachers:

s: *She makes us feel less.*
MC: *What do you mean less?*
s: *Like we aren't as good as the others, we don't play as well.*
MC: *Do you?*
s: *No.*
MC: *Well there you go – but it doesn't mean that your soul, your heart, and your spirit aren't*
     just as good as theirs or better. You don't play well yet. You are here because you are better
     than the students in your grade, the top of the class. I bring you here so that you will
     see and understand that there is so much more you're going to have to do to be the best
     everywhere.

As an aside to me, Mrs. Cartier explains: *We (African Americans) always have to be*
nicer, play better, mind our manners, not rock the boat, and on and on! We have to be so careful
all the time because we bear the wrongs and/or evils that anyone who looks like us have ever
done. The hardest thing for our kids who go to college is across the board racism – Whites against
Blacks and, surprisingly, Blacks against Blacks. My students tell me that they often see other
Black students hanging out with White friends. These are usually Black students from afflu-
ent homes. When White friends tell "Black" jokes, the Black students will laugh. My students
wonder, "Why does this happen?" It happens because often when you are one Black to many
Whites and you become friends, the Whites no longer see your color. Soon you don't either.

Oh, my goodness. I'm so sick and tired of being sick and tired!!!! Earlier today I was
watching a flute and harp duo of two ladies who have always supported me at conferences and
we see each other every now and again. As I listened to them play, it brought tears to my eyes
thinking how thankful I was for my life and for these people who actually studied harp with
me. And then my kids say – "She makes me feel less."

My response

As a Black music teacher, Mrs. Cartier has spent her life helping students learn to cope with racism in a White-dominated country. She knows that to succeed in life, her students must confront the realities of marginalization and become leaders, rather than victims, in their journey through life. I've been in her classroom many times. She is strict, expects high achievement from every student, and cares about their well-being. I've seen her take a crying student into her office and listen patiently while also giving this student tools for handling the situation. I've also seen Mrs. Cartier insist that every student shake hands and introduce themselves to guests in or out of the room.

Her classroom is filled with harps and adorable gadgets like an electronic clock that tells time by flashing colors on a horizontal line. She keeps all kinds of candy, food, and drink for students that are in need or students that assist her in the classroom. She shows her commitment to students every day by greeting them warmly or giving them a warning: "Take off that baseball hat." Mrs. Cartier has used her own money to buy concert clothes and shoes for her students so that they look and feel professional.

Essentially, Mrs. Cartier is determined to give her students life skills, whether they choose to pursue a music career or not. Mrs. Cartier is the kind of teacher that inspires, motivates, and, most importantly, gives hope to those under her care. She is a firm believer that, despite the turbulence of a storm or two, there is always a clearing in sight.

Part 2: The good teacher

If I saw a section titled "The Good Teacher," my first inclination would be to ask myself, "Am I a good teacher?" What does it mean to be a good teacher? Are good teachers in urban schools different from those in other locations? Is there a list of attributes that distinguishes good teachers from not-so-good teachers? Is being a good teacher *good* enough? Perhaps the question "Am I a good teacher?" is misplaced. What distinguishes good teachers is not a focus on themselves but rather on their students. Lisa Delpit suggests that teaching is both for and from the children: "I pray for all of us the strength to teach our children what they must learn, and the humility and wisdom to learn from them so that we might better teach."[1]

As beginning or experienced teachers, we often put all the emphasis on teaching *for* the children when, in fact, our orientation to teaching should also come *from* the children. If a large part of learning to teach comes from the children themselves, then it seems reasonable to explore good teaching in terms of what students need the most. From that point, the attributes of good teaching emerge on their own. For if we are working to meet the diverse needs of our students, then we are engaging in the act of good teaching. Because the needs of students differ in accordance with who they are, where they live, what they dream about, the significant adults in their lives, the struggles they face, and their imagination of the possibilities for themselves – good teaching will look different in particular contexts. According to Delpit:

> Good teaching is not thought of in the same way in all communities. Just as what is considered to be good teaching in Harvard Square differs radically from the same in rural Georgia, beliefs about what constitutes good teaching vary across different cultural communities. Mainstream thinking holds that teaching begins with teachers' awareness of and ability to transfer knowledge. . . . However, I have learned from interviews and personal experiences with teachers from communities of color, that many of these individuals believe teaching begins instead with the establishment of relationships between themselves and their students.[2]

Relationships between teachers and children/adolescents are more complicated than one might initially think. On one hand, there is a power differential that cannot be overlooked. Teachers have authority that students do not. According to Erika Daniels and Mark Arapostathis,

> A delicate balance exists between authority figure and advocate in the teacher-student relationship. Motivating a student to become an independent learner should never inhibit teachers from doing their job in the fear that a student will see them as only an authority figure who wants to control his or her life.[3]

On the other hand, teachers must learn to balance this authority in a way that neither befriends the student nor forces abject compliance. The ultimate goal is to forge relationships between the teacher and student that help advance academic and social skills needed to participate in a democratic society.

There are many examples in the literature that identify traits, dispositions, or actions of a "good" teacher. These are, as Delpit contends, contextual. What makes a good teacher with a majority of indigent students in Alaska looks very different from a good teacher in the low-economic areas of New York City who works primarily with urban African American and Latino youth. There are, however, certain teaching behaviors that seem inclusive of good teachers in any school. In terms of urban teaching, the style of discourse and the teacher's approach to the unique learning needs of the students make all the difference in terms of creating a nurturing urban classroom.

The following list is an attempt to tease out some of the teaching dispositions that seem important for all students, especially urban students.

1. Students need to know you care about them

L. Janelle Dance spoke with many urban teenagers about their school experiences in the course of her research. She asked them what characterized a good teacher.

Their responses are particularly interesting in that students, not adults, had an opportunity to express their views:

> According to the students in my study, the qualities that gave a teacher favorite-teacher status included having a good sense of humor, which makes learning fun yet educational, understanding and encouraging students, being someone whom students can talk and look up to, being concerned about students and having time for them, and believing in students' ability to meet academic requirements. The one characteristic that all favorite teachers have in common is the ability to convince students that they genuinely care.[4]

A strong relationship between you and your students is foundational to all things that you can offer as a teacher.[5] Knowing students by name is the first step toward showing that you care about their identity. While this may seem obvious, it is a challenge for general music teachers who may see as many as 300 or more students a week or ensemble directors with similar scenarios. For White teachers, many of the names will be unfamiliar, thus making them more difficult to remember, e.g. Destiny, Precious, or Deshaun. Make it a priority to learn at least six children every class. In elementary school, you can ask the homeroom teacher to borrow a composite of the class picture for learning names. In middle school or high school, find ways to connect with students regarding something interesting that they might be wearing or a specific school/community event in which they participated.

Meet students at the door, look them in the face, and greet them warmly. Let them know, through this greeting, that they are important to you. Joe Kincheloe remarks, "The more a teacher knows about students' experiences, contexts, dreams, passions, and hurts, the better equipped she will be to engage them in a meaningful educational experience."[6]

How do you find out more about your students? For adolescents, you might give out an "Introduction to You" sheet that they can fill out. Think of questions that will tell you about their musical taste, their home language, their family, their home country (for those who may be immigrants), and what they would like to do in music class this year. For younger children, sing or play games that provide opportunities for individual students to respond. An elementary school colleague of mine ends each class with a "wishing activity" where students close their eyes and think of something they wish for (e.g. a new toy, a sister to feel better when she is sick, a friend to eat lunch with). With the lights low, the teacher has children share their wishes if they choose. It is a special time for both the teacher and the student, while also preparing them to transition to their homeroom teachers.

Music composition, individually or in small groups, allows students to express ideas, feelings, and their sense of musical logic – an activity that is particularly illuminating for students reluctant to speak in class. When young students create a snow piece with percussion instruments, you can suggest that they listen to the mood of the piece: Is it a gentle falling of snow? A raging blizzard? A spirited escapade to build a snowman? What is it like to experience a snowstorm in the city? Is it magical or a major inconvenience? The composition, in its musical form as developed by the students, becomes a prompt for learning about students' lives beyond the school. Likewise, for adolescents, a composition based on "life in the city" creates other avenues for learning about students and their identities. Richard D. Lakes describes the arts for urban youth as "democratizing influences that create communities of like-minded students engaged in the creative process." . . . Furthermore, "the arts offer anti-elitist message derived from the positionality of youth on the margins of society."[7]

Authentic caring asks the questions, "Who are you?" in its broadest sense and "How can I empower you to be all that you can be?" The counterpart is not only sharing stories about yourself but helping students understand that knowing each other is a two-way street. Caring is not, however, feeling sorry for students with challenging home lives or expecting less from them academically. It involves empathizing with their struggle and giving them the encouragement they need to move forward. "This informed empathy," states Gloria Ladson-Billings,

> requires the teacher to feel with the students rather than feel for them. Feeling with the students builds a sense of solidarity between the teacher and the students but does not excuse students from working hard in pursuit of excellence.[8]

Teacher must be cautious, though, as some students are reticent to share their lives with a teacher. Moreover, the teacher represents an authority figure who can be perceived as a positive or negative force. Based on her research with urban high school youth, Dance suggests the following:[9]

1   Get to know, personally, street-savvy students on their own terms.
2   Learn to value the ethnic cultures of street-savvy students.
3   With respect to the *few* students who move beyond posturing to fully internalizing gangster-like beliefs, become familiar with the complexity of social-structural forces that constrain and negatively affect urban communities and become sensitized to the code of the streets that ensues from such force.
4   Read biographies that portray the complex realities and constraints of inner-city life that may influence some urban youths to become "hard" kids
5   Approach statistics about urban crime with skepticism.

"Down" teachers (a term that students used to identify teachers who care about them and made an effort to learn about their world on the streets) recognize that many of these conditions are beyond their control; rather than focus on these incidences, they concentrate on helping students learn about what they can control.[10]

2. Students need to feel that they are part of a community

The good teacher understands that urban students, in particular, need a sense of belonging. Learning communities form when students are working toward the same goals and recognize that each person is central to that mission. In the beginning of my own urban teaching, I found that students had priorities for everything except what I had to teach. It seemed like an impossible task to build a learning community where students did not respect each other enough to listen, participate responsibly in active music making, and share ideas without feeling stupid or attacked. They did not need a traditional music class. They needed a collaborative project where each person had a stake in its outcome. Confirming this, Daniels and Arapostathis state, "One of the themes that ran throughout the student interviews was the need to be interested in and see the value of the tasks in which they are asked to engage."[11]

For my class, *West Side Story* offered a perfect solution – it had elements of street language/behavior, it had love, and it had tragedy. We broke the class into three groups with the task of creating a modern version of *West Side Story*. Students decided how they could best contribute (e.g. playwright, actor, staging/marketing, dancers, and technical engineers) and created imaginative stories based on the musical. They performed their plays for their parents. Were they perfect productions? No. Did they always agree on how to proceed? No. Did they collaborate as a community of learners along the way? Yes, without question.

This project brought us closer as a community of learning than many of the other music lessons that I presented. Here's why: everyone had familiarity with the themes of *West Side Story*; students created their own versions of the story, which created a sense of ownership; each person had a choice in deciding what role to play in the production; I was free to work closely with different groups as they worked together; and students had a stake in the final production because it involved a public presentation. "The teaching of aesthetics in urban education," states Roymieco A. Carter,

> is better understood if tied to lived experiences within the urban environment – its people, languages, homes, neighborhoods, families, authorities, actions, and exchange that take place between these and other facets that illustrate experience as the reflection of understanding for the urban student.[12]

Building learning communities is easy to talk about but difficult to accomplish. Sometimes it takes a particular goal that involves everyone's interest (as in the story above). Sometimes it takes a series of non-threatening music activities that give rise to individual strengths that garner respect of the class. Most important, it takes an enormous amount of modeling on the part of the teacher to get students working together in a meaningful way.

As music teachers, we can't do anything well without a level of trust between and among the students. According to Bill Ayers,

> I believe that people learn best when they are nurtured as well as challenged. . . . We learn when we feel good about ourselves and others, when we trust the environment and the people in our lives, when we are safe."[13]

When the environment is one in which students feel "good," they feel safe to talk about their world inside and outside of the school. Students need to feel that their lives matter and that their motivation to learn leads to even greater possibilities.[14]

Some adolescents, in particular, face heartbreaking decisions regarding gang membership. Gangs provide a sense of family that adolescents crave. And they are "invisibly present" in the community. Not only do gang members hang around outside the schools; there is a level of prestige for those who join. It would be naive to say that a music learning community will offset the power that a gang holds over students. However, it is not so unreasonable to believe that when adolescents find a sense of belongingness in school (not only in music but in other school organizations as well), they may be less tempted to look for that feeling of belonging on the streets.

3. Students want to be held to high standards

In an effort to manage a class, many urban teachers turn to worksheets, videos, and lecture formats to keep the students quiet, giving the false appearance that they are learning the material. The students, "in exchange for not being driven too hard . . . will 'allow' the teacher 'control' of the class, despite the fact that, secretly, many would prefer a teacher who pushed them to achieve."[15] Unfortunately, for many administrators, this environment indicates good teaching. On top of that, there is often rampant grade inflation, which gives students inaccurate information about their achievement. Mrs. Gordon-Cartier has often said that an "A" in her urban school is worth a "C" at the university level. While her students may be able to meet the audition requirements for a university music program, they often fail miserably in their academic courses.

Teachers make all kinds of excuses for demanding less from urban students – ranging from "they refuse to do any kind of work that is challenging," "they don't do their homework," and "their families are not interested enough to help" to biased-related claims about intelligence. Consequently, when students are not pushed in other classes, it is actually quite difficult to request that they work hard in music class. For instance, students who have not experienced the satisfaction of solving a hard problem expect teachers who spoon feed information, often resisting any other style of teaching. From my experience, just because you have a great lesson with music problem solving and reflective discussion does not guarantee that students will immediately rise to the challenge. Some may refuse to participate, and many will complain that the work is too hard.

Nevertheless, "authentic leaders never give up. They refuse to give in to apathy and defeatist attitudes. They are as tough and obstinate as the challenges that unfold around them. The urban setting is rampant with such tests of character."[16] Good teachers know that students take ownership of their learning when they have a say in planning the curriculum and engage in activities that are fun and interesting. They rise to the challenge when the classroom environment becomes less of an individual power play and more of a learning community. "In reality," states Haberman "ultimately [good teachers] cannot force anyone to learn."[17] Whether the student responds now or in a few months, at least they know that you care enough to keep trying.

4. Get to know the language of the inner city

Many students will use terminology from the streets in their communication with you and each other. According to Dance (2002):

> Regardless of how well a teacher knows his or her subject matter, unless she (or he) can relate, or cares to relate, to the demands of urban street culture, she may not be able to acquire and maintain the interest of the students who must navigate the streets on a daily basis. When teachers are unable to structure caring and viable information about street culture into their relationships with street-savvy students, they may undermine urban students' access to important forms of social capital that facilitate positive educational outcomes.[18]

Although derogatory words are never acceptable, it is important to respect the familiar language that students may use despite the fact that it may not conform to standard English. To respect the students' language is to "incorporate it into teaching by welcoming slang, colloquialisms, and 'nonacademic' expressions, and then uses them to introduce new topics, knowledge, and conversations."[19]

Learn the unique ways that students greet each other and look up terminology that you don't understand. Urbandictionary.com is one source that stays current with the fluidity of evolving terminology, although it is a crowd-sourced platform and should be approached cautiously. The teacher who does not accept or follow street language trends is likely to misunderstand important messages that students try to communicate. In fact, Dance states, "Urban students are more likely to trust teachers who talk openly about street culture and give viable advice about avoiding the illicit activities that take place on urban streets."[20]

Certain gestures and postures also communicate information to the teacher. Christopher Emdin talks about the power of a particular handshake as a greeting and suggests that teachers learn and use this handshake whenever appropriate. He also identifies the Black church as a place to observe good teaching techniques for African American students. In a Black church, the preacher often engages with the parishioners in a call-response pattern. There will be places in the sermon when he/she calls out for response (e.g. "Can I get an Amen?"). Likewise, parishioners will call out an assurance or confirmation (e.g. "Oh, yes!") when so moved. Emdin identifies this style of teaching as Pentecostal pedagogy. The point is not that music teachers should copy this style of teaching in the classroom but recognize the nuances and techniques that preachers use to teach their congregation.[21] According to Emdin, Rappers and MCs use similar techniques to engage an audience:

> The ability to guide without controlling, to create the best context, to be flexible, and to make the crowd move is found in both the black church and

in hip-hop. Rappers, who are often described as the teachers of the hip-hop generation, referred to as MC's when they have demonstrated that they have the ability to teach. To MC, or to move the crowd is to be able to share information, spark thinking, invoke dialogue, and keep an audience engaged. . . . They both use call-and-response (e.g., asking the congregation the question "Can I get an amen!" and waiting for the audience to put their hands up and respond) to ensure the crowd is engaged, use the volume of their voice to elicit certain types of responses, actively work the room, and make references to contemporary issues or respond to cues in the immediate environment to enliven their planned/scripted sermons and performances. I argue that the use of these techniques, which fall under the umbrella of Pentecostal pedagogy, is necessary for teaching urban youth of color.[22]

Emdin's observations reflect a unique perspective on culturally responsive teaching with African American students. No doubt a teacher would also learn special teaching techniques from observing rituals or family meeting places with Latino, Asian, or Native American cultures. The message remains the same – that teachers can learn a great deal about communication styles that engage students of color by looking to the community as another source of teacher education.

5. Students need hope

Good teachers strive to provide the means for liberating students from hopelessness. The arts are a significant means for bringing hope into children's/adolescents' lives. Music composition, among the many forms of art, offers students a space for sorting out problems, finding artistic form for expression, and reflecting on the world in which they live. Learning to play an instrument helps students experience tenacity and persistence, two life skills that advance confidence in solving complicated problems. Participating in an ensemble, whether traditional, pop, or non-Western, creates a sense of solidarity and connectivity to other human beings.

We teach the arts because they provide a portal to the human conversation. Giving voice to the voiceless is a powerful gift for our urban youth. They see inequity all around them – in their homes, in their neighborhoods, and in their schools. It doesn't take long to recognize that in a world of wealth, power, and elitism, they drew the short straw. Thus, empowering students through the arts, whether painting a mural to an otherwise lifeless hallway or performing at a school board meeting to energize those in attendance, creates opportunities for expression that urban youth don't often experience.

Pamela Lewis, a former Black teacher in Harlem, is not a trained music educator. Yet, she recognized the impact that participation in the arts had on her young students. She found many ways to engage her students in arts productions involving singing, dancing, etc. during her time as their classroom teacher. She writes:

To succeed in life, my students needed a means of escaping their present mindset without abandoning their communities. The performing arts offered one such means. These roles gave my students a sense of who they were, an appreciation of who they are now, and ambition for who they might someday become. I wanted to give them different eyes to see with, eye that would let them look past the realities of their neighborhood to see that life there wasn't always so dismal.[23]

Melissa Salguero teaches music at P.S. 48, in one of the poorest neighborhoods in New York City (Bronx), where 85% of the children qualify for free lunch.[24] She started her music program with a guitar and a song, "Don't Stop Believing." Now in her seventh year, Ms. Salguero has a thriving music program where students who want to learn instruments start before the school day begins. "At the end of the day, it's not going to be Carnegie Hall, you know, but that's not what we want," says Ms. Salguero. "What I want is – I want the kids to get the experience of working hard." Ms. Salguero's students work hard because she gives them hope and unconditional love. Her student, Luis Galvez, says, "She makes us feel special about ourselves. She doesn't care how we sing." Ms. Salguero won the 2018 Grammy Music Educator Award, and it is not surprising that she finds greatest happiness in watching her students work hard at something they love.

Teaching hope in urban schools is not often addressed in teacher education programs.[25] Yet, it is hope that urban children desperately need to succeed in a space where everything seems stacked against them. "You can do this!" "I believe in you"; "You have what it takes" – these are statements that permeate the classrooms of the most special music teachers. It is a worthy challenge, writes Lakes, to "assist young people in developing optimism in the face of hopelessness."[26]

As music teachers, we always have a choice in the way we teach. We can approach music learning as something that students must endure, or we can teach music as something that brings even the smallest spark of joy in a long school day. Good teachers know that to create hope, they must model it as well. There will be many days that music teachers come home after a hard day at school (e.g. a fight in the hallway, a defiant student, a student who shares a difficult personal story) and wonder, "Did I do the right thing? Is teaching worth it?" The teacher who remains hopeful will know that change comes in small steps and that a new day offers a multitude of possibilities for finding inspiration from their students and forging relationships that give students the strong adult in their lives that they deserve.

Returning to the teachers who contributed to this book

It seems fitting, in this chapter about good teaching, that we return to the teachers who shared their stories about teaching music in the urban school. When I interviewed each teacher, I tried to ask questions that a teacher education student might want to know when considering a professional position in an urban school. Three of these questions are highlighted here:

What are the special skills that urban music teachers need to feel successful?

*   Ms. Foreman, Instrumental Specialist, Middle School (Chapter 2)

    Persistence. You're not always going to get it right, and you may have to fight a little to get kids to try. If you believe that everyone is teachable, you see potential in students beyond the class. Establish an environment that's home – like having lunch with them or letting students hang out in the music room, eating lunch and listening to music. This is a difference between teachers who care and those who keep them at bay.

*   Mrs. Sweet, String Specialist, High School (Chapter 3)

    Flexibility, strength, and sensitivity. Flexibility in being able to move with the kids. For instance, if there were a shooting in the neighborhood, you have to be flexible – not to feel helpless but to help them every day to cope with this. Have the strength to listen to these stories if it hasn't been your experience. For me, personally, you have to have a genuine care for the students. They have enough people in their lives who don't care. Sometimes it is being really strict, "Oh, she cares because she called my mother." Some may not like me, but I need them to respect what I do.

*   Mrs. Skinner, String Specialist, Elementary/Middle School (Chapter 4)

    Perseverance. I think a lot of people let the circumstances and the brokenness of the district get to them and they don't fight because it is too hard. I'll do rehearsals even when I don't get paid. There's always a creative way around it, but it takes work.

*   Mr. Tamburro, Choral Specialist, Middle School (Chapter 5)

    Patience. The kids need you to give extra for everything. When the kids want to fight, they must get the last word. You have to know that and patiently wait. Yelling has no effect, especially from a White teacher. Sometimes I use a stopwatch and click it when they get loud of talkative. They know that they lose minutes from their free day on Friday when they get to play "rock band," piano, etc.

*   Ms. Gopal: Choral Specialist, High School (interviewee, High School Choral Specialist)

    Sacrifice. Passion. Dedication. Commitment. Energy. Time.

What tips do you have for first-year music teachers in the urban school?

*   Ms. Foreman

    Remember that every kid is teachable. You have to figure out a way to get to them and be open to the fact that music might not be their favorite subject. Go to a basketball game and then comment on that. Show up to something that they're doing. Each marking period, I look at their grades for all subjects and if they aren't doing well, I might talk to the subject teacher and then have a conversation with the student.

I always do it in a caring way. When they see that you care about them, they will try or at least stay under the radar and not give you problems. Don't be afraid to ask for help from everyone, not just music teachers. Everyone has the same students. If you are having a problem, communicate with their teachers to find out if they are having problems there as well.

- Mrs. Sweet

    Set up your classroom and be organized with your procedures. Plan all of that ahead of time. You learn this over the years. You really have to find what works for you and your style. Make sure you know who to contact when there's a problem. You don't have to handle this yourself. You need to communicate and reach out to colleagues. When you go into urban teaching, don't think: "I'm going to save these kids." Remember that you're replacing someone who they knew or had transient teachers that they didn't trust. Get to know everyone's names. Make eye contact. Plan several plans, not just one lesson, because things might completely change based on what happened that day. Have students do an information card with updated information because the office doesn't have all the information.

- Mrs. Skinner

    Be willing to learn from anyone – whether they've had experience in the field or not. You don't know it all, and you never will. Don't let "Oh, it's my first year" be an excuse for not doing great things. Don't be afraid to give it your all. Sometimes people are afraid to rock the boat, but there are opportunities to do that in a good way. Also, it's not the goal to be best friends with a kid. The kid will respect you more if you act like an adult because they can trust you with their problems. Being cool and buddy-buddy does them no favors. How you sit with the instrument, you don't talk, your posture – the kids like that there are rules. They like structure. They don't need a friend; they need someone to be strong for them. You have to expect that you will have to put in extra work and extra time in what you do. It's going to involve great sacrifice.

    Performing arts programs are always on the line – we have to step it up and make the school proud. It's especially important for performing artist teachers to show off our kids. It involves hard work. Especially in urban areas because testing is so emphasized and kids struggle with such basic concepts. Principles are hesitant to let students go to the arts. When the principal respects you and your program, he/she realizes that these music experiences that are just as important as the other academics.

- Mr. Tamburro

    Do your work, be on time, and no one will bother you. There is so much freedom to do what you want in the classroom as long as you are handing your work in on time. Try to meet the students halfway. Find something they like, not just something they have to learn. For example, for classical music, I will try to start with something upbeat and something they might recognize from cartoons or something. For pop music, I try to choose music that crosses into other genres. They love acapella music like the Pentatonix; any time I can highlight the music of people of color, they are more interested. If something in technology is blocked, like YouTube, the kids know how to get around it. You can always count on the kids to know how to circumvent the system.

- Ms. Gopal

  When you go into an urban school, the most important thing to find out is who are the most successful teachers and why. Get to know them and observe their classrooms. You can't live in the bubble. I observed the best teachers in English and science. Different successful teachers use techniques in different ways. You look for good teachers who have respect from the students.

  When I started here, I was a veteran teacher already, so I came with a bag of tools. But, every school is its own little society. You have to find out how the society works. It took a while to be happy here – it doesn't happen overnight. We have such a high attrition rate of teachers that has nothing to do with the kids whether the school is urban or suburban. It has everything to do with the politics, mounds of paperwork, and red tape. This is why there is a high attrition rate for first-year teachers. Unfortunately, kids are used to being abandoned.

What are the rewards of teaching music in an urban school?

- Ms. Foreman

  The reward is knowing that I'm touching them beyond music. All of the students I taught fall in love with band; they don't always continue, but they always stay in touch. It goes beyond the music.

- Mrs. Sweet

  It's the enthusiasm and real love and appreciation that the students have for me – that I'm doing something for them. It's usually after performances when they realize all the hard work I do. It's the daily hugs I get. My students are very open-minded; they have had a lot of life experience. They are very grown up in some ways, so you can teach them things that are controversial, like race. I've learned more about what prejudice is – I have a more in-depth idea what people of color have to go through. It's made me more aware of the world. It's been a journey of stretching and growing. It's always a challenge.

  Some days they will be perfectly normal, and sometimes they have a really bad day. I have to either cater to that or keep them going. It made me stronger and able to deal with problems that they brought into the classroom. I've learned to channel the energy and have them move forward or stop and have a discussion. It's the kind of challenge that I love because I'm doing more than teach music. Music teaches you about life and hard work. It teaches about community and working together, critical thinking, and understanding.

- Mrs. Skinner

  The rewards for me are to see the students overcome the challenges they face and that, despite the challenges, they can still make music at high level. A lot of the kids have family issues and money issues; when I see kids that are successful and proud parents – that's the biggest thing for me.

- Mr. Tamburro

   I think the rewards are giving the kids something for the very first time – a music group or composer or taking them for their first roller coaster ride (class trip). Kids are fiercely loyal. Every year I go back, it's better with the kids because they experience so many teachers leaving.

Conclusion

In this book, we covered many topics in urban teaching, such as how music teachers commit to caring for their students; what it means to be culturally responsive; how to take a poorly budgeted music program and turn it around to your advantage; understanding the shifting, changing patterns of the school day, White teachers and students of color; and the role of democracy in cultivating a supportive educative learning community. I end this book with a chapter about the good teacher because, although there are ideas for good teaching throughout the foregoing chapters, it seems important to pull these ideas together in one place to serve as a reference for teachers who will and are teaching music in the urban schools.

To be sure, there is nothing easy about teaching in the urban school and no prescriptive methodologies to guide you along the way. That doesn't mean that one enters the urban classroom without a thoughtful plan – "anything could happen so why prepare?" On the contrary, students *need* good teachers – those who will offer themselves as active listeners, be faithful companions in learning, and create a safe learning space where everyone is valued.

Most of all, music teachers give the gift of music as a form of new life to those who suffer from poverty or neglect, bullying, lack of confidence, poor academic achievement, anger, frustration, or hurt feelings. Mrs. Sweet says, "Music teaches you about life and hard work. It elevates you to be your best self. It teaches about community and working together, thinking, understanding, and critical thinking."

We know the power of music because we have experienced this in many ways. But, have the students? Have they experienced the joy of creating music, or have they listened to music only to complete worksheets? Have they experienced the thrill of applause when a performance went well, or have they slogged through drills and skills only to extinguish the spark they had when they first met their instrument?

What is the point of teaching something for which students have no interest or enthusiasm? Too often, there is a large disconnect between school music and the music they love. There is rarely a child/adolescent who says, "I want nothing to do with music." But there are plenty of students who find music class insufferable yet spend enormous amounts of time on their iPods and in their makeshift garage bands.

In essence, teaching is always political and infused with moral dimensions. We can isolate ourselves from the inequities that exist in our students' lives, or we can look to music as a form of empowerment and transformation. Urban students placed in our care come with complicated personal stories and undue public scrutiny. It is our job, as music teachers, to advocate for the voiceless. It is our job to teach music with rigor and quality because urban students deserve no less.

Discussion questions

1   Reassess your thoughts and feelings about teaching music in an urban school. Would you be open to taking a job in an urban setting?
2   Good teaching in an urban school may look very different from that in a suburban or rural school. What are some of the needs that urban students, in particular, have?
3   What could you do, before you graduate, to be more prepared for teaching in an urban school?

References

1 Delpit, Lisa. 2006. *Other People's Children*. New York: The New Press: 183.
2 Ibid., 139.
3 Daniels, Erika and Mark Arapostathis. 2005. "What Do They Really Want? Student Voices and Motivation Research." *Urban Education, 40* (34): 52. doi: 10.1177/0042085904270421
4 Dance, L. Janelle. 2002. *Tough Fronts: The Impact of Street Culture on Schooling*. New York: Routledge: 75.
5 Lind, Vicki R. and Constance L. McKoy. 2016. *Culturally Responsive Teaching in Music Education*. New York: Routledge; Ramsey, Patricia G. 2004. *Teaching and Learning in a Diverse World: Multicultural Education for Young Children* [3rd ed.]. New York: Teachers College Press.
6 Kincheloe, Joe. 2007. "City Kids – Not the Kind of Students You'd Want to Teach." In *Teaching City Kids*, edited by Joe Kincheloe and kecia hayes, 3–38. New York: Peter Lang: 32.
7 Lakes, Richard D. 2007. "Urban Youth and Bibliographical Projects." In *Teaching City Kids*, edited by Joe Kincheloe and kecia hayes, 71–83. New York: Peter Lang: 77.
8 Gloria Ladson-Billings. 2008. "Yes, But How Do We Do It? Practicing Culturally Responsive Teaching." In *City Kids, City Schools: More Reports from the Front Row*, edited by William Ayers, Gloria Ladson-Billings, Gregory Michie, and Pedro A. Noguera, 162–177. New York: The New Press: 165.
9 Dance. *Tough Fronts*: 146–147.
10 Ibid.
11 Daniels. "What Do They Really Want?" 45.
12 Carter, Roymieco A. 2007. "Can Aesthetics Be Taught in Urban Education." In *19 Urban Questions: Teaching in The City*, edited by Shirley R. Steinberg and Joe L. Kincheloe, 229–244. New York: Peter Lang: 243.
13 Ayers, William. 2001. *To Teach: The Journey of a Teacher* [2nd ed.]. New York: Teachers College Press: 60.

14 Richert, Anna Ershler. 2012. *What Should I Do? Confronting Dilemmas of Teaching in Urban Schools*. New York: Teachers College Press: 53.

15 Murrell, Peter C. Jr. 2008. "Toward Social Justice in Urban Education: A Model of Collaborative Cultural Inquiry in Urban Schools." In *Partnering to Prepare Urban Teachers: A Call to Activism*, edited by Francine P. Peterman, 41–57. New York: Peer Lang: 44.

16 Flagg, Michele A. 2006. "Five Simple Steps to Becoming a Music Teacher Leader in an Urban School." In *Teaching Music in the Urban Classroom: A Guide to Leadership, Teacher Education, and Reform* [vol. 2], edited by Carol Frierson-Campbell, 35–44. Lanham, MD: Rowman & Littlefield: 40.

17 Haberman, Martin. 1995. *Star Teachers of Children in Poverty*. West Lafayette, IN: Kappa Delta Pi: 7.

18 Dance. *Tough Fronts*: 76–77.

19 Emdin, Christopher. 2016. *For White Folks Who Teach in the Hood . . . and the Rest of Y'all Too: Reality Pedagogy and Urban Education*. Boston: Beacon Press: 54.

20 Dance. *Tough Fronts*: 83.

21 Emdin. *For White Folks*.

22 Ibid., 52.

23 Lewis, Pamela. 2016. *Teaching While Black: A New Voice on Race and Education in New York City*. New York: Empire State Editions: 76–77.

24 Kowalski, Sandra. 2018. "Melissa Salguero: 2018 Grammy Music Educator of the Year." *School Band and Orchestra Magazine*. April 6. http://sbomagazine.com/featured/6141-melissa-salguero-2018-grammy-music-educator-of-the-year.html; *2018 Grammy Music Educator Award Goes to Bronx Teacher*. January 26. CBS Interactive Inc.

25 Duncan-Andrade, Jeffrey M. R. 2011. "The Principal Facts: New Dimensions for Teacher Education." In *Studying Diversity in Teacher Education*, edited by Ametha F. Bell and Cynthia A. Tyson, 309–326. Lanham, MD: Rowman & Littlefield.

26 Lakes. "Urban Youth." 76.

APPENDIX

Online resources

Chapter 3

Bullying Intervention: www.stopbullying.gov

Chapter 4

Playing for Change: https://www.youtube.com/watch?v=Us-TVg40ExM
The Landfill Harmonic Orchestra: http://www.landfillharmonicmovie.com

Chapter 5

Coalition of Grieving Students: http://grievingstudents.org
GLSEN Safe Space Kit: www.glsen.org/safespace (downloadable copy on right sidebar)
Diverse Harmony Chorus
    (Google: LGBTQ Chorus for a listing of choruses around the country)
Diverse City Youth Chorus
https://www.facebook.com/pg/diversecityyouthchorus/about/?ref=page_internal
    (contact for repertoire ideas and choral resources)
about grief is *After a Loved One Dies: How Children Grieve and How Parents and Other
    Adults Can Support Them* (http://www1.newyorklife.com/newyorklife.com/
    General/FileLink/Static%20Files/Bereavement-bklet-English.pdf)

INDEX